Forgotten Pioneers

Forgotten Pioneers

The Story of the Original English Lady Cricketers

Giles Wilcock

First published by Pitch Publishing, 2024

Pitch Publishing
9 Donnington Park,
85 Birdham Road,
Chichester,
West Sussex,
PO20 7AJ
www.pitchpublishing.co.uk
info@pitchpublishing.co.uk

© 2024, Giles Wilcock

Every effort has been made to trace the copyright.
Any oversight will be rectified in future editions at the
earliest opportunity by the publisher.

All rights reserved. No part of this book may be reproduced,
sold or utilised in any form or transmitted in any form or by
any means, electronic or mechanical, including photocopying,
recording or by any information storage and retrieval system,
without prior permission in writing from the Publisher.

A CIP catalogue record is available for this book
from the British Library.

ISBN 978 1 80150 688 5

Typesetting and origination by Pitch Publishing
Printed and bound in India by Replika Press Pvt. Ltd.

Contents

Introduction	11
The Ambitions of Mr Michell	19
The Players	42
Preparations for the Show	61
Liverpool and Beyond	71
Miss Daisie Stanley and the *English Lady Cricketers' Gazette*	81
The Show Must Go On … and On	102
'Should Women Play Cricket?'	119
In the Evening	140
Signs of Trouble	151
The Second Season	161
Crisis	178
The Star, Sympathy and Benefits	193
Recrimination and Revenge?	215
The Last Gasp	228
The Ghost of a Forgotten Idea	233
Whatever Happened to the Original English Lady Cricketers?	246
A Place in History?	268
Appendix 1: Biographical Information on the Players	273
Appendix 2: Matches Played by the OELC	286
Appendix 3: Averages for the OELC	304
Acknowledgements	310
Bibliography	312
Index	315

For Francesca

Note: In pre-decimal British currency, there were 12 pence (d) in one shilling (s) and 20 shillings equalled £1.

Converting the value of money from the 1890s into a modern equivalent is notoriously uncertain. Fairly precise values can be found on the website www.measuringworth.com, but a rough equivalent can be ascertained by multiplying by one hundred: so £1 in 1890 would be worth just over £100 today; one shilling would be around £5 and one pence around 50p.

Where contemporary newspaper reports have been quoted, the spelling and wording have not been altered but punctuation and capitalisation have been made consistent.

Introduction

ON 19 July 1890, Turf Moor – usually the home of Burnley Football Club – hosted an event which would have been unthinkable 12 months earlier but which had become almost commonplace. Around 5,000 spectators had paid upwards of 6d (pence) to watch an exhibition match between two teams of professional women cricketers. The two teams, the 'Reds' and the 'Blues', were collectively known as the Original English Lady Cricketers (OELC).

Throughout the summer of 1890, the teams had been touring Britain, captivating audiences with their performances and generating substantial publicity. While women's cricket was not unheard of at the time, this experimental team had no precedent. People simply did not pay to watch women – who had a carefully defined and restricted role in Victorian Britain – play cricket, nor any other sport. And the more high-minded members of society deeply disapproved of professionalism in sport; for women to be *paid* for playing cricket was scandalous.

Despite their revolutionary nature, the teams had proven a huge attraction. When they reached Burnley, the Original English Lady Cricketers had been touring for three-and-a-half months, midway through a gruelling seven-month itinerary that included locations as varied as Edinburgh, Penzance and the Isle of Man. Large and sometimes enormous crowds came to see them wherever they went, while their very existence drove the press into an outraged frenzy which kept headlines and free publicity coming.

Most of the women were under 20 years old – the youngest was 15 – and came from a variety of backgrounds. One particular point of fascination was their costume. They wore dresses – which although they came below the knee, were short by the standards of the time – edged with patterns of red or blue and with 'OELC' sewn near the collar; the outfit was topped off with caps and sashes in their team colours.

The date in question at Burnley – the second day of a two-day game, the first of which had been curtailed by rain – was fairly typical although, owing to a good pitch, higher-scoring than usual. When play began around 2pm, the Reds resumed their innings, having been 119/4 overnight. Their captain Violet Westbrook, by far the best cricketer on either team, was unbeaten on 63. Although wickets fell around her to the steady medium-pace of Ada Heather and Georgina Sheffield, Westbrook moved smoothly to her century, the first scored by any of the OELC (although Westbrook had come close several times before, including one innings in which she was run out for 99, attempting her 100th run from the last ball of the game). When Bianca Seymour gave a return catch to Georgina Sheffield, Westbrook declared the Reds innings closed at 177/8; she was left unbeaten on 104, having hit one five, two fours and eleven threes. She received an excellent reception and, as was the custom everywhere after a good performance by a professional cricketer, a collection was taken for her among the spectators.

Introduction

When the Blues batted, Westbrook and Louisa Daly each took three wickets to bowl out their opponents for 126. Ella Heather made 55, sending several cut shots to the boundary, and Alice Grey hit 26, but there were four run-outs, including the captain Daisie Stanley. Most of these details were recorded by the scorer, a 16-year-old who sometimes called herself Katie Letine. In total, £115 was taken at the gate. But that was just one part of the programme provided by the Original English Lady Cricketers.

When play finished at 6pm, the players relocated to Burnley's Gaiety Theatre where they put on a show featuring a musical drill, songs, fencing displays, a trick cyclist and performances on instruments. Doubtless many of those who had watched Westbrook wielding a bat in the afternoon were equally intrigued to see her wielding a fencing foil that night, or to see Seymour swap her bat for a banjo.

Among those accompanying the team was their coach (and umpire) William Matthews, and at least one matron. Probably also present was their manager, a man calling himself Edward Michel. His name was emblazoned over most material associated with the team, and no advertisement was complete unless it ended with the reassurance: 'Manager: Mr E. Michel'. Quite often, he included his address, which was initially 13 Chesterfield Grove, South-East London, before changing to 11 Queen Victoria Street, Central London. Mr Michel, in a widely published interview, claimed the credit for coming up with the whole idea of a touring women's team despite having no prior knowledge of cricket. Or so he said; Mr Michel had an interesting relationship with the truth.

For newspaper readers, the OELC became a familiar topic over the summer of 1890. If more respectable publications either ignored the team completely like *The Times* or were content with one or two minor stories like the *Daily Telegraph*, local newspapers gave full rein to their fascination with the women cricketers. *Sporting Life* regularly listed the team's itinerary and brief versions of their scores, and theatrical publications such as *The Era* kept a close eye on their activities. This curious mixture of the sporting and the stage might seem unusual to a modern audience but was not entirely without precedent.

* * *

On 6 July 1891, the OELC returned to Turf Moor and played another game. There were fewer runs, fewer spectators, no evening performances and much more rain. Around a thousand people watched the single day of play, but the eagle-eyed might have noticed that neither team had a full complement of players as influenza swept through their ranks. In the interval, a group of female cyclists put on a performance. The Reds scored 74, a total easily passed by the Blues, who had scored 121/5 when play ended. Westbrook made 23 for the former and Ella Heather – now the Blues captain – an unbeaten 55 for the latter. The 16-year-old Lizzie Sanders – who also at times captained the Blues that season – scored 27, bowled effectively and was clearly a vital part of the team, which might have surprised those who had seen her largely anonymous contribution the previous season.

Returning spectators might have noticed other changes in the team since 1890, but were likely unaware that just a few weeks previously the tour had come close to collapse and new management had taken over. Soon after, the OELC fell apart in acrimonious circumstances. There would be no third match at Burnley, and the final press stories about the team concerned a court case between players and management. After that, the OELC faded from sight and memory.

But there is no question that the OELC made a huge impact in 1890, becoming part of what today might be called 'popular culture'. If never quite attaining the fame of W. G. Grace in the cricketing world nor Marie Lloyd in the theatrical, and if neither Westbrook, Heather, Stanley nor Sanders became household names, even at the height of the OELC's popularity, the whole idea of a women's cricket team permeated consciousness enough to inspire music hall satire, cartoon mockery and a fancy-dress trend. None of this has made much impact on the historian, neither the cricket nor the mainstream kind. Aside from a few throwaway lines, the OELC has long been forgotten.

* * *

In the modern world, the growth and professionalisation of women's cricket has been one of the biggest success stories of the last two decades. The sport has attained unprecedented popularity and support. And yet few people realise that today's internationally famous players had Victorian counterparts, nor that professional women's cricket began so long ago. The short-lived nature of the OELC did not lend itself to a lasting legacy but the reason that the story is not more widely known is more complicated than that. And after the final collapse of the team, it would be over a hundred years before women could again play cricket professionally.

With women's cricket firmly established around the world, this is a good time to look back at those who went before. But this can never be a straightforward tale of a cricket team because there is one important question before we begin: whose story is being told? Different answers can change the narrative considerably.

Are we trying to tell the story of the team itself? That is difficult because except for a few fragments from 1890 and 1891, dubious testimony from the 1892 court case and a short but invaluable interview in 1956 with one of the surviving players, we have no first-hand accounts from the women involved. Although it is possible to list their scores with the bat and say where they played almost every day of the 1890 and 1891 cricket seasons, we know little about them. Their motivations, their lives and in many cases their real names are mysteries about which we can only speculate. For some of the players, facts are abundant but answers are meagre.

Depending on how it is told, this could be a tale of triumph – women who overcame the resistance of the cricketing world, the press and the public, and in many cases escaped from a background of poverty and deprivation – or disaster – the OELC disbanded in acrimony, none of the players continued in sport and most (but not quite all) descended into obscurity, submerged beneath the restrictions and expectations of Victorian society.

Or are we telling the story of the men who ran the team? With one short-lived exception, the managers were male. We know a little more about them than we do the players, but again motivations are a mystery. Were they trying to promote women's sport, or simply trying to make money from a spectacle for other men to enjoy? If this is the tale being told, the end becomes important because although the circumstances of the mid-1891 collapse are unclear, financial mismanagement (possibly fraudulent) was a factor. This version of the story becomes one of inevitable decline and failure; there is also more than a hint of exploitation, not least when it emerges that one manager married a 16-year-old member of the team.

If we cannot quite tell the story of the players or the managers, should this be the story of the public, and how they perceived this team of women cricketers? Perhaps it is the story of the elderly gentleman spluttering into his tea while reading the latest exploits of the players over breakfast. The story of the spectator either cheering or barracking depending on his or her views. The story of those who queued outside the ground or waited in the theatres. Or the fashionable young men known as 'mashers' who provided plenty of unwanted attention wherever the women went.

But again we have a problem. None of these people left us their views. We only have what the newspapers reported: facts carefully chosen, filtered and interpreted by (male) journalists. If we are not careful, we are left with the story those writers wished to tell, shaped to fit their own opinions and biases: great fielding could be described as poor fielding; applause could be twisted into mocking laughter; enthusiasm could become derision. Or indeed, vice versa. We do not know what the onlookers thought. It is possible to make some educated guesses, and there are ways to peel back the layers to get some glimpse of the truth. But we have nothing like a full picture.

* * *

Untangling truth from fiction and seeing where the facts might have been changed (accidentally or deliberately) is hard, but just about possible. But what cannot be escaped is the all-pervading misogyny which permeated Victorian society. Many women were forced to conform to male expectations, to keep to their place and to accept their supposed inferiority. However, these views were increasingly being challenged by women themselves; male society was faced with a series of worrying changes to the status quo. It was against this background that the OELC appeared, and such considerations were important to those writing and to those who read their words. And maybe to those who watched or played.

In trying to understand the full picture, small details become important. Those fragmentary interviews and throwaway anecdotes become gold dust.

In the end, we cannot tell anyone's tale as fully as we might wish. But we can tell a little bit of everyone's: the players, the managers, and those who followed closely or from a distance. And perhaps the experience of those people who read of the OELC next morning in their newspapers most closely matches ours: reading a filtered version of the truth from which we might discern just a little of what was truly happening at those cricket grounds.

The Ambitions of Mr Michell

BY THE time the Original English Lady Cricketers played at Burnley in July 1890, the concept of women who played cricket by day and performed in theatres by night had become firmly established. It was radical and scandalous – but undoubtedly successful. How did the idea emerge? Where should we begin our story?

Perhaps the best starting point is one London street. Most of the early advertising for the concept that evolved into the OELC named the organisation's manager as Mr E. Michel of 13 Chesterfield Grove in East Dulwich. That particular house had been vacant at the time of the 1881 census and was empty again in 1891. But in the meantime, Chesterfield Grove was the location of some unusual business enterprises. Advertising sections of newspapers allow us to build up an interesting picture. For example, the unnamed occupant of 17 Chesterfield Grove offered the rental of an unspecified house for £24 per annum during September 1887. In June 1888, a man calling himself Edward Ludwig at the same address claimed to be the manager of 'Snell's Australian Giants', an Australian family which toured England several times to 'exhibit' their oversized children. This latter case is curious, because a few weeks earlier other advertising had listed number 17 as the address of an auctioneer called Edward P. Michel (or Michell).

A few doors along, another resident of Chesterfield Grove also placed regular adverts in newspapers across the country. 'Mr Sanders' at number 23 ran a 'matrimonial introduction agency' which invited respectable men and women to apply for a list of suitable people for 'introduction'. This agency operated from around 1884 until at least 1891, but the adverts peaked between 1888 and 1890.

The common denominator of these two addresses was a pair of siblings. 'Mr Sanders' at number 23 was in reality Joseph Sanders Michell, a 'Confidential Enquiry Investigator' who lived with his wife and children at that address at the time of the 1891 census, when he was 39. His younger brother – who lived at number 17 before moving to number 13, and who probably used the pseudonym Edward Ludwig – was called Edward Parsons Michell.

The two men were the only children of Henry Michell and Mary Parsons. Their parents originated from Cornwall; when Joseph was born in 1852, the family lived in Wapping but had moved to St George-in-the-East, part of Tower Hamlets, by the time of Edward's birth in 1859. The 1861 census records Henry as a licensed victualler who ran the Royal Crown public house on St George Street; several live-in servants helped him run the establishment.

Edward's early life was unremarkable; when the 1871 census was taken, he was listed, under the name Parsons Michell, as a boarder at High Field Lodge School in Winchmore Hill, Enfield. Our next glimpse comes in 1881, four years after the death of his father, when he was lodging with a family in St George Hanover Square, working as a 'General Architect and Surveyor'. Later that year, he married Clara Caroline Fowler – giving his occupation on their marriage certificate as an auctioneer – and 12 months later they had their only child, Henry. Given that Edward Michell gave two different occupations on official documents in 1881, it is hard to be certain how he earned a living, but those newspaper adverts in the 1880s support the idea that auctions were his main livelihood.

There is, however, one other possible appearance of our man in newspapers. In 1885, an actor was charged at Marlborough Street Police Court with 'feloniously obtaining seventeen dresses, valued at £14, belonging to Mr Nathan, costumier, of Castle Street'. His name was given as Edward Michel. He persuaded the magistrates that he had not intended to steal and arranged to pay back the amount. Could this be our Michell? Possibly, but we can't be sure.

Although we might be light on detail about Edward Michell – aside from an impression that both he and his brother might generously be described as entrepreneurs – he was happy to fill in some of the gaps while promoting the OELC. As interest in the team grew, many newspapers printed an interview with its manager. The origin of this piece need not concern us yet, but in giving the interview, Michell invented a whole fictional background and lost a letter from his surname.

The feature described 'Mr Michel' – 'the man whose fertile brain first evolved this quite new departure in the natural game' – as a 'dark-complexioned, good-looking, knowing sort of gentleman of about forty years of age'. He claimed to have French parents, to have been raised in America, and never to have played cricket: 'If I had been a cricketer, I never should have thought of such a thing as a lady team like the one now on tour. A cricketer would have had no confidence in the idea of girls coming to any degree of proficiency in the game.'

Maybe, like his brother's adoption of the pseudonym 'Mr Sanders' for his dubious matrimonial agency – and perhaps his own use of the name Edward Ludwig if he was the manager of the 'Australian Giants' – a new role required a new identity. But something very peculiar indeed was going on here, far more than the slight alteration to how he spelled his name. Why would he claim to be French? It seems an oddly specific deception, but there is a remarkable parallel at the heart of it; perhaps too remarkable to be accidental.

Living in London at this time was a railway manager called Louis Edouard Michel (usually known as Edouard/ Edward Michel), born in France around 1839, who had moved to England in the 1880s. The 1891 census records him living with his wife Grace, whom he had married in 1886, his six-year-old son George Edward and two servants at 4 St John's Wood Park, his residence from around 1885 until his death in 1896. Despite the similarities with the story given by 'Mr E. Michel', Louis Edouard had no apparent connection with the OELC, and his job would have left little time to run a cricket team. Furthermore, a photograph printed in the *Railway News* at the time of his death shows a man bearing no resemblance to the OELC manager, who was pictured in several publicity photographs in 1890 and 1891. And the only legal document to survive concerning the OELC is signed by Edward Parsons Michell of 13 Chesterfield Grove, making it certain that he was the manager, not Louis Edouard.

But if this was not a coincidence, what possible reason could Edward Parsons have for stealing the identity of Louis Edouard? He would clearly not have sounded French, something which he presumably explained away through being 'raised in America'. Nothing obviously linked the railway manager with Michell, nor anyone else associated with the OELC. The only gossamer-thin connection is that William Dennison, who lived at 15 Chesterfield Grove in 1891, was a railway porter. Perhaps the background of the Frenchman just seemed suitably exotic to Edward Parsons Michell.[1] Perhaps Louis Edouard's name brought some kind of cachet as he was several rungs up the social ladder. But we simply do not know.

* * *

Our second major character is a solicitor called Walter Henry Bosanquet. He was born in Bloomsbury, Middlesex in 1839 and came from a distinguished family. His uncle, James Whatman Bosanquet, was a renowned biblical scholar (and more prosaically, a banker); his distant cousin was the philosopher Bernard Bosanquet; and over ten years after the heyday of the OELC, his first-cousin-once-removed Bernard James Tindall Bosanquet invented the googly and played Test cricket for England. Walter Bosanquet had been married since 1866 and by the time he enters our story, he had four children. The family lived a comfortable life in Bromley, Kent, alongside several servants.

Bosanquet had built up a reputation – doubtless through his family connections – as an expert on banking. His wealth and expertise had enabled him to invest money in several projects, charitable and otherwise. And he was also a cricket lover: as an amateur club cricketer, he had

---

1   There may even have been an earlier attempt by Edward Parsons Michell to link with Louis Edouard Michel. If Edward Parsons was indeed the Edward Ludwig who was the manager of 'Snell's Australian Giants', it might not be coincidental that Ludwig is the German form of the French name Louis.

played for Richmond in the 1860s and was still playing for Bromley in the 1890s. By the time that the OELC came into existence, he had offices at 11 Queen Victoria Street in central London, a prestigious address. He was hardly the type of man to frequent Chesterfield Grove or avail himself of Mr Sanders' matrimonial introduction agency.

Yet somehow, in the autumn of 1889, Bosanquet and Michell between them created the idea that evolved over the following months into the first professional women's cricket team in the world. By late 1889, advertising had begun to appear in newspapers and early in 1890 the organisation that came to be called the Original English Lady Cricketers was attracting a lot of attention. How did the rich solicitor and the ambitious surveyor/auctioneer come together in such an unusual venture?

While at first glance there was little to connect them, the most likely explanation is that Michell either worked for or was closely connected to Bosanquet's firm of solicitors. Maybe he surveyed or auctioned buildings with which they were involved in some legal capacity. And between them, these two men developed the idea that became the OELC, probably around autumn 1889.

* * *

We can just about trace the genesis of their scheme. The most crucial piece of evidence is the surviving paperwork that brought into existence the company that ran the whole operation.

On 26 October 1889, a Memorandum of Association was filed at Companies House under the Companies Act of 1862 to incorporate a new company which was to be limited by shares – the English Cricket and Athletic Association

Limited (ECAA). In simple terms, this created a company which had a separate legal identity to the shareholders who owned it; a loophole through which the creators of any company had to jump.

More importantly for our purposes, it listed the shareholders – how much money they had put into the newly formed company, their occupation and their address. The capital of the new company was stated to be £1,000, divided into 1,000 shares of £1. The original plan, 20 shares of £50, has been crossed out on the document. The majority shareholder and managing director was Walter H. Bosanquet, who had 843 shares; all the paperwork had been drawn up by his company, Mullens and Bosanquet of 11 Queen Victoria Street. The other major shareholders were a merchant called Alfred L. Shaw, who held 100 shares, and Henry Frith – listed on the documents as a 'gentleman' but better known as a writer of boys' stories and the translator of the works of Jules Verne into English – who had fifty shares. Clearly, under the initial plan Bosanquet would have held seventeen of the £50 shares, Shaw two and Frith one. But for whatever reason, Bosanquet wished – presumably after the initial Memorandum of Association had been drawn up – to involve more people and therefore opted to split the shares up to be worth £1 each.

The other seven shareholders were men with far more humble backgrounds, each possessing one single – and probably merely symbolic – £1 share. Their identities do not tell us much. There were four clerks, a solicitor's clerk and an accountant; it is not unreasonable to guess that all were employed by Bosanquet and received their share for working in some capacity with the ECAA. But the most notable shareholder was Edward Michell, listed as a surveyor. Nothing distinguishes him on the paperwork; he is not even listed first after the majority shareholders. When he signed the Memorandum of Association in October 1889, his address was 13 Chesterfield Grove, but on a list of shareholders dated November 1890, he was living at 28 Shirlock Road. It is only the existence of these lists which enables us to identify 'Mr E. Michel' as Edward Parsons Michell.

What we don't know is the story behind these documents. Whose idea was it? The interviews given in 1890 by 'Mr Michel' plainly set out that he was the initiator of the scheme, and later advertising described him as the 'sole originator and business manager'. Bosanquet's only public comments on the issue appeared in a letter to the *Bromley and District Times* in May 1890, in which he claimed that his involvement was for 'the promotion of cricket and other athletic exercises among women'; while he admitted being the director of the company behind the OELC, he stated that 'Mr E. Michel' was the source of the 'whole scheme'. Yet if the idea was Michell's, surely he would have been marked as more important than the lowly clerks on the Memorandum of Association. If he was to be manager, why was this not listed as his occupation? If he was so central, why did he not hold more than one share?

But there is a linked, and perhaps more important, question. When Bosanquet and Michel conceived of the scheme in the autumn of 1889, what was their initial plan? What was their vision of what the ECAA would do? The Memorandum of Association does not help, even though it set out the aims of the ECAA. The most important was the first: 'To advance and promote the exercise, pursuit and development in the United Kingdom or elsewhere of all or any of the following games, sports and pastimes.' There followed an exhaustive list of sports, headed by cricket, football and lawn tennis but also including bicycling, musical drill and dancing. For anything left out, there was a catch-all 'or any other game, sport or pastime of an athletic nature or similar in kind or character or analogous to any of those above mentioned.' The other aims in the memorandum were mainly practical ones: purchasing property or equipment; lending, borrowing or investing money; the awarding of prizes or payments to 'promote the objects of the company'; and various other legal necessities which need not concern us here.

Nowhere in more than two pages of aims, provisions and legal language was any mention of women or women's sport. Just the promotion of games, sports and pastimes.

What, then, was the ECAA planning? One answer appeared even before the paperwork had been filed. In early October 1889, an advertisement appeared in theatrical publications such as *The Stage* and *The Era* for 'The Original English Female Athletic Troupe', offering 'complete entertainment for parks, cricket grounds, fetes, or large halls.' This advert was opaque – probably deliberately so – in giving little indication what might be involved except that it would be provided by 30 women and would be 'highly attractive, and refined picturesque entertainment'. It also mentioned 'Roman sports and old English games' – which probably left the reader baffled – and promised that the troupe would be 'splendidly equipped'. They were available for booking from Easter 1890, and enquiries were directed to their manager: E. Michel of 13 Chesterfield Grove.

It is almost as if the aims of the ECAA and the aims of this Original English Female Athletic Troupe were completely different; all that apparently linked them was the occupant of 13 Chesterfield Grove. Only with his interview from May 1890 did Bosanquet suggest that the aim all along had been to promote women's cricket; neither his company's Memorandum of Association nor the early advertising made any such claim.

We do not know how successful this initial advertising campaign was, although it made no impression on the press, nor do we know if the Athletic Troupe even existed beyond the 'fertile brain' of Mr Michel. But the next time the concept was tentatively aired in public, it had been refined. And this time, there was a considerable reaction.

*　*　*

In January 1890, an advertisement appeared in the *Daily Telegraph*: 'Lawn Tennis: Lady Players Wanted for select exhibition matches. Training and costumes free. Small salary and all expenses. No premium. Applicants must be of good address and appearance, respectable, strong, active, not under 5ft 6in in height, over 22 years old. Long series – Address fully (letter only), etc. Parents and guardians invited to communicate.'

Initially, such a novel request was taken to be a joke, so a follow-up letter appeared underneath later versions of the advertisement, stating:

> The vacancies occur in the above troupe (the Original English *Lady* Cricketers), the members of which will also study lawn-tennis, Swedish drill, etc, for the purposes of playing public

matches from Easter to October. Tennis tuition and match costumes free. Members find hose, gloves, etc. Salary 10s [shillings] per week during training or practice, and from £1 to 30s during the time of public matches. Travelling expenses paid the whole time.

There was to be six-and-a-half hours of practice each day, anyone under the age of 21 needed the 'consent of their parents or guardians', and 'references as to character, etc, are also required'.

It was this advertisement which lit the spark of publicity that burned throughout 1890. It came to the attention of a journalist, who penned a rather dismissive article which concluded: 'The managers of this extraordinary venture may possibly intend to add another to the many novelty shows on view in this country, but it is to be hoped that they will not succeed. It is not altogether pleasant to see feminine acrobats, but exhibitions by professional female cricketers and lawn-tennis players will be positively painful.' And, as was common in the Victorian press, local newspapers took the article and reprinted it; the result was that the story rattled around the country for a couple of weeks.

Although that advertisement received a lot of attention, smaller ones passed unnoticed, such as those in *The Era* during January which wanted 'managers of recreation grounds, winter gardens, cricket grounds, and other large places of amusement to know that the Original English Lady Athletes' still had 'seven weeks vacant during the ensuing summer seasons'. They offered: 'Cycling, Sports, Athletics, Drill, Fencing, Assault-at-Arms, &c' and were 'trained by leading professors [professionals]'. 'Dressed, and provided with Pictorial and other, Billing equalled only by Barnum and Bailey.' The terms offered either a fixed fee or a share of the profits. There was no mention of any cricket. Enquiries were directed, inevitably, to E. Michel at 13 Chesterfield Grove, or in some adverts at St George's Hall, a theatre in Wandsworth. In February a feature published in the *South Wales Echo*, which aimed to secure bookings for the 'English Cricket and Athletic Association', said that they were 'open to accept engagements for cricket, flat racing, Roman sports, &c'. Another advertisement in *The Era* in March listed a range of attractions provided by the group now known as the Original English Lady Cricketers: a 'complete day show', an 'assault-at-arms' by night, cricket, 'crooketta', cycling, fencing, boxing and Swedish drill.

Around the same time, another series of advertisements quietly appeared in *The Era*. No connection was made to the ECAA, nor any variant of the 'Original English Lady Cricketers', nor to cricket, nor even sport. The only link was a very familiar address. For example, a January advertisement requested second-hand 'stage dresses, hose &c, suitable for principal boy or girl's parts, complete; also lady gymnast's dress and girl's leotard'. Details and the 'lowest cash price' were to be sent to 'F. H.' at 13 Chesterfield Grove. Also that month, a request appeared for a 'lady, used to bicycle troupe; also girl knowing something of trapeze work and flying rings. State experience and lowest terms for two months engagement.' Again, details were to be sent to 'F. H.' at 13 Chesterfield Grove. In February, another advertisement appeared: 'Wanted, lady bicyclist, good for trick work. Six months' tour. No turn shows. State lowest terms, age, and photos.' Details were to be sent to 13 Chesterfield Grove, but this time to 'Wheeler' (presumably a pun).

The dizzying shifts of emphasis displayed in the advertising might betray confusion or disagreement behind the scenes. Two possible scenarios could have led to this point in early 1890. Maybe Bosanquet (and the other two major shareholders) conceived of the idea of an organisation to promote cricket (which was central to the name of the ECAA and was first in the list of sports outlined in the Memorandum of Association), and appointed Edward Michell as manager because they had previously worked together. In this scenario Michell decided to make it an organisation to promote *women's* sport and drove the subsequent direction into the confusingly wide range of activities promoted between October 1889 and February 1890. Another possibility is that Michell was the driving force all along: he thought of the idea and approached Bosanquet to bankroll it; Bosanquet and the others saw potential in the idea and became involved hoping to make some money.

In either case the advertising in late 1889 and 1890 reflected Michell's original conception before his troupe transmuted into a cricket team. The spectacle being promoted was only loosely tied to the world of late-Victorian sport. The adverts were suggesting a different world, an implication that would have been grasped by anyone who read them: the world of athletic and cycling displays; the world of 'Barnum and Bailey'; the world of gymnasts wearing leotards. In other words, the world inhabited by readers of *The Era*: the stage, theatre and music hall.

Music hall was at this time approaching the height of its popularity in Victorian Britain; for example, the number of music halls in London had trebled since the 1860s, and the venues had made considerable efforts to become more 'respectable'. Audiences flocked to see performers in halls around the country; acts included song, dance, acrobatics, magicians and comedy. Also popular was burlesque, in which the stars – wearing revealing outfits by the standards of the times – parodied highbrow entertainment or mocked the upper classes. Many of the biggest stars were women. Even if male audiences may have been lured in by skimpy costumes, and the beauty of performers was probably of more interest than their talents, music hall was an opportunity for women to succeed on their own terms.

Just a hint of this world can be seen in the advertisements section of *The Era*. There were requests from all over Britain – not just London but places such as Bolton or Morley – for pianists, violinists and other musicians; vocalists; dancers; acrobats; clowns; horse riders; actors; illusionists; trapeze artists; puppeteers. And these come from just one page of one issue. Another impressive demonstration of the variety of acts available was seen in late 1889 at a tribute to the trick cyclist George Gorin, who had been killed earlier that year. An extremely well-attended tribute at the Canterbury Music Hall in London involved over a hundred acts including Gorin's own cycling troupe, a ventriloquist and 'Captain Pike and his performing fish'. Women played a sizeable role in proceedings; Miss Vesta Victoria and the 'Sisters Bushling' appeared, Miss Nelly Moore performed a sketch from *The Burglar* and Miss Jenny Hill gave a recital 'with considerable feeling' of a tribute written by Fred Bowyer.

Such a world would have held little attraction for Bosanquet and was more likely to have appealed to Michell, a man who may have worked briefly as an actor and who probably managed the 'Australian Giants' as they toured venues in 1888. The only difference between the early vision of those advertisements and the usual spectacle of music hall was the emphasis on athletic pursuits and the hint that events would take place outside. Perhaps the originator of the idea hoped that this would be sufficiently different to stand out in a crowded market. The unique twist: recruit women with the skills to put on a theatrical performance and train them in various disciplines such as cricket, tennis and athletics to provide a sporting exhibition as well. If this might seem unlikely to a modern audience, the 1890s were a different world. And this vision of breaking into music hall became a reality with the frequent evening appearances of the OELC in theatres, where the women not only performed, but were supported by other theatrical stars.

* * *

If music hall had been the plan, something clearly changed in March 1890. The nebulous proposals were replaced in the advertising with something more concrete. Stories appeared in the press with an emphasis on cricket. Several reported pieces of information, such as the names of coaches and the location of practices, were accurate enough to detect the hand of a publicist pushing information at willing journalists. One of these, reprinted in several newspapers, revealed that the parent organisation of the women's team, the English Cricket and Athletic Association, had been registered the previous October for 'the purpose of instructing ladies in "cricket's manly toil".' This can only have come from someone with knowledge of the ECAA.

In March 1890 more details emerged in a lengthy advertisement printed in *The Era* to publicise 'The Original English Lady Cricketers', which it assured readers was a registered trade mark. They would provide 'sport, not clowning' at venues throughout the summer. Various products would be on sale at these exhibitions, including photographs. and after a 'complete day show' there was to be an 'assault-at-arms' by nights. The sporting demonstrations were to include 'cricket, crooketta, bicycling, fencing, boxing and drill'; readers were assured that the women were 'Refined Lady Athletes, not Burlesque Masqueraders.'

In another vertiginous shift, the ECAA had gone from promoting a show 'equalled only by Barnum and Bailey' – in other words a circus – to promising 'sport, not clowning' and 'athletes, not burlesque masqueraders'. From this point, cricket became the priority, possibly because the idea of women cricketers had received most attention in newspapers. But it may also be connected to the syndicate behind the ECAA. Perhaps the shareholders were uncomfortable with the drift towards music hall. Here, the words of Bosanquet to the *Bromley and District Times* in May might be important: 'I insisted, at the outset, on two most important stipulations, as conditions of my co-operation, viz, that there should be, throughout, perfect respectability, and that the cricket should be as real and good as it could be made.' It may also be relevant that around March, the correspondence address of the manager of the OELC listed in the advertising materials switched to Bosanquet's offices at 11 Queen Victoria Street.

The likeliest explanation is that Bosanquet – the man holding the purse strings – had reined in some of the wilder elements and insisted on 'perfect respectability'. The change around March might reflect Bosanquet taking more control. Even so, he was reluctant to claim any credit, as reflected in the interview he gave in May and the frequent public assurances that the idea had come from Michell. But there is reason to suspect that Bosanquet was far more involved than he wanted to admit: he funded the operation, umpired several games, took a paternal interest in the women and – most importantly – his was the only name on a set of rules issued to the players. Was Michell merely his employee? A man to be the public face of an entertainment spectacle which was beneath Bosanquet's immense respectability? Probably not, but it is unfortunately not possible to pin down the precise nature of the relationship between Bosanquet and Michell, nor how much control each man had.

Whatever the balance of responsibility, what made Bosanquet and Michell decide that women's cricket would be the vehicle for their ambitions? What was their inspiration (apart from Bosanquet's love of the game)?

One possibility was an idea from half a century beforehand. In the 1840s and 1850s, teams of male professional cricketers toured England playing matches against local teams. This idea, begun by William Clarke with his 'All-England Eleven', has been credited with increasing the popularity of cricket in England and introducing it to areas where it had rarely been played. Maybe that is what Bosanquet envisaged: a pioneering tour which spread the gospel of women's cricket, just as Clarke had done for men. He certainly gave that impression in his letter to the *Bromley Times*, in which he suggested that the OELC were 'the first serious attempt to promote the game of cricket amongst the members of the weaker sex'. He observed that 'there is a great deal of ladies' cricket in this country', against which there were 'great prejudices' to be overcome, 'more especially in the southern counties'.

Through their cricket, he hoped that his OELC would 'convert' these opponents.

* * *

Bosanquet's summary of the state of women's cricket in England in 1890 was fair but not quite the whole picture. Women's sport in general was emerging from a dark period during which it had been actively discouraged. In pre-Victorian times, it was quite common for women to play cricket, even with elements of pseudo-professionalism; several matches between 1790 and 1835 were played for prize money or involved collections for successful players. However, the lack of leisure time for most women following the Industrial Revolution meant that access to the game became restricted to the upper classes.

By the late 1830s women's cricket had effectively fizzled out, and Victorian moralists suppressed any possibility of a revival. A widely accepted argument was that strenuous physical activity such as that involved in cricket and other sports could harm women – a notion which found echoes in some press reactions to the OELC – or in some way 'defeminise' them. The stereotypical Victorian view of women as weak, vulnerable and overly emotional convinced those with the power to make decisions that female sport should not be allowed. In cricket, women were reduced to mythical supporting roles: the legend that overarm bowling was invented by Christine Willes, who found the prevailing underarm style impossible owing to the width of her skirt; or the idea that Martha Grace coached her son William Gilbert Grace into the great cricketer that he became.

For most of the Victorian period, cricket was something that women watched, not played. The first glimmer of progress came in schools. Education available to girls was rooted in the notion that a woman's place was at home; therefore, it bore no relation to the equivalent experience for boys, which had a heavy emphasis on sport. For many years, physical education played little part in girls' curricula because the men who drew them up believed women were too weak and fragile for such activities.

During the 1880s such orthodoxy began to be challenged as physical education and fitness began to assume greater importance in the minds of educators. The growing obsession in public schools with the cult of games, comradeship, fair play and a healthy body began to seep into girls' education and was adopted by female educationists. Despite the reservations of male commentators, several influential women – such as the Swiss-born Martina Bergman-Österberg, the Lawrence sisters who founded Roedean School, or Frances Dove at Wycombe Abbey School – won a reluctant acceptance that girls could take part in sport at school without lasting moral or physical harm, and might in fact benefit from it.

From there, the introduction of team games into girls' schools was the logical step, and cricket, having a particular association with moral decency, was an obvious choice. In contrast to boys' schools, any competitive element was discouraged, and there was that ever-present concern that cricket could be 'de-feminising'. Even so, the sport proved popular and there were occasional matches between girls' schools, although there remained an expectation that girls would stop playing once they left formal education. For example, W. G. Grace's only daughter Bessie was a good cricketer but he would not let her continue playing once her schooldays were over. However, a growing number of women's cricket clubs formed in the 1880s, the most famous (but not the first) being the White Heather Club, which had 50 members by 1891. However, these clubs were generally the preserve of the upper classes, not ordinary people.

Not only cricket but women's sport in general grew in popularity towards the end of the 19th century. Lawn tennis, for example, became popular not least for the social opportunities of mixed doubles. However, men constantly – often mockingly – dismissed the notion that women could ever be good at sport, and eyebrows would have been raised at any participant taking matters too seriously. There was also a hierarchy of respectability: cricket, tennis and hockey were reasonably acceptable, but athletics was questionable among the upper and middle classes. As Richard Holt wrote in *Sport and the British*, his historical survey of British sport: 'Appearing scantily-clad in public in a sport which was cheap and therefore open to lower class participation was regarded as unsuitable for girls from "good homes".' Such an attitude might explain why Bosanquet – the epitome of the 'good home' – would have had reservations about some of the plans advertised for 'Original English Lady Athletes' and why the focus switched to the far more acceptable sport of cricket.

But Bosanquet had one major reservation – expressed in his letter to the *Bromley Times* – about contemporary women's cricket. The most common and popular games involved female cricketers playing against teams of men who batted, bowled and fielded left-handed to even up the contest. Bosanquet noted that this led to matches which were 'from a cricket point of view, very melancholy functions indeed'. Instead, Bosanquet seemed to want genuine competitive cricket for women; as such, he held a view which most men of his class would have vehemently opposed.

Perhaps more importantly though, he wanted to create a good spectacle because the revolutionary part of the scheme was that spectators would pay to watch the games. For female players, this was unprecedented; there had never been genuine professional women cricketers, even in pre-Victorian times. Professionalism was anathema to the male cricketing and sporting establishment, and to amateur club cricketers like Bosanquet. For him to embrace it was remarkable, although his radicalism was quite likely motivated by the desire to make a profit from the spectacle.

Therefore, his wish expressed to the *Bromley Times* that the cricket played by the women should be 'as real and good as it could be made' was not as altruistic as it might first appear. His anticipation of criticism – which would not be disappointed – betrayed the simple fact that the largely male consumers of booming spectator sports such as football and cricket viewed the women's version of these games as inauthentic. If the OELC were to be commercially viable and attract crowds, the cricket had to be of a standard good enough to persuade people it was worth seeing. Nothing like that had ever been attempted. Therefore, Bosanquet engaged professional coaching and Michell arranged for extended practices to produce the desired authenticity. In his own words, the entrepreneurial solicitor spared 'no pains or expense'.

* * *

Bosanquet's use of the word 'real' is slightly double-edged because there had been attempts in this period to produce cricket as 'entertainment' rather than sport. Some theatres had worked with cricket clubs in the 19th century to provide 'gala benefits' for professionals and in the late 1880s there was at least one team of 'lady cricketers', comprising theatrical stars such as Vane Featherstone and Maude Millett, which played against male artists and journalists.

But the most notorious example of cricketing entertainment was the bizarre and little-discussed late-19th-century phenomenon of 'clown cricket'. Although good cricketers played for the teams of clown cricketers – including the county players Tom Emmett, Edmund Peate and Walter Gilbert, who appeared under pseudonyms – the games were intended to provide farcical amusement. Batting and bowling were taken relatively seriously, although there were sometimes trick bats that allowed balls to pass through; it was only in fielding and during breaks in play that the 'clown' aspect predominated, for example through the performance of acrobatics and comedy routines. But in a foreshadowing of what would happen with the OELC, visits of touring clown cricket teams were highly anticipated in many places; and like the OELC, the players often featured in local theatres in the evenings.

Clown cricketers continued to operate into the 1890s, as did clown footballers; however, the number of teams declined over the years from their height in the 1870s. Such enterprises were unsuccessful and faded when it transpired that crowds wanted to see genuine cricket. The echoes with the OELC are numerous enough to suggest that someone was familiar with the old format but it clearly did not appeal to Bosanquet, whose commercial instincts might have warned him that the cricket of his OELC needed to be high quality to attract audiences and avoid the fate of clown cricket. And he was doubtless aware that many people would have placed women's cricket on the same level as 'clown cricket'.

* * *

Bosanquet's vision was some considerable way from the spectacle being offered in the early advertising for the OELC, making it likely that the final format was driven by his twin desires for 'perfect respectability, and that the cricket should be as real and good as it could be made'. Michell's music hall aspirations survived but were subordinate to the sport; a considerable reverse from what originally might have been planned.

So much for where – or from whom – the idea of the OELC might have arisen. There is much that we do not know. But the team quickly took on a life of its own because the plan required players.

These must have been recruited over the course of several months around January 1890. Presumably most responded to the adverts in the press, and by the time the cricket season started the OELC had enough recruits to fill the two teams of Reds and Blues, as well as some reserves. And it was these players who brought the OELC to life. We know little about many of them, and we can only guess why most applied to become part of the strange troupe.

But we should begin with the story of one woman whose motivation was clear: she joined as the consequence of a shocking murder.

The Players

ONE NIGHT in June 1889, a man called George Gorin was stabbed to death outside the Canterbury Music Hall, a large establishment catering to the middle classes, on Westminster Bridge Road in Lambeth. Gorin's attacker made no attempt to escape, but unsuccessfully attempted suicide; although badly hurt, he was taken into custody and charged with murder. To the shaken world of the music hall, Gorin had been known as 'Professor Letine', the manager of the 'Wondrous Letine Troupe' which consisted of his wife Olga ('Madame Letine'), three young girls and a nine-year-old boy, all of whom gave displays of trick cycling and acrobatics. The Letines were one of the most famous of a growing number of cycling troupes providing entertainment in music halls and theatres in the late 1880s. At the time of Gorin's death, his troupe were performing several shows each night. But the involvement of young children created a whiff of exploitation which is how Gorin came to meet his very public demise.

His killer, Nathaniel Curragh, believed Gorin to be responsible for the death of his daughter Beatrice, who had signed with the Letine Troupe in 1886 at the age of 13. She died from illness – possibly tuberculosis – late in 1888 but her father suspected she had been ill-treated by Gorin. This belief might have reflected Curragh's disturbed mental state rather than the reality. At the trial, he was found to be unfit to enter a plea on the grounds of insanity and sent to Broadmoor prison, where he died in 1915.

A tribute to Gorin was held at the Canterbury in August 1889 and raised over £200 for his widow Olga – 'Madame Letine' – who expressed her thanks in an advert taken out in *The Era*. The other cyclists of the 'Wondrous Letine Troupe' faced a far more uncertain future. One of their number was the 16-year-old Katie Tatton, a horror-struck witness to her employer's murder, who had testified at his inquest.

Born in 1873,[2] Catherina Tatton was the daughter of William Tatton, a copper plate printer from Lambeth, and Harriett O'Grady from Limerick. Baptised as a Roman Catholic at St George's Cathedral in Southwark, Tatton went to Walnut Tree Walk School in Lambeth, but her life is otherwise a mystery until she testified against Curragh in 1889. She subsequently performed at Gorin's tribute and continued to live with Madame Letine, but clearly needed a new job.

The solution arrived in the form of the advertisements placed by Michell in early 1890 looking for an experienced cyclist who could perform 'trick work'. These could almost have been designed to appeal directly to Tatton; it is not hard to see why she leapt at the opportunity. Did she know she was signing for a sports team? Possibly not as there was no such indication in the advertisements. In fact, Tatton never seems to have lifted a bat in anger during her time with the OELC.

---

2   Her birthdate is a little uncertain. When she was registered at Walnut Tree Walk School, her birthdate was given as 27th March 1874 but she was baptised on 10 March 1873.

***

If we can trace the circumstances which led Tatton to join a sporting organisation, the motivations of her colleagues are more of a mystery. Around 40 women played at least once for the OELC in 1890; owing to the inaccuracy of newspaper reports, we cannot be more precise.[3] Although we can identify many of them, some players remain nothing more than a name on a scorecard. Only a handful can be traced confidently enough to give a reasonable picture of their lives, and there are just five women for whom we have surviving accounts in their own words. This makes it a challenge to understand why, or indeed how, they came to play for the OELC.

But if the women rarely spoke for themselves, their manager was more than happy to talk on their behalf. In the 1890 interview which transformed him from a lowly surveyor into a French-born entrepreneur, Edward Michell invented similarly fabricated backgrounds for his players. By this stage, he had a clear picture that he wanted to present to the public and therefore made some grand claims on their behalf. According to Michell, the 'girls' were of a 'superior class': two were daughters of 'West End physicians', two were daughters of a dentist and two were daughters of an architect. He stated: 'It is of vast importance to us that the respectability of the girls should be above suspicion, because a good deal of their work will be to play in private matches among the gentry.'

---

[3] In the two seasons the OELC operated, 61 different names are associated with the club but some of these could be duplicates or mis-transcriptions.

Each claim was an outright lie with a clear purpose: in Victorian England a person was judged on their background, making the occupation and 'class' of the players' fathers a reflection of their own respectability. To attract audiences with a higher social status, and to convince prospective hirers of the legitimacy of the OELC, Michell needed to place his players 'above suspicion'. In reality, none of the players' fathers were doctors or dentists and, with a couple of possible exceptions, none came from the 'superior' background advertised by Michell.

Most of the women were working class and some lived in obvious poverty. We can confidently trace 22 of their fathers, who held a variety of skilled and unskilled jobs. And buried in various records – the census returns, the birth certificates, the marriage certificates, and a few other sources – there is just enough information to tell us why these women might have risked joining such an unusual and potentially disreputable enterprise as the OELC.

Several appear to have suffered considerable hardship; for them, the financial incentive must have been extremely attractive. Elizabeth Talitha (Lizzie) Sanders was only 15 when she joined the OELC but her father had died before her second birthday. Lizzie lived with her mother and older sister, both of whom worked as dressmakers; her brother had joined the army. At the time of the 1891 census, the three women shared a house with two other families, a common arrangement in Victorian England whereby landlords maximised their property: the Sanders family had three rooms between them, presumably representing a floor of the three-storey house. It is not a stretch to imagine that they were poor, and an opportunity to join the OELC must have seemed a heaven-sent opportunity.

There are other players for whom escaping poverty could have been the motivating factor, prompted by the death of a family member. The family of Susan Fletcher Shemmonds had moved from Staffordshire to London following the death of her father, a druggist and grocer, in 1884. Their declining fortunes are illustrated in the censuses: the family had a servant in 1881 but by 1891 Shemmonds, her mother and her widowed sister (an insurance clerk) were, like the Sanders family, renting rooms alongside two other households. It may have been a similar tale for the Scottish-born Allina (Lena) Parsons, whose father (a surveyor) had been dead for some years when she joined the OELC at the age of 19; her family had moved from Inverness in Scotland to London, where she and her sister Mary were admitted to Thanet Street School in 1881. By 1891 Lena and her mother lived with Mary and her husband. There is much that is unclear; her aunt ran a jewellery shop in Aberdeen, where Lena had lived with her family for a time. Why did they choose a more difficult life in London?

Changing family circumstances may also explain why the 21-year-old Mary Louisa Daly joined the OELC; her father had been a Metropolitan Policeman but by 1891 he was working as a milk carrier and supporting six children. The census records three lodgers living with them in a property which held another three households, one of which occupied a single room (although the Daly household was spread over at least five). Another player accustomed to cramped conditions was Annie Hampson, who was originally from Somerset but had moved with her parents to London. Her father was a mason; the 1891 census shows the family living in a single room of a house in St Pancras.

The backgrounds of other players indicates that their families might have had more financial security, even if life was not exactly comfortable. Sophie Blanche Charles was one of six children; her father had been a fishmonger but by the time of the 1891 census was a general dealer. Perhaps the need to keep a roof over so many heads prompted her to find work, aged only 17. Other families were involved in jobs which carried little social status. Florence Emma Hardwick was the daughter of a dairyman and might have worked for him before she turned to cricket. Emma Georgina Sheffield's father was a fishmonger. And the sisters Eliza (Ella) and Ada Heather came from a family of lightermen.[4]

It is likely that the Charles, Hardwick, Sheffield and Heather families had steady incomes and in 1891 they all lived in private houses which they did not have to share with others, even if the properties might have been small or crowded. For these women, it is less obvious why they would have needed to join the OELC but money was still probably a driving factor.

Slightly different was the case of the 19-year-old Elizabeth Margaret Dempsey, born in Ireland in 1871. She was the daughter of William Dempsey, a sergeant in the 43rd Foot Regiment of the British Army. The nomadic lifestyle of the family is illustrated in the birthplaces of the Dempsey children: Elizabeth's siblings were born in places as varied as Jersey and India. William died in 1886 in Portsmouth, after which Dempsey's mother married a publican.

---

4 Lightermen carried cargo along the River Thames in flat-bottomed barges called lighters; they were required to hold a licence, for which they had to serve a five-year apprenticeship.

Nellie Wadkin also had a stepfather who was a publican. Her father, Samuel Charles Wadkin, had been a timber dealer (although he seems to have worked more in the building trade) but had been admitted to Bethlehem Lunatic Asylum in February 1878, and died there just under four months later. Could Dempsey and Wadkin have been driven into cricket through being unwanted stepdaughters? Or had the changing family circumstances made additional income necessary?

At least two of the players were married when they joined. Annie Emma Light (née Nicholas)[5] was the daughter of an agricultural labourer and wife of a coal porter, whom she had married in 1887. It is quite likely that the extra money would have been a strong motivation for her. The other married player seems to have been Marie Lisle, whose identity cannot be established with certainty, although it is likely that her husband was an actor.

But it would be inaccurate to say that all the women came from impoverished backgrounds. For example, Annie Adele Matthey was the 19-year-old daughter of a Swiss-born restaurant manager who in 1891 lived on Agar Street opposite Charing Cross Hospital. Beatrice and Flora Barefoot were daughters of a timber merchant who lived in a terrace located in a prosperous area of Camberwell. Similarly privileged, living in a terrace in a well-to-do part of Lewisham, were Grace and Violet Lyon, the daughters of a stationer (who had also been the manager of a mill

---

5 Annie Emma Nicholas was almost certainly the player known as Beatrice Light, who according to publicity material was born in Southampton in 1870. This matches with Nicholas. The other possibility is a woman called Beatrice Light, but she was born in London in 1868, making her a less likely candidate; her father was a railway goods manager wealthy enough to employ servants.

and an auctioneer). Elizabeth Moss was the daughter of a bookbinder and her family lived in a Tottenham terraced house.

And some of the women did not quite fit into any category. Mary Willett was the daughter of a coachman and domestic servant, living with her large family in a small terrace in Beckenham. The father of Daisy Berry was a clerk of works who lived in Ramsgate. And the most curious recruits were Edith and Florence Woodward, the daughters of a prominent music dealer in Cheltenham.

Despite Michell's grandiose claims on their behalf, this disparate group of women, whose ages ranged from 15 to 26, spanned the working and lower-middle classes. And while we cannot be certain – not least because they never discussed the issue publicly – it was likely the prospect of a good salary that convinced the majority to pursue an unlikely career in cricket. The initial contracts were for two-year engagements, although many of the first recruits dropped out after less than a year and the OELC folded before the contracts could be fulfilled. There is no question that the wage was generous. The January advert said: 'Salary 10s per week during training or practice, and from £1 to 30s during the time of public matches. Travelling expenses paid the whole time.' These figures were largely confirmed in the 1892 court case. The team trained from roughly January to March and played from April to October. Therefore, the maximum wage would probably have been around £50, although most players would presumably have received a lower amount; there was also a small bonus if their team won.

This was a surprisingly good salary, although it did not quite match what was available in men's cricket. For comparison, professional county cricketers at the time earned anywhere between £70 and £250 during a season, excluding winter pay, benefits and collections for good performances. This was roughly between £3 10s per week for a member of the groundstaff to £12 10s for a leading player. Other male professionals in this period earned varying amounts: northern leagues offered over £3 per week in some cases, but 30s per week would have been a fair wage for a male professional at a local level. Bosanquet – who provided the money – and Michell were (probably unintentionally) paying a very competitive amount; for a woman to earn the same as a man in the 1890s was highly unusual. In other spheres, the average annual wage for men in the United Kingdom in 1890 was just over £50, but this varied depending on the kind of work and the location. A male manual worker in London might earn up to £100, agricultural workers received around £40, wool and cotton workers even less. Women were usually paid less than half of those amounts; members of the OELC, in contrast, earned more than many working men.

* * *

Although no one ever commented publicly on the OELC wages, it is unlikely that men would have approved of such radical equality. Victorian England was a male-dominated, misogynistic society in which women had few rights: they could not vote; they were expected to give up a job – if they had one – when they married in order to become a 'housewife'; they were infantilised and treated with condescension. Enormous areas of life taken for granted by men were closed to them. But in the period leading up to the end of the 19th century – known at the time and to historians since as the *fin de siècle*[6] – these traditional attitudes were increasingly challenged as society changed rapidly in ways which made many men uncomfortable.

The legal status of women had gradually improved – for example with the Married Women's Property Act of 1882 or the Guardianship of Infants Act of 1886 – and there was growing political pressure to make further reforms. An attempt to bring about women's suffrage was defeated in 1884 but there were demands that women be admitted to universities and that female wages should be increased. There was even a sense – perhaps more in the imagination of men than in reality – that there could be a 'revolution of women'. Female writers questioned what it meant to be a woman and a new word emerged: feminism. Part of this maelstrom was the idea of 'New Women', a term not coined until 1894 but a familiar concept by 1890: women who were increasingly unwilling to play the roles assigned to them by men.

In this context, a team of mainly working-class, independent and well-paid women would have embodied many fears, and instilled terror among upper- and middle-class men, who quite possibly perceived them as an existential threat. That the cricketers were single – or at least believed to be – would have heightened these concerns. Feminist thinkers had begun to argue that marriage should not be the only aim in life, and it was possible to have freedom as a single woman. These unmarried women – known as 'odd women' – were viewed with suspicion and contempt by the male establishment.

---

6 For those living through it, the term *fin de siècle* often carried negative overtones of social degeneration and change for the worse.

The reaction in wider society to 'New Women' was predictable: the fear that masculinity would be destroyed prompted the deliberate exclusion of women from male life. As the literary critic Elaine Showalter put it: 'As woman sought opportunities for self-development outside of marriage, medicine and science warned that such ambitions would lead to sickness, freakishness, sterility, and racial degeneration.' The ideas of 'New Women' were blamed for an apparent growth in 'nervous disorders'. Some of these notions find an echo in the dire warnings of what would happen to women who took part in competitive sport and were always in the background when male writers continually complained about, belittled and dismissed the efforts of the OELC. If cricket was seen as a reflection of all that was best about Victorian England, it was inevitable that the encroachment of women would provoke fear.

But could any of the OELC recruits have been inspired by the movements of the *fin de siècle* or the idea of 'New Women'? Did any of them have a desire to strike out independently? Perhaps, but the 'New Woman' was often a product of men's fevered concerns; how much ordinary women subscribed to these ideas, or were even aware of them, is uncertain. 'New Women' were more likely to be found in fiction than in the streets; if 20th-century feminists saw in them the seeds of their own movement, their 19th-century contemporaries were less enthused.

Players like Sanders and Tatton clearly had more pressing concerns than abstract notions of 'New Women'. Nevertheless, it is just possible that one or two of the players *did* subscribe to some of these notions; there is no direct evidence, and we do not have any relevant testimony from the women themselves, but some of their actions *might* just hint at some sort of political ideology.

* * *

If one possible motivation to join the OELC was financial and another political, there were other considerations that might have affected individuals. There are several women who had some kind of link with theatre and music before they joined. For example, Florence Woodward, one of the older players at the age of 26, had been working as a musician's assistant since the age of 17. In later years, she and the man she married worked as actors, while her sister Edith Woodward became a dance teacher. Other potential theatrical connections can be found in the lives of Lena Parsons, whose brother-in-law was a theatrical manager, and Marie Lisle, who was probably an actress. Similarly, the roles that the women went on to take in the OELC's evening performances might give a hint why they joined: Daisy Berry, Sophie Charles, Emma Hardwick, Adele Matthey and Bessie Moss took part in fencing displays; Ella Heather and Violet Lyon performed single stick (a once-popular martial art in which competitors used a stick); and Bianca Seymour (who is hard to identify with certainty, but who might have come from a theatrical background) performed capably on the piano and banjo. Maybe for them, the OELC was simply about giving performances and they saw it as just another theatrical or musical venture; perhaps the cricket side was incidental or even unwelcome.

And some could have come just for the sport. Elizabeth Dempsey might have been a proficient sportswoman if the reference to a Lizzie Dempsey who took second place in a swimming competition at Portsmouth in 1886 refers to our cricketer (who almost certainly lived there at the time). Mary Willett, the only member of the OELC who ever spoke of her experiences in later years, told Netta Rheinberg in 1956 that she had applied after a friend showed her an advertisement offering 'a professional engagement to women interested in cricket'. Willett said: 'I had played the game as a youngster and ... I was always a very fast runner and used to win all the races at school.' Perhaps it was athletics as well as cricket that attracted her.

Both Willett and her friend applied for the OELC but the latter was turned down. Rejection was the fate of many applicants, if we can believe the claims in newspapers that around 200 women applied, of whom 30 were selected. But this might be one of Michell's pieces of propaganda, because the number 30 was mentioned in the earliest advertisements in 1889, before any players could have been recruited.

We know nothing about how the numbers were whittled down; was there a cricketing trial that involved demonstrating their batting, bowling or fielding ability? Willett, for example, merely said that she was accepted. Was there an audition of their musical or theatrical abilities? Was Bosanquet involved, was the decision Michell's alone or did they recruit coaches or theatrical performers to advise them? We simply don't know. The only certainty is that the players cannot have been recruited only for their cricket ability.

We can only guess at their feelings at being involved in such a scheme – at least until the events of 1891 made their opinions very public – or what they thought about Michell and Bosanquet. The high turnover of players might be our only hint that some were less than enchanted with the OELC.

***

If the answer to the question of who the players were remains cloudy, the means of their recruitment opaque, and their motivations impenetrable, we have a much clearer picture about what happened to the women after they were accepted.

Once cricket became the primary focus, for the spectacle to be as serious as Bosanquet wanted, the women had to be trained. To this end, someone – either Michell or Bosanquet – engaged professionals to do the job. The main coach, who remained with the OELC throughout 1890 and into 1891, was a man called William Matthews. Almost nothing is known about him, and he has proven impossible to locate on the census or any other records. One report called him 'an old member of the Surrey club', another 'a well-known school coach', and a third said that he had formerly played for Kingston Town. There are no definite traces of him in the pages of *Cricket: A Weekly Record of the Game*; the closest we come are a handful of instances in the 1890s which might be him but equally could be a different W. Matthews playing club cricket in the Surrey area. Similarly, newspapers record someone called Matthews associated with Kingston in 1862 and 1879, but there are no other details and we have no way of knowing if this is our coach.

Whoever he was, Matthews was solely in charge of the cricketing side of the operation. But because he lacked 'star quality', other coaches were employed to get the players up to speed and provide greater publicity. The most famous, mentioned several times in the pre-season advertising, was the Surrey and England bowler George Lohmann, but in reality he seems to have only been involved briefly, as was his brother Stewart. Far more important were George Hearne of Kent and Maurice Read of Surrey. Michell revealed in his interview that Hearne had taken some convincing to become involved; he 'came down eight times before he would agree to train the girls'. Hearne and Read's names were prominent in advertising, providing reassurance that the women had received the best possible training, but others also coached for a time, including Hearne's brother Alec, and Fred Bowley of Worcestershire. Another slightly mysterious member of the coaching group was Charles Billet, who featured on some advertisements in July as one of the leading coaches, but was absent from other publicity material.

When did training begin? The advert from the *Daily Telegraph* might indicate a date around January 1890, and that it comprised daily practice. Reports once the season began – which should be taken with a pinch of salt as they were designed to promote the team – said that the women had begun cricket practice in October 1889. Another hint came from one of the players, who said that Stewart Lohmann had worked with them late in 1889. Michell claimed in his interview that because the women had no prior knowledge, it had taken the coaches six weeks to teach them how to bowl, and the whole enterprise had cost £2,000 in total by April 1890. Whatever Michell's original plans might have incorporated, and if Bosanquet did have to rein him in, cricket must always have been ongoing behind the scenes. In any case, there must have been at least three months of practice for most of the team.

Our one eyewitness to what took place is Mary Willett but, given that she was speaking more than 60 years later, her memories were hazy. We also know that she was one of the later recruits, so her experience might have been a little different to those who were involved for longer. She remembered practising once a week indoors 'on matting in a hall at Wandsworth' – which must have been St George's Hall, a correspondence address of 'Mr Michel' and the main location for training – and outdoors at Balham. She recalled being coached by Matthews, George and Alec Hearne, Read and Bowley.

A more detailed picture emerges thanks to a reporter who spoke to some of the players while they were training in early March, almost a month before they made their public debut on the field. It is not quite clear from the context whether this was an indoor or outdoor practice, but the mention of an incident with a trapeze suggests that he saw them indoors at St George's Hall. The feature was almost certainly arranged by Michell as part of a publicity drive which aimed to make everyone aware of his team of women cricketers; in November 1890, a writer in *Cricket: A Weekly Record of the Game* revealed (in the only mention of the OELC in that publication) that he and 'about half a dozen' other journalists had gone to interview the lady cricketers in Wandsworth earlier that year, most likely during the practices.

The March article stated that 'some of the girls have been practising for months past; others have only had one or two months of it as yet. They practise in neat serge frocks, long enough to be modest, and short enough to be convenient. They wear neat little leg pads, and underneath their loose vests they wear ingeniously constructed breastplate arrangements to preserve them from injury.' The writer watched one woman who had been batting check the clock when she was called off to ascertain if she had received her allotted time. He singled out some players:

Ada Heather, 'a good all-round cricketer [who batted] in a beautiful easy style against the bowling of Matthews, the professional, and several of the girls'; 'Miss Matthey, the little all-round W. G. of the team'. When Matthey bowled Ada Heather, the wicket-keeper Miss Moss – known as 'Mossy' – shouted, 'Yorked her!' But Heather began to bat well, encouraged by Matthews, who coached her to 'keep that left elbow well forward'.

The practice was clearly enthusiastic – although that could have been exaggerated for the journalist – and the women assured him how they did not mind the occasional knock with the ball. One of them revealed how she had been struck in the eye, but it 'serves me right for not keeping that elbow well forward ... we have been told, too, often enough.' Miss Sheffield and Miss Daly had also been injured when they fell from a trapeze, which they had been 'forbidden to touch', while 'skylarking'. The presence of a trapeze raises the question (albeit unasked in the article) of what they were practising apart from cricket. But the journalist mentioned, almost in passing, that 'one or two of the ladies' had a background in gymnastics: for example, Miss Matthey 'has distinguished herself at the Polytechnic'. This intriguing hint, which was never followed up, almost certainly refers to the Regent Street Polytechnic, which is now the University of Westminster. Gymnastics displays – of a very similar nature to those which would be put on by the OELC in their evening performances – were regularly provided by women gymnasts. How many of the players, especially those who shone in the evening, came from the Polytechnic?

The author also spoke to George Hearne and Maurice Read, who were assisting Matthews during that practice.

They spoke appreciatively of how well the women had taken to cricket, although the former criticised their tendency to pull the ball too often. Hearne singled out Matthey for her one-handed catches, while Read observed that the whole team were 'as hard as nails' and it would be impossible for 'an eleven of girls' to beat them. Read praised the ability of Miss Fletcher and Ella Heather to play forward to Matthews, and suggested that they, and Miss Sheffield, were able to handle most of what Matthews sent down to them.

* * *

Aside from their training, there was another form of preparation. Several women adopted pseudonyms. Mary Willett remembered that Matthews *ordered* them to do so, but this cannot quite be correct given that at least 18 players used their real names. We know the actual identities of nine pseudonymous players but the others managed to disguise themselves sufficiently that we do not know who they were.

Katie Tatton had a foot in both camps: publicity material called her Katie Tatton, but some reports called her Katie Letine, suggesting that she kept her old cycling identity. Not a huge amount of thought appears to have gone into alternative names. Mary Willett, for example, adopted the name Beckenham after her birthplace. Violet and Grace Lyon took the surname of Westbrook, after a mill which had once been managed by their father in their birthplace of Godalming.[7]

---

[7] For the avoidance of confusion, from this point we shall mainly refer to all players by their 'stage' names; in a similar vein, we shall refer to the team manager as Mr Michel – the name used by the press – rather than Mr Michell.

What is less certain is why players chose to adopt new names at all. Some of those who did so came from slightly more affluent backgrounds and therefore might have been seeking anonymity; alternatively, it was common practice in theatre to adopt different names and so they may have been following this precedent. Neither explanation satisfies completely and none of the players were especially secretive about their true names. Elizabeth Dempsey was listed as Elizabeth Nora Dare on early publicity material, but she was quite happy to go by her real name on all the scorecards for matches; and Violet Westbrook revealed her identity to a journalist during the season.

But anyone hoping to remain anonymous would have been infuriated by the massive publicity campaign which preceded the 1890 season and put the name 'Original English Lady Cricketers' on everyone's lips.

Preparations for the Show

WHILE TRAINING for the players was ongoing, 'Mr E. Michel' was trying to ensure that they had somewhere to play. Although the first advertisements, which appeared in October 1889, claimed that many games had already been organised, this was probably a fabrication. There were gaps in the fixture list as late as June 1890.

The earliest advertising appealed directly to 'managers of recreation grounds' informing them of the 'Original English Lady Athletes'. Michel offered them 'terms, share or certainty'. Our best evidence of how Michel negotiated comes from Great Yarmouth. In April 1890, he wrote on behalf of the ECAA to the Great Yarmouth Amusement Committee requesting the use of their Recreation Ground. He offered three options: a flat fee simply to hire their ground; a 25 per cent share of the gate receipts in return for the use of the pavilion and other facilities; or a 40 per cent share which further included the provision of police, attendants, local advertising, a band and the posting of advertising bills. The Great Yarmouth Committee opted for the 25 per cent share and reserved the right to provide refreshments. Similar offers were doubtless made to grounds across the country; the option of sharing profits must have been attractive, offering little risk with potentially large returns from even a moderate crowd.

However, the reception was not always so cordial. In March 1890, Michel had written to Leighton Buzzard Cricket Club offering to hire their ground in May at a cost of £3 3s. The committee voted in favour – by four votes to two – but the lessee of the ground, Mr G. L. B. Calcott, protested that they had over-reached their authority; some club members were equally unhappy and a meeting was called to discuss the issue. A lively debate ensued. One dissenter protested that the women had been practising 'in a barn'; another complained that the ground was being used for a 'commercial speculation' which would not benefit the club. But others saw the benefit to the community of attracting spectators to such an event and so the members voted to allow the OELC to use the ground. Calcott would not, however, be moved, refusing even to discuss the matter further, and the proposal fell through. Instead, Michel arranged for the teams to play at the nearby Linslade Cricket Club.

Finding places to play continued to be an issue. Especially in 1890, few matches took place on actual cricket grounds; many were played on little more than fields. For example, at the Cheltenham Petty Session in early June, the proprietor of the Royal Oak public house was granted a licence which allowed the OELC to play in a 'field adjoining Pittville Gardens'. And when Michel's attempt to arrange the use of 'Mr Oldrid's Park' in Boston was unsuccessful, he paid the town's football club to use the Lord Nelson Ground instead.

Some of the venues proved unsuited to cricket. There was often no dedicated cricket pitch; coconut matting was sometimes used, but batting conditions were usually terrible, resulting in extremely low scores. Other problems included the need to keep non-paying spectators out of grounds not designed for such measures, leading to clumsy solutions such as canvas screens to block the view from outside. A regular lack of suitable facilities meant the women often changed in tents. Some grounds had no 'boundary', such as at Chiswick, so that scores were all-run (with no fours or sixes), while at others such as Clifton the small dimensions of the playing area led to frequent fours.

Despite these teething problems, the ECAA were clearly ambitious, arranging a programme which involved travelling the country. Such an operation was too much for Michel to manage alone, and local arrangements were left in the hands of others. Sometimes this would be the people who booked the OELC to appear, such as Edmund Tearle, the manager of the Theatre Royal, who organised the visit of the OELC to the Pitsmoor Ground in Sheffield. But Michel also had a group of regional agents who had responsibility for different parts of the country, such as F. W. Walden of Liverpool. And for a time, he had the assistance of a deputy manager, Ernest Norris, who was an actor at the Grand Theatre in Islington.[8]

These local representatives handled publicity and the organisation for the day of the match. Advertisements, whether paid for directly by Michel or by his agents, appeared in local newspapers as well as national theatrical publications such as *The Stage* and *The Era*. But the manager also hired people to put up fliers where the team were to play. We know that an 'advertising contractor' called Charles Cave was hired in Reigate because he subsequently quoted an 'unsolicited testimonial' from Edward Michel in his own publicity material.

---

8 A feature in *Music Hall* named one manager as 'Mr Hill Sley', almost certainly an error in transcription.

There is one other piece of evidence of how arrangements worked; in late October 1890, a man called Henry Morgan sued the ECAA for around £50 in the Liverpool Court of Passage on the grounds that he had not received wall posters in time for the OELC's second visit to Liverpool. The plaintiff argued that the match was unsuccessful because of this. On 11 June, Morgan had engaged the OELC to appear ten days later; the agreement stated that Michel would provide 'a number of pictorial posters, bills, lithographs, and photographs' by 12 June to allow time for 'distribution to the billposters'. But only a small number arrived before the game; Morgan even had to pay extra because Michel had not covered the costs of delivery. The representatives of the ECAA disputed in court that there had been an agreed delivery date and 'denied that the non-delivery occasioned any loss to the plaintiff'. The claim was settled out of court for £15.

Other organisational matters also went awry. There was a disagreement at Exeter in September when the team refused to play owing to the wind blowing away the canvas screen surrounding the field. The desperate state of the pavilion in which they were supposed to change also dismayed the players, one of whom called it a 'cow shed'. Michel blamed the lessee of the ground, Mr R. Bradley, although the local newspapers were less sympathetic, reasoning that Michel should have checked for himself. And an indignant letter appeared in the local press from Bradley, who cast more light on the process. He had been contacted by 'the person who engaged them for the West of England' around a month before the game. Bradley had recommended another venue, with better facilities, but nothing had come of this and the match had been advertised as taking place at his ground, somewhat to his surprise. Bradley continued, in his own defence: 'The person who brought the teams here did none of the following things which I understand, according to the agreement, he was supposed to do. He brought no tent for the use of the teams, engaged no police, gate men, ground men, or band, and never came near the ground till a few minutes to one on the day of the match.' Michel said to Bradley that both of them had been badly served by 'the party who brought the company into the West of England'.

Another arrangement which left something to be desired emerged the following March, when a printing firm applied for a summons against Thomas Martin, the proprietor of the Bath Hotel in Plymouth, to receive payment of the £6 10s he owed for 'printing and advertising in connection with the team of lady cricketers who were on tour'. The judge, granting the summons, observed wearily that 'Martin's cases came before him half a dozen times at every sitting at Plymouth'. Martin was back in court in April 1891, having still not paid what he owed.

* * *

All this organisation would have been meaningless without spectators for the cricket matches. Therefore someone, probably Michel, organised an impressive publicity drive before the cricket season.

In January and February 1890, various rumours appeared in the press which were sufficiently accurate to suggest their source was close to the ECAA. The cumulative effect meant that well before the cricket season began, the concept of a women's sporting troupe was firmly established in the public consciousness. Disapproving comments – whether written by journalists, muttered at clubs, over breakfast tables, or shared in the workplace – merely served to embed the idea further. In March, the first advertisements which accurately reflected what the OELC would offer appeared in *The Era*, at the same time as the organisers finally settled on the title of 'Original English Lady Cricketers'. These promised 'sport, not clowning' and 'refined lady athletes, not burlesque masqueraders'.

With the plan having settled down, the publicity drive began in earnest. Part of this was the invitation of journalists to the Wandsworth practices in March, but there were two triumphs of promotion later that month. Not long after the report appeared on the practice session, a convenient 'rumour' appeared that 'the first public appearance of the lady cricketers in costume will be on boat race day' – the Oxford and Cambridge Boat Race at Putney. The cricketers duly appeared on 26 March, steaming up and down the river on a yacht in colourful outfits – which at least one journalist took to signify their support for Cambridge – accompanied by George Hearne and Maurice Read. The press obligingly reported the presence of the 'lady cricketers', although many writers did not realise who or what they were.

The biggest coup came in late March, when the team featured in *Lillywhite's Cricketers' Annual*. The frontispiece was a photograph of what it called the 'Red' team, alongside Matthews, most of them looking distinctly uncomfortable in front of a whitewashed brick wall – presumably at St George's Hall where they had been practising. An advert on the following page stated:

> With the object of proving the suitability of the national game as a pastime for the fair sex

in preference to Lawn Tennis and other less scientific games, the English Cricket and Athletic Association Limited have organised two complete elevens of female players under the title of 'The Original English Lady Cricketers'. Trained by W. Matthews, S. B. Lohman and qualified assistants (under the supervision of G. G. Hearne, Maurice Read and other Leading Professionals), equipped with regulation outfit by Messrs Lillywhite, Frowd and Co, and elegantly and appropriately attired. N.B. Every effort is made to keep this organisation in every respect select and refined. A matron accompanies each eleven to all engagements. During the forthcoming season, exhibition matches will be given in the principal towns of the United Kingdom. Colonial tour to follow. Private engagements of one or both elevens can be arranged for a complete match or to meet lady amateurs.

Accompanying the photograph was a brief feature that discussed in positive terms the ongoing growth of women's cricket and which noted that readers would probably be aware by then of the existence of the women's team. Given the well-coordinated campaign, it would have been hard for anyone to miss it.

* * *

Even with all these successes, when the cricket season began the itinerary was far from complete. The advertising had given the impression that anyone interested in engaging the teams should hurry, but requests for fixtures continued to appear well into the season. Scattered evidence suggests that plans were fluid until almost the last moment. The feature which described the practice session gave no indication of what form the cricket would take; at that time the OELC seem to have planned to face other women's teams. But the sheer number of players reportedly in training – most sources said 30 – suggest this was not quite the intention. Later adverts offered 'two complete teams' and exhibition games had become the focus.

The final format was simple. The women were split into two teams, the 'Blues' and the 'Reds'. The initial distinction was supposedly based purely on hair colour – the 'Blues' were brown-haired and the 'Reds' blonde – but there was movement between the teams, especially in the first weeks. For most of the season, they were evenly matched from a cricketing viewpoint so perhaps the players were shuffled until the best combinations were found to provide good games. This separation into Blue and Red must have been finalised by March when the photograph of the Red team appeared in *Lillywhite's Cricketers' Annual*. But up until the last minute, there was still some uncertainty. For example in early April, before the OELC had played in public, a feature said that the Reds were to be captained by Ada Heather, who always played for the Blues and did not lead either team in 1890.

As it happens, the apparently late recruitment of one player made a big difference to the organisation of the teams, and the success of the whole enterprise. Although not mentioned in the report on the practice sessions, and not listed as a captain even in early May, the eventual Red captain was the most significant cricketing figure on either team. Violet Westbrook (whose real name was Violet

Blanche Lyon) was the daughter of a relatively prosperous stationer. She proved to be head and shoulders above her colleagues with both bat and ball and came to dominate matches in such a way as to draw comparisons with W. G. Grace. Westbrook had learned to play cricket long before joining the OELC, being taught by her brothers; although she later credited the OELC coaches with having improved her game the reality is that she must already have been a talented player. Given that her ability must have been clear from the second she picked up a bat – and would have been a publicist's dream – her absence from early newspaper reports (such as the one about the Wandsworth practices) can only be explained if she joined quite late in the day. But her skill made her the obvious choice as the Red captain.

The other team captain was Daisie Stanley, whose real name was Daisy Anita Berry. She had a background in athletics, which was where her sporting skill actually lay, but she quickly assumed a dominant position in the organisation which was out of all proportion to her cricketing ability. Without her, the whole enterprise may have been very different. Her father was a clerk of works (although on some census returns, he was listed as a bricklayer) and despite suggestions in the player profiles produced for the OELC that she was from Chetnole in Dorset, she was really born near Onslow Gardens in London.[9] Although Stanley does

---

9   Daisie Stanley's real name was never revealed in newspapers, and Daisy Anita Berry's birthplace of Fulham contradicted the claims in OELC publicity material that Stanley was born in Chetnole, Dorset. But Berry's birthdate was the same as the one given for Stanley and her father was a clerk of works, the same occupation Stanley claimed for her father. Stanley later admitted in an interview to having been born in London in the region of Onslow Gardens; Berry was born in Fulham and lived in the general area of Onslow Gardens at the time of the 1871 census. This makes it extremely likely that Daisie Stanley was Daisy Anita Berry.

not seem to have spoken to the journalist at Wandsworth, George Hearne was eager to discuss her in that feature. He noted that she had been a gymnastics teacher, could 'run like a deer' and clear a height of 3ft 7in when jumping. Away from sport, according to the 1891 census, she was a dressmaker; one feature on the OELC claimed that she designed the costumes for the team, although this was not repeated elsewhere. She was also described as the editor of the OELC's publication, the *Lady Cricketers' Gazette*, and played a key role in the evening entertainment associated with the tour, choreographing whole routines. In many ways the OELC of 1890 was the creation of Stanley as much as Michel. And, alongside Westbrook, she was the only player to speak at any length to the press during the 1890 season. Unfortunately, she never discussed how or why she became involved.

As March turned into April, after all the practice, organisation and publicity, it was finally time to take to the field. With such a build-up, it was almost inevitable that the OELC would be an immediate success. But even after the novelty value of women cricketers had worn off, something seized the public imagination. For all the focus in the build-up on 'music hall' or 'burlesque', it was the cricket which drew huge crowds. Stars of the team emerged despite attempts by Michel (and Daisie Stanley) to steer the narrative. Even the most sceptical observers were forced to concede by the end of the 1890 season that the answer was yes to the question frequently posed throughout the summer: could women really play cricket?

Liverpool and Beyond

ON EASTER Monday 1890 the approaches to the Police Athletic Grounds in Liverpool were thronged with people. Although the day was bright and sunny, the wind was bitterly cold; this did not deter what everyone agreed was thousands of paying spectators from attending the first day of the opening match of the Original English Lady Cricketers' tour.

The Liverpool press gave the game enormous coverage. As well as the story of the recruitment and training of the players, some new details emerged in newspapers: that the women had only been able to practise on turf two or three times, and that as part of their preparation they had played a private match against a boys' school outside London (which they won). But Liverpool was their first appearance before a paying audience.

The venue was unpromising – an open, windswept ground with a bare, uneven playing surface bordered by drab terraced houses. Violet Westbrook won the toss for the Reds and chose to bat; Beatrice Light (listed on the scorecard as M. Light) and Grace Westbrook (Violet's younger sister) were the opening batters as the Blues, led by Daisie Stanley, took the field at 2pm.

Almost immediately the players' appearance became the focus. The Liverpool newspapers – and almost every journalist who ever saw the teams – became mildly obsessed over their costume: 'Their dress was exceedingly picturesque'; 'they also wore very pretty cricket caps' (*Liverpool Mercury*); 'their "make-up" is exceedingly pretty and attractive'; 'presenting an appearance quite coquettish'; 'a picture altogether novel for a cricket field' (*Liverpool Echo*). The outfits were certainly more colourful and striking than would normally have been seen during a cricket match. They had been manufactured by Stagg and Mantle of Leicester Square and consisted of a blouse – embroidered below the collar with 'OELC' – and long skirt, both of which were fringed with the team's colours.[10] Each player wore a cap with an appropriately coloured ribbon, and had been given her own Ayres International bat.

The game took place over two afternoons – on 7 and 8 April – both of which began with demonstrations by the women of a new sport. 'Lawn crooketta', invented by John D. Horne of Leicester, was a simplified version of tennis played in a smaller space with racquets resembling crooks. The ECAA (which in practice probably meant Michel) clearly hoped crooketta would be popular: the women were photographed playing it at Liverpool, and it featured in early advertising material. But it was quickly dropped from the programme, suggesting that the public were unimpressed. Other attractions for spectators included music played by a local band and a visit from a locally famous athlete called Tommy Burns. As the tour

---

10 The design of the fringe subtly changed quite early on; in at least the first game, and in the *Lillywhite's* photograph, it was a vertical stripe of solid colour. But by early May, this had changed to a two-tone diagonal pattern.

progressed over 1890, musical accompaniment from local musicians was a recurring theme. But it was the cricket which grabbed the attention.

Despite the rugged appearance of the ground, the OELC were lucky that the pitch played well – better than many later ones – for their opening performance. On the first day, the Reds scored 111. The openers Light and Grace Westbrook were the stars, staying at the wicket for over an hour before they were parted; Light scored 24 and Grace Westbrook 30 but once they were out, the batting collapsed until Sophie Charles (16) and Elizabeth Dempsey (17) rescued the innings. The wickets fell to Daisie Stanley (three), Georgina Sheffield (three) and Bessie Moss (three) but there was some press confusion over names: the *Liverpool Echo* said in its report that Violet Westbrook was dismissed by Stanley, but the scorecard named the bowler as Sheffield. When play ended around 5:30pm, the Blues were strongly placed on 56/2. Stanley had been dismissed for nought opening the batting, but Ella Heather was 36 not out. That evening the cricketers, dressed in their costumes, visited the Shakespeare Theatre to watch a play, a publicity coup for both the venue and the OELC.

The next day, the Blues were bowled out for 130, of which Ella Heather scored 63 in around two-and-a-quarter hours. Her sister Ada made the next best score (17); Susie Fletcher and Lena Parsons also reached double figures. Five wickets fell to Violet Westbrook and three to Light; the other two went to Louisa Daly. In the time remaining, the Reds batted again and scored 117/5; among the runs were Grace Westbrook again, with 21, Violet Westbrook with 28 and Adele Matthey with 41. One oddity was that overnight scorecards named Annie Hampson among the Blues, but on the second day Florence Woodward batted in her place.

No one (except perhaps the players who wanted their win bonus) seemed too worried about the result – many newspapers did not bother to report who won – but it was most likely classified as a win to the Blues based on the first innings' scores.

The reaction to the game was – apparently – overwhelmingly positive. The Liverpool newspapers described how spectators were won over by the cricketers' skills. For example, the *Liverpool Mercury* suggested: 'Those who visited the Fairfield grounds expecting to see ladies on the field who would be – as is often the case among the gentle sex – unable to throw or catch a bowl, must have been agreeably disappointed, as the members of the team were exceptionally clever at bowling, catching, stopping, and fielding.' *The Stage* – which took an ongoing interest in the OELC that betrayed the theatrical origins of the group – said: 'Considerable pleasure and interest was manifested by the great crowds of spectators, who seemed surprised at the smartness and proficiency of the ladies, who handled both bat and ball with all the confidence and ability of the sterner brethren of the leather and the willow.' Most enduring was a line from the report in the *Liverpool Mercury* – 'They play and do not burlesque the game' – which was used extensively in promotional materials thereafter.

Watching journalists were impressed by the women's cutting and driving of the ball, but noted that their main shot was 'getting the ball round to leg', at which Ella Heather excelled. The fielding was also complimented. The unrelenting positivity from Liverpool seems slightly implausible; perhaps some kind of financial inducement encouraged such positive coverage. But one hint of a different reaction slipped the net. A fragmentary syndicated newspaper report observed that the crowd at one point mocked the players on account of their reaction to the cold: 'There was a disposition on the part of spectators to chaff the players, who were nipped and pinched by the cold, unbecoming red noses and blue hands being very prevalent.'

Other than this, there is plenty of evidence of the narrative being steered by sources within the OELC. For example, Violet Westbrook scored only 8 in the opening game and would have been unknown outside the team, but the reporter for the *Liverpool Echo* could inform readers that she was the 'W. G. Grace of the party'. Perhaps an explanation lies in the presence on the second day of the larger-than-life Michel, boasting to the *Liverpool Echo* of his 200 applicants and the £2,000 so far incurred for expenses.

The consensus was that the standard of play was far higher than anyone expected, and the game had been an undoubted success. Several newspapers put the attendance in the thousands on the first day; later reports indicated that 15,000 had attended, although these do not make clear if this was a combination of both days or merely on the first day. If such a claim might be questionable, the crowd was certainly enormous and impacted the attendance at a nearby athletics meeting.

One curiosity is that the *Liverpool Echo* said that it expected the OELC to 'meet with more success than did the lady footballers of last year'. There is no record of a team of lady footballers in 1889, unless it was a local venture, but when the OELC visited Newport in June, the *South Wales Echo* similarly indicated that 'the lady cricketers, after the manner of the lady footballers, have undoubtedly "caught on".[11]

* * *

This triumphal opening inevitably led to enormous interest in the OELC. A feature in the *Leicester Journal* in May said that the OELC had arranged 58 matches, but advertisements indicated that dates were still available and over the coming weeks, many more games were arranged. However, the team went into a kind of limbo at this point. Michel told the press that immediately after the Liverpool game, the OELC were to travel to Rugby for a 'private engagement'. But while stories about the Liverpool match echoed around the press for the remainder of April, few new stories emerged from the OELC camp. Given the need to generate newspaper publicity, it is more likely that the team were not playing rather than appearing before private audiences.

According to the lists of fixtures printed in *Sporting Life*, which covered the OELC extensively throughout 1890, the teams did not play again until appearing at Ashford on 23 April. The only advertisements in this period were ones requesting fixtures. After that, there was another week with no obvious games until the OELC reached Slough on 30 April. From then, the teams played almost continuously until the middle of October. There are a few gaps where there is no indication – neither advertisements nor match reports – of any games, but the teams were probably still

---

11 A series of cigarette cards by Ogden's in 1888 depicted the 'Lady Cricket and Football Team'; the accompanying text simply said that the cards showed 'one of the Lady Cricket and Football Team, contemplating visiting India to compete against the English and native clubs'. No other details have been found of this team.

playing. Coverage of the tour was patchy and it has not always been possible to find local newspaper reports of matches which certainly took place; but we can say with some confidence that Michel aimed to play six days a week, and that for the rest of the season he generally achieved this.

Between the Liverpool game and the beginning of May, Michel arranged for photographs to be taken, including a portrait of Daisie Stanley and some 'action' shots of cricket and crooketta at the opening match in Liverpool. Studio photographs were also taken of the Reds and Blues in costume – as Michel and Matthews stood proudly at the back – as well as some outdoor pictures of both teams at a game in London. These photographs were most likely intended for distribution to the press and for sale at matches.[12] One appeared in the *Illustrated Sporting and Dramatic News* on 24 May; drawings taken from one photograph which depicted Stanley and Violet Westbrook also appeared in some newspapers.

There must have been other contact between the OELC and the press. Most newspaper reports were accompanied by a scorecard which must have originated with the team: no journalists would have known the players. The OELC scorer throughout 1890 was Katie Tatton/Letine; she never played a game of cricket and her contributions were limited to keeping score and performing on her bicycle. But scorecards were erratic: initials of the players were

---

12 The members of the OELC may also have received copies; one of the team photographs appears on the inside cover of *Fair Play* by Netta Rheinberg and Rachael Heyhoe Flint. This almost certainly came from one of the players – most likely Marie Beckenham or the daughter of Violet Westbrook, to whom Rheinberg spoke – and it was accompanied by names of the players (which are not included in the actual photograph nor its associated paperwork).

inconsistently reported and their surnames were often spelt incorrectly – for example Lizzie Sanders was often recorded as 'Saunders' – or mangled entirely – Adele Matthey was often listed as 'Matthews'. Perhaps the scores were passed along verbally; or someone's handwriting was illegible. But the result is that we cannot always be certain whether an unfamiliar name represents a new player or a transcription error. Similarly, the appearance of a new initial alongside a surname might indicate either that someone's sister had joined or there was an error printing the name of an existing player.

* * *

And so the tour gradually assumed a shape going into May. The match at Slough was fairly typical. It was not played at a cricket ground but on a field belonging to the Dolphin Hotel; the proprietor was likely involved in arranging the game. Although one report said that 'as good a wicket as can be procured this early in the season had been prepared', it was evidently not easy for batting: in around four hours of play, the Reds scored only 80 in reply to the Blues' total of 69. And in another hint of what lay ahead, only Violet Westbrook seemed capable of scoring runs. She scored 49 out of the Reds' total of 80; the next-highest score was 12, and no one else in the game reached 20. Westbrook also chipped in with four wickets. There were five run-outs in total, and – like in many of the early games – 'bowled' was the most common dismissal (accounting for ten of the 20 wickets). Few catches were taken: two in the field and two 'caught and bowled'. Although no attendance figures were reported, *Sporting Life* noted the presence of a 'fashionable company'.

The next match received much wider coverage. The OELC played on the Antelope Ground in Southampton where Hampshire County Cricket Club had played until 1884.[13] Scores were higher – the Reds scored 117 in their first innings, to which the Blues replied with 128 – but Westbrook was again far superior to the rest: she scored 68 in the first innings (no one else passed 28 in the match) and took five wickets. The Reds collapsed for 50 on the second day, giving an easy win to the Blues, who continued batting after passing the Reds total.[14] *Sporting Life* described the attendance as 'moderate' on the first day, but said that around 4,000 attended in good weather on the second. At this stage, no one other than Westbrook stood out with the bat, although several players had managed to play a long innings. The bowling was dominated by Elizabeth Dempsey for the Blues, Georgina Sheffield and the Heather sisters for the Reds.

Before play on the second day, the women gave one of their final exhibitions of crooketta (although the sport was still intermittently advertised as part of the programme until the beginning of July, there is no evidence it continued to take place). They also visited a local theatre on the first evening and two music halls on the second, occupying boxes on the second night. Doubtless all parties were satisfied by the publicity generated.

---

13 By 1890, it was occupied by St Mary's Football Club – which later became Southampton Football Club.

14 This practice of batting on after passing the opposition total, followed all season, was standard in men's one-day matches at the time; results were often given in two ways when the team batting second won – by wickets (i.e. the number of wickets remaining when the target was reached) and runs (how many more were scored by the team batting second).

But the most significant event at Southampton was the debut of the *English Lady Cricketers' Gazette*, the publication of the OELC edited by Daisie Stanley. It was sold at every match for the remainder of the season and formed the basis of most subsequent newspaper reports. And with its publication, the players suddenly became more than just a collection of names.

Miss Daisie Stanley and the *English Lady Cricketers' Gazette*

SOMEONE AT the ECAA – probably Michel – had quickly identified the potential commercial value of merchandising connected to the OELC. As early as March 1890, advertisements promised that 'elaborate pictorials, blocks and litho[graph]s' would be available to buy, and photographs of the players were being sold from an early stage. Colourful posters publicised OELC games and the image of the team was carefully cultivated.

But from its first appearance at the beginning of May, the *English Lady Cricketers' Gazette* took publicity and promotion to a new level. Edited by Daisie Stanley and dedicated to 'the encouragement of healthy sport, pastime and amusement for women', not only was the *Gazette* another means of raising money, but it also provided a backstory for the players and gave Michel and Stanley the centre stage. More importantly it provided material for regional journalists who were covering the tour. It became the essential source for everything written about the teams in 1890. And newspapers were generally positive about it, regarding it as another in the growing list of achievements by these women cricketers.

Frustratingly, no copies seem to survive: no library or archive even has a record of the *Gazette*'s existence. The number of issues is unknown, although it is likely that there were at least two.[15] But the extensive reprinting and quotation make it possible to reconstruct most of what would have been found between its covers. For example, we know that there were reprints of press reports (which can realistically only have meant reviews of the Liverpool match); and probably one or two photographs – perhaps including the portrait of Stanley taken at Liverpool.

The most important article was a widely reprinted interview with Michel (which we have already encountered several times). His main aim was to demonstrate the propriety of the whole enterprise and to encourage those considering engaging his team: 'It is of vast importance to us that the respectability of the girls should be above suspicion, because a good deal of their work will be to play in private matches among the gentry.' After making his dubious claims about the high-class backgrounds of his players – seized upon and repeated by almost every journalist who set eyes on the *Gazette* – he made other attempts to emphasise the reputable nature of the OELC in another widely reproduced passage. He reassured readers: 'There is nothing in the costumes to which the most fastidious person could take exception. The skirts are long, and the edge is weighted with shots so that they do not lift with the wind.' And as a further reassurance, they 'also wear combination undergarments, made in one piece, so that

---

15 The large number of unchanged articles printed from the *Gazette* suggest that only one issue was published, but updated player profiles (including details of when Westbrook scored 99) appeared in the press from mid-July, which must have come from either a second issue or an updated first edition.

no matter what happens nothing could occur in the least to shock their own modesty or that of the spectators. Then they also wear a sort of armour across the breast, which completely protects them from injury. The armour is made from steel plates, leather, and wadding.' These details were frequently reproduced, being particularly fascinating for many journalists.

Michel also explained some of the arrangements for the tour, again showing how much care was being taken of the players. An 'excellent matron' called Mrs Grant took 'good care of the girls' and 'of course, we keep them in residence together, and take care of them'. In another part of the *Gazette*, Daisie Stanley mentioned that there were two matrons, but we have no other details about them.[16]

Michel explained that the players were 'delighted' with their circumstances and loved playing cricket: 'They are the greatest opponents while they are playing against each other in the field, but they are the best of friends afterwards.' And Michel reminded readers that everything took place with the permission of their parents, who had 'entered into an agreement to allow the girls to remain in our charge for a period of two years'.

The *Gazette* also transformed the players from a list of names into real people. Michel gave a little description of them – 'The average height of the girls is 5 feet 7 inches; the average age 19 years. The tallest girl in the team is 5 feet 10 inches, and the shortest 5 feet 5 inches' – but more importantly they were fleshed out in brief but informative profiles, organised into 'Reds' and 'Blues':

---

16 At least one matron did accompany the team; Mary Willett/Marie Beckenham mentioned a matron in her interview with Netta Rheinberg in 1956.

> **Louise Daly**, born at Marylebone, June 19th 1868. A good, fast bowler …
> **Sophie Charles**, born at Chelsea, November 17th 1872. A fair, slow, underhand bowler, and one of the fleetest runners in the team …
> **Ella Heather**, born at Chelsea, July 10th 1871, one of the best bats, playing in correct style with good defence; a very useful slow bowler …
> **Lizzie Sanders**, born at Chelsea, August 1st 1872. Bats well, with plenty of hitting power …

As far as it has been possible to check, the birthdates were largely accurate, except that some years had been changed. Sanders, for example, was actually born on 1 August 1874. Some players became slightly older, others slightly younger; but it is not quite clear why.

* * *

By the time the *Gazette* was on sale, there were already some standouts in the teams. Ella Heather was recognised as a talented batter, but the 'star' of the early games was Violet Westbrook, whose all-round achievements found little acknowledgement in her original profile: 'Violet Blanche Westbrook, born at Godalming, Surrey, July 23rd 1871. Sound and reliable bat, excellent and thoroughly correct style. Has been appointed captain of the "Reds".' The complete lack of mention of her bowling skill reinforces the suspicion that she was a late arrival in the team, but she was already being described by the press, with an unsurprising lack of imagination, as the 'W. G. Grace' of the OELC.

With the publication of the *Gazette*, Miss Daisie Stanley became the dominant figure of the whole enterprise. For the first time, we hear the apparently unfiltered voice of one of the players. She was prominently named as the *Gazette*'s editor – a fact emphasised in all subsequent newspaper coverage – and featured extensively within its pages. Like Michel, she was the subject of a lengthy interview but she also wrote an article which discussed the red-hot topic of the effect of exercise and sport on women. Unsurprisingly, Stanley argued that it was hugely beneficial and encouraged more women to become involved in cricket.

Her profile was more detailed than the others: 'Daisie Stanley, born at Chetnole, Dorsetshire, October 27th 1870. Successful left hand over-arm bowler. Possesses a thorough knowledge of the technique of cricket and is Captain of the "Blue" Eleven. Was formerly an Instructress at Alexandra House Gymnasium, Kensington Gore.' Given such an abundance of information, it is tempting to wonder if she was also the author of the profiles.

Stanley had more to say about her background in her interview. She claimed to have been a 'teacher of calisthenics' at the gymnasium of Alexandra House – a residence for female students of the Royal College of Music – and said: 'I believe I am the only lady who was ever summoned to Marlborough House by HRH the Princess of Wales[17] to give an exhibition before the Princess and her daughters.' She again expressed her devotion to cricket, which she argued should be 'taught to all girls': 'It affords a larger scope for the development of the muscles of the arms, the legs, and the chest, as well as training the eye and hand. It is an open-air exercise, and not so exhausting as lawn tennis, and not so trying for women as most other exercises.'

---

17 This was Princess Alexandra, after whom Alexandra House was named, who was married to the future King Edward VII.

The very fact that Stanley stated her views on women's exercise publicly – even if they were fairly conventional – made her an unusual figure. Single, apparently independent, and with a dedication to exercise, she bordered on being a 'New Woman'. Whether her words were an act of performance or an accurate reflection of her personality and beliefs, this is the only example we have of a player expressing any kind of philosophy. Journalists certainly found her to be an endless source of fascination. For example, in an article in May, *The Queen* included her in a list of prominent women that month. Misplaced regional pride prompted the *Western Chronicle* – published in Yeovil, near to Stanley's supposed Chetnole birthplace – to comment on the 'present national celebrity' of the 'captain of the now famous lady cricketers'.

Stanley also had plenty to say about the OELC: 'All my [*sic*] girls are sharp and to the point in fielding.' As for Matthews, he was owed 'so much credit … for the patience he has expanded on us'. Questioned by her interviewer (if she had not written her own questions) as to whether the women were 'ballet girls' – presumably meaning having a theatrical background – she 'indignantly' responded: 'Decidedly not. We have no ballet girls in our teams. The whole are daughters or sisters of professional men or respectable tradesmen. Two are daughters of a West End Physician. Two more are sisters of an architect in the City.' If her claims about backgrounds are not quite as grand as those of Michel, she might have been just as untruthful; of players whose families we can trace, there are no physicians nor architects. And we know that several women had some experience of theatre.

Such was the interest in Stanley that she was interviewed several more times. A feature published in June contained so much detail that the source can only have been Stanley herself. It revealed that the 'tall, graceful figure, endowed with considerable physical strength for a woman' was not in fact from Chetnole, but from the West End, near Onslow Gardens, and was not called Stanley at all. After leaving school, she had become interested in athletics and 'in these she very soon excelled all her contemporaries at the local gymnasium, her progress being exceedingly rapid'. It was this which gave her the athletic physique so admired by the newspapers and probably led to her position as 'assistant instructor at this athletic school for young ladies' – by which the author presumably meant Alexandra House Gymnasium. After this, 'looking around for other worlds to conquer', she took to cricket which she 'quickly mastered'. Because of her prowess, she was 'unanimously elected' as the Blues captain,[18] 'a choice she has since fully justified, by her skill as an all-round cricketer and her judgement in placing the field'.

The article is interesting in several ways apart from the shameless promotion of its subject. It was most likely syndicated but can only be found today (via the British Newspaper Archive) in the *Newcastle Courant* in a section entitled 'London Chit-Chat'. But Stanley's words are original – they are not copied from elsewhere; they contradict the *Gazette* (from which they are clearly not taken) and were not apparently widely reproduced in the way that *Gazette* pieces were.

---

18 The claim that OELC captains were 'elected' is unique to this article.

One other article provided some different information about her background. In September, a newspaper suggested that she had 'distinguished herself as a student at the Whitland's [also called Whiteland's] Training College for governesses – one of the best colleges of its kind in London'.[19] And yet the myth from the *Gazette* persisted; as late as October it was being suggested in a Dorset newspaper that 'she comes of one of the oldest Dorsetshire families, having been born at Chetnole ... Her father, who died some five years since, was for many years clerk of the works to one of the most eminent firms of West End contractors.' Her actual father was still very much alive.

But there was no disguising that Stanley's real passion was for gymnastics and athletics rather than cricket. An article in October noted that 'she is probably without a rival as a runner, being considered by qualified judges to possess the fleetest foot ever shown by a lady whilst her "staying" powers are remarkable'. And the author of an article in *The People* in November was impressed by the times she had recorded in 200- and 300-yard races. The same piece claimed that she had 'passed open examinations in scientific and artistic subjects', begging the question of where this information – bordering on the hagiographical – was coming from, and for what purpose.

The stream of stories looks suspiciously like a publicity campaign to position Stanley as an indispensable central figure in the OELC. Some possible reasons for this began to emerge at the end of the season. But there was a backlash in mid-May when an anonymous correspondent to the

---

19 There is no record of anyone studying at Whiteland College called Daisie Stanley or Daisy Berry; nor is there a record of any pupil called Daisy in the relevant period.

Standard revealed that Stanley had never 'been an assistant instructress or pupil' in the Alexandra House Gymnasium. And an advertisement appeared in several publications over the next few weeks in which 'Miss Stuart Snell begs to state that Miss Daisy Stanley, Captain of the Lady Cricketers, has never had any connection with the Gymnasium at Alexandra House.' This does not *necessarily* mean that the Blues captain was lying: if she *had* worked there it would have been under her actual name, not 'Daisie Stanley'. Or perhaps Miss Snell simply wished to disassociate the gymnasium from the cricketers. But typically for the smitten pressmen, this public refutation had no impact and they continued to mention her employment at Alexandra House as they unquestioningly followed what Stanley – through the *Gazette* – had told them.

* * *

So who was Miss Stanley? An artist? A scientist? A governess? A gymnastics teacher? An athlete? A writer? Whoever she was, we can be certain that she was unfortunately not a natural cricketer. In fact, the fascination with Stanley clearly had little relation to her accomplishments on the field. In the matches for which we have a scorecard, she had one of the lowest batting averages (managing just under 4 runs per innings with a highest score of 23). She took 42 wickets in these games (no analyses survive, so her bowling average is unknown) but was overshadowed by several women who took more than 100 wickets. In fact, she all but stopped bowling after mid-July, possibly owing to an injury. By contrast, her fellow captain Violet Westbrook scored over 2,600 runs, averaging over 50 with the bat, and took over

200 wickets.[20] But when an illustration of the OELC by Lucien Davis appeared in the *Illustrated London News* in May 1890, Stanley was the central figure.

At least the ongoing fascination with Stanley provided one of the few descriptions of an OELC member in action. When the teams played at Clifton in early June, the *Bristol Mercury* described her as a left-handed 'round-arm bowler, and though she pitched the balls rather high – as indeed did most of the other bowlers – she kept a very good length'.

But Stanley had another skill which doubtless delighted Michel: she deliberately fanned flames guaranteed to generate column inches. For example, in July she gave an interview to the *Manchester Evening Mail* alongside Violet Westbrook. When the writer of the piece arrived, the two were supposedly discussing an article in the medical journal *The Lancet*. Stanley was loudly indignant about the content: "'I should like the writer of that" – indicating the article with a contemptuous gesture – "to see some of my girls. Why, do I look as if I am being killed? (she certainly did not) Or Miss Westbrook? And yet we have been playing nearly every day for weeks."' Westbrook concurred, more meekly, that if the journalist could see 'the girls', he 'would not write such stuff again'.

The contrast between the fiery Stanley – and her possessive description of 'my girls' once again – and the placid Westbrook could not be plainer, but Stanley's rage was based on a (probably deliberate) misinterpretation of the 'article' in *The Lancet*. In fact, the piece was a

---

20 Violet Westbrook (222), Georgina Sheffield (149), Ada Heather (169) and Louisa Daly (104) took over 100 wickets in the matches for which a scorecard survives. In these recorded games, Stanley was only the eighth-highest wicket-taker.

letter from W. Henry Kesteven of Finsbury Circus, who questioned whether cricket was unsafe for women owing to possible long-term effects of 'the violent impact of a hard cricket ball on the mammary gland'. His concern was not with exercise itself – 'there is no doubt of [women's] muscular capacity' – rather the supposed dangers of being struck. There was no follow-up in *The Lancet*, making Mr Kesteven a lone voice. But the ire expressed by Stanley and Westbrook at the suggestion cricket was 'not healthy' for women – not quite what Kesteven had written – made for good newspaper copy.

Stanley's next target was Lord Willoughby de Broke, an English peer and the president of Warwickshire County Cricket Club (not yet a first-class county in 1890). After the OELC had appeared at Leamington on 18 June, de Broke had written to the *Warwick Advertiser* to encourage support for Warwickshire and to express irritation that instead of concentrating on his county, newspaper coverage was being given to 'that farce of farces, that dismal burlesque on the noble game – a ladies' cricket match'. He also grumbled that 'the aristocracy of the neighbourhood' had attended the OELC game and implored everyone to attend county games at Edgbaston. He concluded: 'To the lady cricketers I would use more in anger than in sorrow the words of our immortal county bard [i.e. Shakespeare], "Get thee to a nunnery – go."'

Reaction to de Broke had been generally unfavourable. The editor of the *Warwick Advertiser* was unapologetic about the column inches he had given to the OELC, regarding it as a matter of public interest even if opinion was divided on the team's merits. And other newspapers paid no attention to de Broke's attempts to promote Warwickshire and, doubtless to his fury, focused purely on his remarks about the OELC. In truth no one had much respect for de Broke's opinions on cricket. But given a platform in the press to discuss his comments, Stanley apparently lost her temper. Her *Manchester Evening Mail* interviewer wrote: 'Miss Stanley has made a scarifying reply to this outburst of patrician indignation.' She believed a team drawn from the best OELC players would probably defeat 'any second-class county' – meaning Warwickshire – and issued a challenge to meet Warwickshire's first eleven; she even suggested it might boost interest in the county team. Stanley suggested that her team believed they could compete against men. Westbrook apparently agreed with all of Stanley's sentiments, although she was not quoted and seems to have been at best a reluctant attendee at the discussion.

The rest of the interview was more orthodox. Michel, apparently present with the two women as a kind of moderator (or possibly spoken to separately), observed that owing mainly to the presence of Westbrook in the team, the Reds had won more games than the Blues at that stage. Stanley also praised Westbrook as the difference between the teams, and thought the best Blues batter was Ella Heather. As the discussion moved on to ordinary cricket matters, Westbrook spoke up more. She noted that her team could not dismiss Heather, but they tried to take advantage of her love of the cut shot by bowling for catches at point. She added: 'That is one great disadvantage of playing together so often. We get to know one another's play too well.'

The piece ended with both Stanley and Westbrook's dismissive remarks about the frequently printed claims that women could not throw. They also ridiculed a notion in the press that some women were using aprons to catch the ball, or that they did not play with a straight bat. Westbrook noted that male cricketers did not always play with a straight bat, while women cricketers 'play as straight as they can, and never drag an off ball over to leg'. Stanley added that, unlike men, the women did not blame the umpire or the pitch or make other excuses for their dismissals.

Stanley rehashed some of the same ideas when speaking to the *Burnley Express* later that month, saying that she could select a team from the OELC players to beat a second-class county. But she conceded that 'as yet they were hardly, as a body, good enough to play against a good team of male players'.

Another interview, closer to the end of the season, appeared in *The Cornishman* when the OELC toured the South-West. But this was a strange article because the writer was obsessed with the players' undergarments. During a game, he was taken into the pavilion to meet Stanley, who had missed several matches with what she told him was a foot injury. She spoke about the health benefits for women in taking part in cricket and told him that she had been involved in athletic activities all her life and, to his embarrassment, invited him to 'feel my muscle'.

But, having already asked Michel whether the 'cricketeresses' wore corsets on the field – the manager asked a player to bring him one of the chest-guards to see – the inquisitive journalist began to question Stanley about the issue. She said that although the women did not wear corsets on the field, they wore them in everyday life and she believed that 'ladies would look very sloppy' without them. Bizarrely, the writer continued to press the point, arguing that women could be 'trained' to not wear them.

He even described her bemused response: '"Ye-e-s," said Miss Stanley, reluctantly.' This went on for some time – taking up the bulk of the article – until he moved on after she stopped answering him and merely smiled instead: 'And then I sympathised with the fair lady and tore myself reluctantly away.' Although he wrote in the rest of the article about how good the players were, and quoted from the *Gazette*, he had not asked her a single sports-related question.

* * *

In contrast to the interest in Stanley, Violet Westbrook received much less press attention although her achievements dwarfed those of her opposite number. But unlike Stanley, we know quite a lot about Westbrook's early life, which was far more comfortable than many of her team-mates'. Her father was William Henry Lyon, who from the 1850s worked at Westbrook Mills in Godalming, an extensive and lucrative business that specialised in oil leather, and by 1867 was its manager. Violet spent her early years living with her family at Westbrook Mills House. Like most such organisations, Westbrook Mills had its own cricket team and it is likely that this is where Violet first saw – and maybe played – cricket. By the time of the 1881 census, the family had moved to Shalford and William Henry was an auctioneer.[21]

In her few interviews, Westbrook revealed some details about her life without giving too much away. For example, in May when she was run out for 99 at Guildford,[22] a brief

---

21 On the 1891 census William Henry called himself a retired stationer, so perhaps he had several jobs after leaving the mills.
22 She was run out going for her 100th run from the last ball of the match.

profile appeared in the *Surrey Advertiser*, the information for which can only have come from the player, which stated that her real name was Violet Lyon and that her father had been the manager of Westbrook Mills before working at the County Court in Guildford. The feature said that she and her sister Grace had been coached by their brother – most likely Frederick, who was seven years older than Violet but had died in 1886.

In June, Westbrook gave an interview to the *Nottingham Daily Express* in which she said: 'I think cricket is a splendid game for girls. I learned the theory and some practice at home at Godalming with my brothers;[23] but could lay claim to no proficiency before I underwent tuition last winter.' The latter suggestion seems unlikely – perhaps a ploy encouraged by Michel to provide prestige for the OELC coaching – not least as she must have joined late in the process; Matthews and company would have had little time with her. In any case, she was far too good to have been a recent convert to cricket. Westbrook said that she had been taught several shots during the 'tuition' but was still developing her defensive play during the coaching sessions which continued to take place during the tour. Although modest about her own skills, she expressed a belief she would be able to play men's fast bowling, having faced it comfortably during practice. She claimed to be a supporter of Surrey but had no plans to qualify for county cricket. Her hope was that the example of the OELC would encourage more women to play the game.

Perhaps the truest account of her cricketing experience came from her updated profile that appeared in the *Gazette*

---

23 As well as Frederick, Westbrook had two younger brothers.

from July – after it had become obvious how good she was – which stated that she had 'played the game from infancy'. But it might have been difficult getting details from Westbrook herself. One journalist, quoted in *Gentlewoman*, joked how hard it was to pin her down: 'What is the use of going to interview Miss Westbrook? When the Blues are batting, she is of course in the field, and when the Reds are in, why she is batting all the time.' More than any other OELC member, it feels as if Westbrook loved cricket; and given the relative prosperity of her family, this was probably her main reason for joining.

The contrast in tone between the interviews of Stanley and Westbrook reinforces the notion that something else – whether it was politics, self-promotion or pure publicity for the OELC – drove Stanley's far more combative and frequent appearances in the press.

* * *

If Stanley's outspokenness and wide range of interests intrigued the newspapers, and Westbrook's weight of runs and wickets made her impossible to ignore, the rest received almost no attention. Unfortunately, this masked several changes behind the scenes. Even by the time the *Gazette* was published, the profiles were out of date owing to the fluid nature of the personnel. Some players had swapped between Reds and Blues and others had disappeared entirely. Newer arrivals, including two particularly long-serving members, Nellie Wadkin and Marie Beckenham, were absent from the original profiles. A revised set of profiles appeared from July onwards, but even these were quickly inaccurate.

The first changes to the team occurred almost immediately. Annie Hampson was one of four 'Odds' (i.e.

reserves) listed in the *Gazette*; she was named in the Blues' team for the first day of the tour at Liverpool, but by the following day had been replaced by Florence Woodward and never appeared again in any of the published scorecards.[24] Equally mysterious is the woman listed as 'A. Robinson', who played at Liverpool but was not included in the profiles and never seems to have played again. Nor can we explain why Nellie Wadkin – another absentee from the first edition of the *Gazette* – played that first game and then disappeared until the end of May (after which she played regularly).

Fortunately, not every change is inexplicable. Beatrice Light, listed in the profiles among the Reds, was another whose only (very successful) appearance came at Liverpool. By the time of the next game for which a scorecard survives, she had gone forever, although she was still listed in the *Gazette* until the profiles were revised. There was a simple explanation. Away from the cricket field, she was almost certainly Annie Emma Light (née Nichols, born in Southampton in 1870, matching the *Gazette* profile[25]), whose second child, George Thomas Light, was born in late July 1890. During her only appearance she was almost six months pregnant; even if she had hidden the pregnancy until then, there was no way she could have continued.

A similar explanation might account for the

---

24 Hampson could feasibly have played in the private game at Rugby, and possibly at Ashford at the end of April as we have no scorecards for these.

25 There was a Beatrice Light living in London in 1891, the daughter of a railway goods manager, but neither her birthdate nor birthplace match that listed on the player profiles, which were usually reasonably accurate. Incidentally, this Beatrice Light was baptised alongside her sister on the day the OELC played at Maidenhead in May, but while it might be tempting to imagine a wealthy family rescuing her from the clutches of the OELC and saving her soul, it is highly unlikely that this was our cricketer.

disappearance from the team of Marie Lisle, who played regularly until late May, after which she and her sister Annie (who returned for a few games in September) vanished. We cannot be certain about the identity of Lisle; her profile in the *Gazette* says that she was born in Harborne, Staffordshire, on 27 January 1868. The most likely candidate was a woman called Marie Lisle, born in England (the town was unrecorded) in 1868 and living in Scotland at the time of the 1891 census with her Sunderland-born husband Joseph Carter Lisle. She was listed as a 'theatre actress' (her husband is a 'theatre actor'); similarly on the 1901 Scotland census, a Marie Lisle was listed as a 'dramatic actor'. By the time of the 1911 census, the Lisle family were back in England, living in Shropshire (Marie's birthplace was given as Wolverhampton, Staffordshire, the same county as listed in the *Gazette*). Both Marie and Joseph were workers for a 'Portable Theatre'.[26] Given the diverse range of the birthplaces of their children on that census – Limerick in Ireland (Joseph in 1899), Irvine in Scotland (James in 1901) and Brownhills in Staffordshire (Gladys in 1903) – they may have been touring for many years. The theatrical link is good circumstantial evidence that she was our missing cricketer.

Marie Lisle's youngest daughter Dorothy was born in England and was just one year old on the 1891 census. If Marie had been pregnant during the 1890 season, it would explain why she stopped playing. But there are problems with definitively matching the actress to the cricketer even though so many of the jigsaw pieces fit; there is no obvious

---

26 A portable theatre company toured the country, assembling their literally portable theatre building each time they arrived at the location where they were to perform.

record of her marriage (even though the 1911 census reveals that she married in 1888) and therefore we cannot identify her before 1891 or locate her family to see if she had a sister called Annie.[27]

We are on more certain ground in identifying other women who disappeared despite having a profile in the *Gazette*. Edith and Florence Woodward were sisters from Cheltenham who came from a musical family; their father George Woodward was variously listed on census returns as an 'instructor of music', a 'professor of music', and a 'music seller', and seems to have been a combination of all these things; an obituary for Edith in the *Gloucestershire Echo* in 1947 said that her father 'dominated the musical life' of Cheltenham. Both sisters followed in his footsteps, pursuing lives dedicated to music. Neither of them achieved much in their brief time with the OELC, although the *Gazette* described Florence as a 'very good all-round cricketer'. Perhaps they had applied for a musical role advertised by the ECAA. Their early departures might have been a result of a lack of enthusiasm for cricket – quite likely not what they had expected when they signed up – or perhaps they were summoned back to Cheltenham when their eminently respectable, and presumably horrified, family discovered they were playing professional cricket under their real names. But they may have continued to play; when the OELC visited Cheltenham in June, the *Cheltenham Chronicle*, although

---

27 There are other problems with the Lisle family such as inconsistencies between census returns. For example, the 1911 census stated that Marie and Joseph only ever had three children but the 1901 census (of which only a transcription is readily available online) lists six. These could, however, be the result of recording or transcription errors (either at the time or when they were digitised).

ignorant of their departure from the side, mentioned in its report: 'Two of the team are Cheltenham young ladies, and one of them played at Guiting the other day in an ordinary [presumably meaning men's] cricket match, making one in the first innings.'

The most high-profile disappearance was that of Louisa Daly who, by the time of her final appearance at Bradford in mid-August, had taken over 100 wickets. At the beginning of the month, a newspaper had described her as 'the best bowler in the team', although it also suggested that she had lost form recently. Even so, there is no indication why she stopped playing; it might have been injury or she may have simply decided to leave the team. But she was not done with cricket: she still listed herself as a 'Lady Cricketer' on the 1891 census, although as we shall see there are several possible reasons for that.

There was one final mysterious departure, followed by an equally mysterious reappearance. Susie Fletcher played at the start of the season, and like the others stopped playing early – in her case, after the Southampton game in early May. Unlike the others, she returned in mid-July and remained a regular until the end of the season; somehow, she managed to be included in both versions of the profiles.

We do not know what lay behind these disappearances. Nor do we know what led to the recruitment of new players. Marie Beckenham first played on 15 May, after which she was almost ever-present; like Wadkin, she was an addition to the revised profiles. Other newcomers included several women who called themselves Gordon – their real name was Barefoot, making them sisters of the players going by the pseudonyms Beatrice and Flora Fane – but only Eva Gordon made it on to the second version of the profiles.

Was there trouble within the team? The lack of stability in those first weeks might suggest so. But unfortunately, no explanation survives.

The Show Must Go On
... and On

ONE POSSIBLE explanation for the high turnover is the heavy workload demanded of the cricketers. Between April and October 1890, they appeared in around 80 exhibition matches – over 100 playing days – across the length and breadth of Britain.[28] A comparison with male professional cricketers is revealing. George Lohmann, the occasional OELC coach and one of the leading (and best-paid) cricketers in England, played 32 three-day matches during the 1890 season. Both the OELC and their male counterparts generally played six days of cricket each week. For the men this meant two matches but for the women – who mostly played a combination of one- and two-day games – it was often three, involving a greater amount of travel.

And for any professional cricketer, it was travel which made the lifestyle so exhausting: an endless succession

---

28 From newspaper reports and advertisements, we can reconstruct a list of 77 fixtures between the Reds and the Blues in 1890, 22 of which were played over two days and two over three days (103 days of cricket in total). There were almost certainly other games for which no record survives. As one newspaper said in August, 'Since [the start of the season], with the exception of two days' rest, the teams have been playing without intermission.' Although this is not quite accurate – it does not account for the quiet period in late April – it seems a fair summary.

of railway stations, trains, long journeys and nights in unfamiliar hotel rooms or other lodgings.

Perhaps the only way in which the lives of the women were easier was in the hours on the field: their games usually began at 2pm and ended at 6:30pm, whereas men played from 11am until 6:30pm. But the women also had to perform at theatres in the evening, which more than offset the shorter cricketing day. The men's season was also briefer; Lohmann's last game was in mid-September but the women played for another month, an unusually late finish.

Nearly seven months in each other's company must inevitably have created tension among the players. Furthermore, their lives were far more constrained than those of male cricketers. Mrs Grant (or the other matrons) constantly supervised them and Matthews travelled with them. He also umpired their games, usually alongside a local official such as the captain of the hosting cricket club, meaning that they never escaped the attention of their employers. It is unclear if Michel attended all the games, but he was certainly frequently around the team, and Walter Bosanquet was sometimes present: for example, he umpired games at Slough on 30 May and at Catford on 15 October. Male professionals never endured such ongoing scrutiny.

To exacerbate the issues, the women had no other outlet. When county cricketers grew tired of their team-mates, they had the prospect of facing different opposition every few days, making or renewing friendships and rivalries across the country. The members of the OELC could only look forward to a series of interminable matches – the same teams, the same batters, the same bowlers, the same shots, the same tactics, the same evening routine – almost every day from April until October.

The monotony of the cricket was the biggest drawback to the format of Reds against Blues. As Violet Westbrook hinted to the *Manchester Evening Mail*, it must have become predictable and tiresome for the batters constantly to face the same bowlers. Maintaining motivation must have been a struggle, with the only incentive for victory being a small financial bonus.

To make matters worse, many of the women struggled with the cricketing side of the operation. Good cricketers like Violet Westbrook, Ella Heather, Georgina Sheffield and Louisa Daly were the exception. The overwhelming majority of players – even supposedly specialist batters – had a batting average in single figures and only eight women were regular bowlers.

It simply cannot have been fun. In Birmingham, one member of the team spoke – a little indiscreetly – to a journalist to express their dissatisfaction with the sport they were playing: 'From a few hints which one of [the players] allowed to drop, however, I should not gather they are very enthusiastic about the game, and, excepting to two or three of them cricket is much a matter of work. They would rather be in the field than batting, although batting is what they most easily take to, very few of the girls being able to bowl a straight ball, but in the field they think they are the objects of more attention.'

Glancing through the available scores, it is striking how similar many of the games were and how the same players dominated. There was no narrative to the season: no championship at which to aim, no important match on which to focus. Instead, the teams just had to turn up at the next venue, hope for a good crowd, and go through the motions of another meaningless fixture. This problem had an obvious solution: the OELC needed to play other teams, and this seems to have been the initial intention. However, outside opposition never materialised.

Violet Westbrook told the *Manchester Evening Mail* in July: 'We are doing our best to get up matches with lady amateur XIs and XXIIs. Already several fixtures of this kind have been made. When we were at Taunton a team of lady amateurs practised on the ground we played on.' But that was as good as it got. Early advertisements had offered games against local women's teams as an alternative to exhibition matches, and there is some evidence that tentative arrangements were made. Two months before the OELC visited Douglas on the Isle of Man, the local newspaper called for 'local young ladies' to come forward for coaching at the cricket club so that they would be ready to face the visitors. But when they arrived on the Isle of Man in July, the OELC put on their usual exhibition match.

There were other attempts to play other women's teams. For example, the *Manchester Times* reported that when the OELC were in Cambridge, they had challenged Newnham and Girton – the two all-female colleges – to a game, but neither establishment had a cricket team.[29] There were even attempts to organise games against men, despite the reservations of Bosanquet about such cricket: a prospective match against a men's team at Dover fell through, and at Newton Abbot in September, the OELC would have played a local men's team but decided quite late in the day that they were not yet ready for such a challenge.

---

29 Or perhaps they did not want to admit having one to the OELC. There is evidence that women were playing cricket at Girton from the 1870s onwards.

But there is a possibility that games against other teams *might* have been squeezed in. A newspaper in Northampton stated in June that 'the Lady Cricketers have arranged matches in many towns with High School and Ladies' Amateur Clubs'; although there is no record of any such games, they may have taken place. Similarly, *Sporting Life* regularly included the OELC games on their list of weekly fixtures and these were not always Blues v Reds; for example, on 1 August, *Sporting Life* said that the Lady Cricketers (Blues) were to play Twenty-Two Amateurs at Glasgow. The teams *were* in Scotland at the time, playing as one of the attractions at the Edinburgh International Exhibition, but never apparently ventured further afield. Nor was *Sporting Life* necessarily accurate: it stated that during the week commencing 4 August, the Lady Cricketers (Reds) were to play 22 Amateurs at Newcastle, but the OELC spent that week playing two-day games at Barnsley, Sheffield and Derby. Something similar happened at Plymouth in September; originally scheduled to play Plymouth Ladies and then Plymouth Ladies' High School on 17 and 18 September, the OELC instead played exhibition games in Teignmouth and Newton Abbot.

Amateur women's teams certainly existed in 1890 and the press – alerted by the OELC to the phenomenon of women's cricket – took more notice of them than usual. Additionally, there seems to have been a growth in the number of women playing – even if the press were loath to credit the OELC. The *Cheltenham Looker-On* asked: 'How long will the craze for Ladies' Cricket Clubs last? Just now there are no less than eleven in the South of England alone, and a still larger proportion to be found in the North. The new mania is affecting the popularity of tennis not a little.'

But coverage of this growth perhaps betrayed why these clubs did not want to play the OELC: reporters emphasised the purity of amateur teams, unsullied by the commercialism and professionalism of the OELC. Therefore the middle- and upper-class members of the clubs had no wish to associate with lower-class professional women. For example, an article in the *Manchester Times* in July, which discussed the growing interest in cricket among women, stated: 'The craze for cricket among ladies has done some good; though, since it has been taken up by professionals, the ardour for it among more fashionable folk has considerably cooled.' Similar sentiments were expressed in *The Lady*, a magazine aimed at women, which said in June that 'the introduction of the professional element into any games played by ladies is much to be regretted; therefore it is impossible to read with any pleasure of the various successes achieved by the lady cricketers during their season which is now in progress.' The writer believed any achievements by the OELC would be outweighed by the 'evil' of their professionalism:

> Professionalism is most decidedly the great evil of cricket as it now exists, but the existence of the male professional element is a trifle compared to the introduction of a female compeer. So long as girls confine themselves to playing with friends and relations before an audience of friends, neighbours, and tenants, there is no harm done, and this healthy exercise will probably do them an immense deal of good. It is impossible, however, not to regard with grave disapproval the introduction of systematic tours of professional lady cricketers who are willing

to exhibit themselves to an undiscerning crowd willing to pay the necessary entrance fee, and whose principal object is a share of the gate money.

Opposition was also expressed in *Woman*, a publication about which little information survives. This particular piece was widely reproduced in 1890: 'Let it be granted that female cricketers may achieve a fair amount of success at the great English game. After all, is it worth the candle? A quiet game among girls in a country village, "just for the fun of the thing," may be well enough; but when we hear of "professional lady cricketers," of "touring," of "gate money," and such like abominations, it is high time to protest against a craze which passes the ridiculous and verges on something even worse.'

A similar point was made, rather less pleasantly, in *The Graphic* in September, as part of an article marvelling at how 'the columns of the sporting papers at this time of year are full of the doings of lady cricketers'. But it explicitly stated: 'We do not mean those "lady cricketers" who are touring the country making money out of their skill; we have little sympathy with them.' Instead it praised the numerous games being played in the country houses of the upper classes: 'In the late summer … it is quite an institution; and a very harmless amusement it is. It is not harder work than lawn tennis; it gives opportunity for the wearing of some very pretty costumes; and it amuses the other sex. We fear it is not always the excellence of the play which attracts the male creature.'

A different view was expressed in the *South Wales Daily News*, which noted the excitement being generated by a forthcoming visit of the OELC – advertising hoardings around Cardiff had been displaying 'The Lady Cricketers are Coming' for several days – and suggested that the equivalent of the Gentlemen v Players matches – the famous fixture in which a team of leading male amateurs faced the best male professionals – might be possible given the number of amateur women's teams, although it conceded that the OELC would be too good for any such opposition.

In the absence of outside opposition, the weakness of the Red v Blue format was soon noticed. An 'Amateur Lady Cricketer', writing to the *Daily Graphic* in September, was cautiously positive about the OELC, but thought that matches between the Reds and Blues 'cannot possess a tenth of the interest that county or local engagements would occasion', and that it was 'difficult to feel any enthusiasm' for the matches, as spectators had 'no reason for caring whether Red or Blue wins'. Nevertheless, she was moderately impressed by the OELC and argued that 'the real interest of the example of these or other professional lady cricketers will begin when we have county or local teams of ladies, who will call in professional help as men do now. A match between, say, Ladies of Middlesex and Yorkshire, or between Girton and Newnham, would really raise some excitement.'

Even journalists who were enthusiastic about the OELC conceded that a continuation of Blue v Red would soon lose its appeal. One writer said: 'As a novelty it was worth seeing, but probably few would care to make a second visit, unless with a considerable interval.' And another suggested that the management should consider 'whether an occasional contest with masculine opponents would not add to the excitement of the game; otherwise it is to be feared the new entertainment will be but a nine days' sensation.'

***

Fortunately for the success of the team, the novelty of seeing women play cricket was enough to attract spectators in the short term, and the OELC held their lustre well enough throughout the 1890 season to guarantee attendances that were always respectable and sometimes spectacular. From the opening game at Liverpool, with its reported audience of 15,000, crowds flocked to watch. The management claimed that the first Liverpool game and those at Leicester, Nottingham and Scarborough resulted in the biggest gates. We only have partial figures for the Nottingham game (between 1,500 and 2,000 spectators on the second day) and nothing for the other two. However, other matches seem to have had impressive attendances.

These figures need to be treated with caution because they can only be sourced on the rare occasions when the press reported approximate numbers of spectators. Some attendances seem to be based on information provided by the owners of the ground or the associated cricket club but others appear to be based on estimates by journalists. It is unlikely that such calculations were wildly inaccurate; but nor should they be relied upon too much. For example, reports of the same game could give different numbers, such as when one newspaper said that 1,200 watched the OELC at Newport but another said that the attendance grew to 15,000 by the end of the day (both of those could be correct if the crowd increased substantially).

With these qualifications, the numbers indicate how many people watched the OELC and which games were especially attractive to the public. There were at least 32 days of cricket (across 22 games) which drew audiences of over 1,000. Four matches were reported to have had audiences of over 10,000: at Chelsea (between 12,000 and 16,000 as part of the Royal Military Exhibition), Newport (possibly 15,000), Liverpool (15,000, though it is not clear if this a combined figure for both days) and Manchester (13,000 across two days). While not all attendances were so impressive, there were few occasions when the crowds were poor. One of the exceptions was at Preston where only around 50 spectators saw the first day. Canterbury also saw a 'very small attendance of spectators'.

There is, however, one surprising indicator of the relative appeal of the OELC. During the 1890 season, the Australian men's team visited England, playing a three-Test series and 37 other games between May and September. Such tours were generally popular and spectators flocked to watch. And yet several of the OELC matches had an attendance surpassing that for games featuring the Australians. More people watched the OELC at Leicester and Nottingham than the equivalent Australian games against the county teams, and on 8 September, 5,000 watched the Australians play MCC at Lord's on the same day that 7,000 watched the OELC at Crystal Palace. There are some caveats: it was the seventh visit by an Australian team to England in 13 years and the tourists were defeated far too often to be an attractive spectacle for the public. But it was still remarkable for a professional women's team to draw some bigger crowds than an Australian Test team.

Another interesting phenomenon was the composition of these crowds; many reports observed that the proportion of women spectators was far higher than was usually seen at a cricket ground. It was also frequently noted that the 'better classes' eagerly attended the games, which was quite a boost to their respectability. More orthodox cricket spectators also attended: the Yorkshire county team watched one match, and some of the touring Australians were among the crowd at the Royal Military Exhibition in September. However we look at it, there is absolutely no question that the OELC were an enormous hit.

But perhaps more important than the reality was the *perception* that the OELC were hugely popular. The *Northampton Daily Reporter* looked forward in some anticipation to the arrival of the OELC in June: 'Great interest will attach to the visit of the Original English Lady Cricketers ... on Monday and Tuesday, and should the weather be fine an extraordinarily large gate is anticipated, though Northampton will probably not rival the 20,000 and 15,000 who witnessed the matches in Liverpool and Cambridge respectively [both of these figures are wild exaggerations; only 1,000 attended the match at Cambridge]. From all over the country come reports of a most successful tour, and critics of cricket speak in praise of the manner in which the game is played.' Similarly, the visit of the OELC to Newton Abbot in mid-September was keenly anticipated.

And dotted throughout local newspapers were stories of individuals eager to see the OELC: an account in the *Hastings and St Leonards Times* of a lethargic Hastings Town Council meeting in September which stated, perhaps sarcastically: 'A gloom hung over the Chamber suggesting that the members wanted to be out with the lady cricketers'; a man – appearing before Warrington magistrates in July after drunkenly attacking a policeman – who his companions insisted had only come into town to watch the lady cricketers; and the annual outing of the Shepton

Mallet Church Choir to Weymouth in October during which several people went to watch the OELC.

But perhaps not everywhere was quite so welcoming. One strange article in November, of uncertain reliability, stated that 'when the Lady Cricketers recently proposed to visit [Worcester], their match was interdicted by the police on the score of decency'. This was somewhat dubiously sourced to 'a friend of mine' by the author, and no similar story appeared elsewhere except as a reprint of the original. As it was part of a story which sought to emphasise how unreasonable the police were in Worcester, it may not be reliable: for example, the article also claimed that nursemaids could be fined £5 for 'gossiping' or 'loitering' in the streets, and that there were also fines for anyone walking 'two abreast thereon with perambulators or other carriages, with or without children therein'.

* * *

If the popularity of the OELC in 1890 is unarguable, how did this translate into financial success?

Despite a paucity of direct evidence, we can be certain that the 1890 tour made a profit, possibly a big one. This was the impression given by the end of the season, although as so often we must be aware that we may simply be parroting what Michel and the ECAA wanted the press to believe. For example, an article in *Gentlewoman* observed in November 1890: 'The wet summer was not very favourable for money-making, but the autumn brought a very satisfactory harvest.' *The Sportsman* noted in September that, 'The financial aspect has been decidedly promising considering the amount of prejudice that has had to be encountered, and overcome, and the expenses of taking the girls about the country, while their payments – be they two pounds or four pounds per week – mount to a goodly sum.' *The Globe* described the tour as 'a great success, from a monetary point of view, notwithstanding a summer unfavourable for outdoor sport', and *The Stage* observed that the gate money made from the tour would tempt others to copy the format.

No kind of financial accounts have survived, so we must speculate. Many advertisements give admission prices, generally a minimum of 6d (although at some grounds it was at least a shilling to watch). On top of this, spectators could pay a little more (sometimes an extra 6d, sometimes up to 2s) for a better seat, depending on the venue's facilities – perhaps within an enclosure, grandstand, or a pavilion – or even to have a carriage admitted on to the ground. At several locations it was also possible to be admitted for half-price at 4pm. It would not be unreasonable – and would perhaps be conservative – to assume an average payment of one shilling per spectator.[30]

The uncertainty over attendances – figures were not reported for more than half of the games – make estimates of gate receipts hazardous. But even if no one had attended those games for which no figures survive, between 90,000 and 100,000 people in total would have paid to watch the OELC in 1890; therefore the real number must have been considerably higher. And if all those spectators paid one shilling for admission, that would have seen gate receipts of between £4,500 and £5,000. To speculate a little further: if the average attendance at each day's play was 2,000 (which is not unreasonable based on the surviving data), that would

---

30 For some matches – such as their appearances at the Edinburgh Exhibition or the Royal Military Exhibition – the OELC most likely were given a flat fee as the gate money would have gone to the organisers.

be a total attendance of around 200,000 people and gate receipts of around £10,000. However, even here we are on uncertain ground as small differences in assumptions lead to substantial variation in figures, and this is as far as the evidence can safely take us.

However, there were deductions to be made. Michel, in negotiations, offered the ground owners either a share of gate receipts or a fixed amount. We have a few examples in which we can see how much money each party received. The Great Yarmouth Amusement Committee accepted Michel's offer of a 25 per cent share of the gate receipts in return for the ground, pavilion and other facilities. That match was played on 25 and 26 August, and although no indication was given of the attendance, a local report said that £127 was taken at the gate. Therefore the Great Yarmouth Amusement Committee would have taken just under £42, and the OELC would have taken £85. We have similar details from a game at Hastings, revealed at a committee meeting the following April: the Hastings Central Cricket and Recreation Ground had received just over £51 as their share of the profits from the OELC appearance there. Depending on their agreement with Michel, this meant gate takings of between £125 (if they had a 40 per cent share) and £200 (with a 25 per cent share); therefore the ECAA took away between £75 and £150 from Hastings. For any games where the ECAA paid just a flat fee (we don't know how frequently this happened) the profits would have been even greater.[31]

Visits were certainly beneficial to clubs. Chesham Cricket Club, which had insisted on a guaranteed fund

---

31 If the ECAA made an average of £70 from every game, that would have been a total profit in excess of £5,000.

of £25, made £85 on the gate against expenses of £50, giving them a healthy profit to boost their 'empty coffers'. Some clubs cashed in shamelessly; the members of Burnley Cricket Club were not happy at having to pay for admission to watch the OELC as they usually received free admission.

* * *

For the ECAA, there would have been expenses to offset the gate money, but there is little evidence to suggest how great these might have been. Presumably a cut of the receipts went to local agents. There is one clue in this area; Henry Morgan of Liverpool sued the ECAA for £50 on the grounds that their non-delivery of advertising material had resulted in poor attendance. Not only does this indicate that he received money from the gate rather than a fixed amount, but it also suggests that £50 was a fair expectation (although he settled out of court for £15).

Other deductions from the profits might have included refreshments, advertising and staffing. But the major outgoing for the ECAA would have been wages. According to advertising, the players were paid 10 shillings per week during training (roughly January to March) and between 20 and 30 shillings per week during the season (April to October). The maximum wage would probably have been around £50, although most players would have received less.

Despite the claims in publicity material that 30 women had been recruited, and although 26 people are named in the original player profiles, it is most likely that there were no official reserves. When the teams visited the Isle of Man in July, one player was 'indisposed' and as no replacement was available, the teams played ten-a-side. And other women stepped in throughout the season for one-off appearances before disappearing forever, suggesting that they were temporary recruits to cover absences. The most likely scenario is that the ECAA employed just 22 full-time players (plus Katie Tatton, who never played a game and remained the scorer throughout) who travelled from venue to venue, with replacements drafted in (although there are no clues as to where they came from) when necessary. Therefore, the total wage bill was probably something in the region of £1,200.

The only other available figure we have regarding expenses was mentioned by the press soon after the tour began in 1890: that the ECAA had spent £2,000 before anyone had even set foot on the field. This presumably included training expenses, the purchase of equipment and clothing (including for the evening performances), and any costs involved in hiring venues.[32]

Going by the overall numbers, the money generated by the team seems to have been considerably greater than the cost of running it. This backs up the newspaper suggestions that the OELC made a good profit in 1890. So what happened to this surplus?

In 1891, Michel said, in a slightly suspect account, that the ECAA decided, at the end of 1890, 'to devote the entire profits realised to the expenses of continuing practice during the winter. This was done, and the then-members received a weekly salary when practising, although there was, of course, no income.' He also claimed that much of the money

---

32 Cricket bats were advertised in *Cricket: A Weekly Record of the Game* for around 12s 6d each in 1890, which seems to have been a representative price (meaning that purchasing 22 bats would have cost £13 15s). Cricket balls seem to have cost somewhere between 5s and 6s, but we do not know how many the OELC used in a season; it is unlikely they used a new ball for each game.

for the tour came from Bosanquet, who 'from time-to-time advanced various sums to the association' when money ran out during the season. At the time Michel was writing, none of this money had been returned and Bosanquet had 'lost very considerably by the speculation'. Michel, in this letter, was defending himself from accusations of financial misconduct and wanted to demonstrate that there was no money for him to take. Nevertheless, even he conceded that there was a profit in 1890.

And it is likely, despite his protestations, that the profits were distributed among the shareholders – including to Mr Michel, the proud owner of one share.

'Should Women Play Cricket?'

ALTHOUGH WE know that tens of thousands of spectators flocked to watch the OELC in 1890, we know little about the standard or style of cricket that they saw. Apart from one photograph of the first game in Liverpool – which shows two Blues fielders running a little stiffly towards the viewer, chasing a ball while the two Reds batters turn after completing their first run – we have no images of the players in action. Such photography (rather than posed shots) was tricky at the time owing to the limitations of technology; at Liverpool the camera was positioned too far from the pitch – square on, roughly in line with the direction of point – to identify anyone and therefore it does not tell us much. Nor do we have any moving images: film was still an experimental process in 1890 and commercial recordings some years away.

Nor can we particularly rely on the limited statistical evidence from scorecards. There are many games for which no individual scores survive or for which we only have details for a single day of a match lasting several; and there are games that we know took place but which went unreported. Nor can we compile accurate or comprehensive statistics about the games for which details survive: the published scorecards are littered with errors such as individual scores not tallying with the stated totals, misidentified players, mistaken initials (often making it impossible to distinguish between sisters) and an almost universal lack of bowling figures.

Given the lack of other evidence, we are forced to rely on newspaper reports to get a sense of how the women played cricket. But much cricket writing lacked sophistication in 1890; there was little analysis and less description even for the highest levels of the sport. Reporting rarely ventured beyond bland details of bowling changes and scoring shots. The local journalists who covered most OELC games lacked the expertise of those who wrote about cricket regularly. As a result, we know almost nothing about how Violet Westbrook batted, how Ada Heather bowled, or how Elizabeth Dempsey fielded. Nor can we evaluate how good the players were, relying on the subjective accounts of non-experts. Did Westbrook score over 2,000 runs in 1890 because she was an exceptional player or because she faced poor – and painfully familiar – bowling?

To add to the frustrations, we must be careful in using the newspapers to understand what was happening on the field. Although vast numbers of articles about the OELC were published, the writers were hardly impartial. The need to untangle the biases of an author is hardly unique to the history of the OELC, but issues are multiplied here because of the prejudices of male Victorian journalists against women and women cricketers. We are left with a situation – familiar to the historian but less so to the cricket follower – in which we cannot trust the written sources that we have.

However, despite this litany of caution and despair, it is possible – if we are careful – to get an impression, however fleeting, of what might have been happening on the field and ascertain the opinions of spectators.

* * *

The coverage of the opening match at Liverpool was atypical of what followed; the overwhelmingly positive tone seems more than a little suspicious; perhaps there had been a financial inducement. For example, the *Liverpool Echo* gushed:

> They can wield the bat with all the defensive skill and hitting powers of a veteran professor [professional] of the art, and would certainly put to shame many a gentleman amateur … The young ladies bat with considerable freedom; they knew the art of "cutting" and "driving" and their chief prowess consists of getting the ball round to "leg" … The fielding of the whole party is exceedingly smart and skilful, and they can "take" and "return" a ball on the run with considerable grace and ease … A feature in their play is the excellent running and shieing [shying] of the ball.

Similarly, the *Liverpool Mercury* said: 'Those who visited the Fairfield grounds expecting to see ladies on the field who would be – as is often the case among the gentler sex – unable to throw or catch a ball, must have been agreeably disappointed, as the members of the team were exceptionally clever at bowling, catching, stopping, and fielding.' And the *Liverpool Courier* made the oft-repeated comment that the teams 'play and do not burlesque the game'. This quote was often accompanied in publicity material by one from the writer George R. Sims, who supposedly said when he attended a match: 'I came to scoff and remained to applaud.'

Writers outside Liverpool did not take the OELC seriously at first. For example, the *Weston-super-Mare Gazette* commented: 'It is, of course, amusing to see ladies play cricket, but interest in the novelty cannot be long sustained.' Even late in the season, when it had been grudgingly accepted that the OELC had been a great success, the *Suffolk and Essex Free Press* dismissed the team as 'little more than an elaborate and rather ridiculous joke'. The *Middlesex Independent* took a similar view, suggesting that it would have been more interesting 'had the representation partaken of the form of a burlesque of the grand old game' rather than attempt to play seriously.

There were frequent unfavourable comparisons to men's cricket. A writer for the *Leamington Spa Courier* made clear that he considered this to be an inferior version of the game. He observed that the field placings were 'in strict accordance' with cricketing convention, but the fielders stood closer than men would have done. The bowling he classed as 'not of an order that would severely test the ability of any competent [presumably meaning male] player', although he made an exception for Daisie Stanley. He suggested that several bowlers were throwing, complained that the ball was delivered too slowly, grumbled that not enough fours were struck and mocked the fielders as too ponderous and liable to drop the ball: 'It was very amusing to watch some of the girls run. They did it with a will, certainly; but not with much grace – in fact one young lady decidedly "wobbled".'

Even praise could be condescending, such as when the *Manchester Courier* printed a cautiously favourable article in July: 'As to the quality of the cricket thus newly thrust upon us, it is excellent – for ladies. Judged by the ordinary standards it is, perhaps, a little slow, and one longs to see now and then such vigorous drives as sometimes startle visitors to Old Trafford ... But although better cricket might be desired by the critical, there is that in the ladies' play which sustains interest fairly well.' The writer also described 'little feminine weaknesses' such as 'a batsman, or shall we say batswoman, stamping her foot when her wicket is razed to the ground'. He suggested that the laughter at such occurrences 'in no way disconcerts the cricketers, but spurs them on to greater activity'.

There were frequent comments about the slow nature of play. An article in the *Middlesex Independent* in May suggested that the crowds quickly became bored by the 'funereal' pace of the game at Chiswick: 'As soon as the novelty had worn off, the 'milk and watery' character of the whole proceedings became to those who had been accustomed to watch genuine sport, painfully apparent.' Some writers perceived a lack of intensity in the games, but others thought the problem was *too much* intensity and expressed surprise at how focused the women were on the field.

But perhaps the most surprising aspect of the coverage was that it betrayed fear: that women playing cricket was somehow a threat to men. Readers were frequently reassured that women simply weren't as good, or those who succeeded did so through playing in a masculine style. For example Violet Westbrook, as the best player, was often compared to male cricketers (usually W. G. Grace) rather than judged on her own merits. Even the women seem to have fallen into this trap: the reporter at Weston-super-Mare noticed that 'some of the girls regularly answer to the names of "Charlie," "Jack," and "Tom," whilst others are distinguished only by their rightful names.' And when Lena Parsons took a good catch at Clifton, there were calls (either from the crowd or her team-mates, the report does not specify) of 'Well caught, sir!'

Most interesting was the defensiveness stirred up when it became clear how successful the OELC were. A journalist for the *Lancashire Evening Post* took issue with a claim in the *Women's Penny Weekly* that there had been a lot of interest in the OELC, suggesting that the writer – presumed to be of 'the feminine sex' – was 'not strictly correct'. The *Evening Post* writer attributed the large crowds to 'amused interest', although he grudgingly conceded that 'most people who have seen the players have been surprised by their performances' and that 'male journalism has, of course, given them an ungracious snub or two'.

Other writers used the OELC as a vehicle to discuss changes in society which meant that women were now allowed to do activities once considered unthinkable for the 'weaker sex'. Of course, such fears were a growing feature of the 1890s far beyond the world of sport. Even if the cricketing journalists were not explicitly echoing concerns about 'New Women', there could have been some subconscious association of the cricket team with the growing feminist movement. How much did these concerns distort the opinions of the journalists, and how much does that warp our evidence?

* * *

From those writers who tried to judge the play on its own merits, there were some positive remarks. For example, an article in the *Nottingham Evening Post* said of the batting: 'There were some very clever "cuts", and the ball was driven to a distance which showed that there was no lack of muscular strength on the part of the players.' Even more fulsome praise came from the writer in the *Weston-super-Mare Gazette*, who enthused that bowling was the team's 'strongest point': 'Several of them are exceedingly good left-hand bowlers, although, of course, some are yet very erratic.'[33] The *Nottingham Evening Post* said that they 'bowled well (nearly all overhand) and bat still better'. *The Globe* commented that the players could 'hit hard' with the bat and that the bowling was 'better than could be expected', while the *Warwickshire Herald* praised the batting and bowling as 'extraordinary'.

But when it came to fielding, no one quite seemed to know what to think. Most writers agreed that the fielding was the OELC's least strong discipline; for example, the *Weston-super-Mare Gazette* was fairly typical in its judgements: 'The fielding is perhaps the weakest point in the game, but this is probably due to the ladies having practised under cover, and they will no doubt improve.' Some writers narrowed the weakness down to throwing whereas others condemned the women as outright poor in the field. For example, the *Globe* stated: 'The fielding is – we should say, incurably – bad. The young Amazons cannot "return" the ball with sufficient velocity. It is the old story

---

33 The same writer misunderstood Michel's remarks to the *Liverpool Echo* that it had taken over six weeks to train the players how to bowl effectively, believing that it meant that 'great difficulty was experienced at first in inducing the teams to bowl overhand'.

– they cannot throw.' This view was shared by the writer for the *Leamington Spa Courier*, who snidely commented that the umpires 'had very little to do except dodge the balls thrown in by the fielders'. And yet some thought that the fielding – and throwing – was good. The indecisiveness is best illustrated by two reports on the same match. When the teams played at Old Trafford in July, a writer for the *Manchester Courier* judged: 'The throwing, by no means bad or inaccurate, is quite characteristic, being of the nature of shying; the fielding is a strange mixture of grace and contortion.' But an article in the *Manchester Weekly Times* stated: 'The worst feature of the play was the fielding, the picking up being wretched and the throwing-in execrable.'

There was a similar lack of consensus when journalists gave their Olympian Judgements on the whole concept of the OELC. Many viewed it as positive. For example, the *Nottingham Evening Post* thought that 'it was very good fun, and everyone was astonished at the ladies' display'. When the OELC appeared in Aston, a writer for the *Warwickshire Herald* had 'expected great things, and I was not disappointed. They are really first-rate players;' he concluded that 'if one can master the objection of ladies appearing in dresses very little shorter than ordinary walking costumes have frequently been, and their indulgence in exercise more vigorous than orthodox, there does seem little to object to in girls playing cricket.' But once again two critics could form extremely different opinions from a shared experience; the *Smethwick Telephone* called the same match a 'farce' in which 'these so-called lady professional cricketers' were 'frishing about … looking like so many freaks of nature'. And in doing so, they were lowering 'woman's dignity' and lowering themselves 'in man's estimation'. The writer continued: 'If it had been announced as a petticoat display, I could have understood it better, but to advertise it as a cricket match was an insult to that noble game.' He did not think that women should even be permitted to play privately, let alone in public.

The Aston match was one of the few in which the OELC responded to what was written. The *Birmingham Daily Mail* recorded that 'the lady cricketers are, I am afraid, hardly likely to come to Birmingham again, for they went away somewhat disappointed with the criticism they met with in the newspapers. The manager declared that he would rather they had been downright abused than chaffed.' Although Daisie Stanley put on a defiant front in her interviews, this snippet is an indication that some of the criticism might have affected the other players.

Another feature of the press coverage was an obsession with the appearance of the players. There were comments on their attractiveness, whether expressed in general terms – for example, one newspaper feigned coy delicacy in declining to state 'whether the young ladies are good-looking or not' while another suggested that lady cricketers 'must be young if they are to be attractive' – or about individuals, for example calling Bessie Moss a 'pretty little damsel' or describing Katie Tatton as 'the bright-eyed intelligent little maiden, who officiates as scorer'. The *Leamington Spa Courier* even complained that the women had acquired a suntan from having their caps at the back of their heads. The main focus was doubtless the costume, whether on specific items – for example, their 'short skirts of white cricketing flannel, reaching about four inches below the knee, and weighted with shot' – or the overall effect – described by one newspaper as 'picturesque, and exceedingly modest' while another said that 'their abbreviated white skirts, their ribbons, and their turn-down collars ... make an appearance which is decidedly pleasing'.

It was these costumes which made the biggest impression. For example, the Leamington writer observed that the spectators had gathered early, 'watching the young lady cricketers passing in and out of the dressing tent' to see their transformation from 'fashionably dressed young ladies into something not unlike the light and airy beings who take part in what theatrical proprietors, in their pantomime announcement bills, term "A Cricket Ballet".' When the OELC played at Scarborough, two 'popular dramatists' called Pettitt and Sims even made enquiries whether they could obtain versions of the costumes.

* * *

Most reports give the impression that the writer arrived at the games with clear opinions about women's cricket and left with those impressions – whether positive or negative – firmly reinforced. Their writing was often concerned less with the game of cricket in front of them and more with broader philosophical issues about whether women should be playing at all. For example, a writer in the *Burnley Express* said that women should stick to sports such as tennis: 'Ladies are bewitching at tennis, but I must confess the spectacle of a dainty miss "batting like a man", and of a ball flopping into petticoats, is not edifying.'

The most vicious criticisms of the OELC came in the *St James's Gazette*, which covered the OELC extensively but with decreasing respect. An article published in May conceded that the cricketers could 'pile up a high total of runs – largely because the fielding of the opposing team of ladies is excessively bad' – and complimented their costume. However the rest of the piece attacked not just the OELC, but women in general.

> The whole business is very silly and very vulgar. A band of good-looking young women between eighteen and twenty-three, who ought to be at home learning how to boil a potato and to make a cup of drinkable coffee, are instead travelling about the country exhibiting their physical strength and their ankles to anybody who can pay a shilling to see the delectable sight. If a number of frolicsome girls like to play a game of cricket in a quiet meadow, nobody shall say them nay; but the professional lady cricketer is rather too much. Already we have the professional lady tennis-player, and she is not so agreeable a product of civilisation that we need desire to have her multiplied. Presently we shall have the professional female footballer, if not the professional lady boxer.

This article, which the editor later claimed to be 'tongue-in-cheek', provoked an angry reaction from Lady Florence Dixie, a prominent feminist who later became involved in women's football. She wrote a letter suggesting that 'there is just a smattering of spite and envy in your ridicule' and that 'you were brought up to believe women slaves, idiots and nonentities, only fit to boil potatoes and make coffee for such noble beings as yourself'. She wrote at some length about feminist ideas. In fairness to the *St James's Gazette*, although it referred to Dixie's letter as a 'tempestuous epistle', it published it apparently in full and with no editorial comment or rebuttal.

The relationship between the *St James's Gazette* and women's cricket further deteriorated when a letter was published in early June which quoted Doctor Samuel Johnson's reaction to hearing a woman speaking at a Quakers' meeting: 'Sir, a woman preaching is like a dog's walking on his hind legs. It is not well done; but you are surprised to find it done at all.' The author of the letter concluded: 'It would be refreshing to hear the Doctor's views upon the professional lady cricketer.' Later that month, the *St James's Gazette* published a mock debate between fictional schoolboys on the topic 'Should we let girls play cricket?' It was just an excuse to restate the view that women should be kept in their place.

But some felt that the *St James's Gazette* had taken matters too far; the *Western Times* in September said: 'A great deal of objection has been raised in some quarters to ladies playing cricket. The *St James's Gazette* notably has affected to be greatly shocked at the feats of these ladies. But to my mind there cannot be a more healthy outdoor exercise … At any rate, the lady cricketers have already proved that they can play the national game.'

Indeed, there was, by the end of the season, an acceptance even in national newspapers – albeit grudging in some quarters – that the OELC had been a distinct success. As the tour drew to a close, *The Globe* suggested that 'although the suggestion of a venture of this description was received with considerable disfavour, the girls by their modest demeanour in the field and their genuine attempts to play the correct game, have disarmed even the most severe of their earlier critics.'

Sporting Life judged the tour to have been an 'unqualified success'; the *Pall Mall Gazette* said: 'Without seeing them, it can scarcely be realised how well they play, some of their fielding and batting being really excellent'; and the *Manchester Weekly Times* even questioned why the umpires were men rather than women.

* * *

So much for the opinions of the newspapermen. What did everyone else think? Did the readers agree with them? This latter question is impossible to answer, although the views must have struck a chord or they would not have continued to be printed. What about those who went to watch? What did the viewing public think of it all? Spectators were certainly interested enough to attend in large numbers, attracted by curiosity, advertising or word of mouth, but what was their opinion of what they saw?

Our only source of information here is the newspaper reports. And writers were not averse to denying the popularity of the OELC if it suited their purpose. Depending on the biases of the journalist, cheers could be reported as jeers; rather than finding out their real thoughts, the writer could use 'artistic licence' to impose his own opinions on the spectators.

But underneath, we can sometimes detect occasional signs of what the crowd really thought. An article in the *Manchester Courier* revealed that there were many women in attendance when the OELC played at Manchester who 'quite naturally' were appreciative of 'their fair sisters' work'. In fact, the author thought that the audience, if anything, gave the players too much credit. When the teams played at Aston, the writer for the *Warwickshire Herald* observed that the crowd, mainly consisting of men, 'appeared to be lost in admiration, and a specially brilliant piece of play did not fail to produce a burst of enthusiastic applause'. But that same author also sat for a time with a group who made frequent sarcastic remarks about the players, until they lost interest and turned their attention to a nearby policeman instead.

There are other suggestions that the women sometimes faced mockery. An article in the Portsmouth *Evening News* about the OELC's first appearance in London lamented that the games were open to the public: 'No woman can stand ridicule, and when lady cricketers tumble head over heels in endeavouring to reach a "skyer", or flop down on the popping crease to escape a run-out, or punch the umpire in the ribs to avoid a hard return, we suspect they will not relish the laughter of the crowd.' But the writer was not worried about the effect of this 'ridicule' on the women themselves; instead, he expressed concern for the feelings of their fathers, brothers and prospective husbands.

Some journalists suspected that many male spectators were present for reasons other than the cricketing abilities of the women. While a writer for the *Smethwick Telephone* was walking among the crowd at Aston, he heard 'observations of a very debasing character'. He added: 'To see the lady wicket-keeper pose in the position which is necessary for this masculine game was quite sufficient, I should think, to make any of the ladies present blush for their sex.' This particular 'debasing observation' was perhaps the author's own. Another writer expressed sentiments that might similarly have betrayed his personal thoughts when the OELC played at Chiswick: 'The curiosity of the crowd to obtain a nearer inspection of this costume led some inconvenience. The ladies might take the hint. The crowd would pay to see the costumes without the play. Without the fatigue of the cricket, abundant gate money ... might be realised by the two elevens simply by exhibiting themselves in their flannels!'

They may have had a point about the intentions of the audience. There are a few reports of the women receiving unwanted attention. At Maidenhead, several young men purchased photographs of the players, but their attempts to chat and 'flirt' with the women were rather coldly rebuffed. At the Military Exhibition in Chelsea, *The Sportsman* reported that some 'mashers' – young men, usually fashionably dressed and supremely confident, who often made unwelcome approaches to women – 'were unusually eager to "see the girls dontcherknow", quite a mob awaiting their departure from the pavilion after the conclusion of the game.' More positively, at Great Yarmouth a group of around 90 young men known locally as the 'Lambs' provided various entertainments for the crowd, including at one point 'serenading' the players, 'to whom they had given a morning concert on the sands'. The report said that the players had not received such attention elsewhere and had enjoyed the experience.

If we cannot always trust the journalists, are there other ways to gauge the public reaction? One indication of the genuine popularity of the OELC was the reaction to their appearance at the Royal Military Exhibition in September; they were such a success that the organisers booked a return appearance in October.

A less obvious demonstration of success was that, from an early stage, they became a target of satire. From

June, Nellie Navette, a star of the music hall, advertised herself as 'Burlesque Artiste and Specialite Dancer, and the "Lady Cricketer" (Pirates beware)'. A large part of her act throughout 1890 was a song, 'The Lady Cricketer' (which debuted on 9 June) for which she dressed up in an outfit resembling that of the OELC. She later recalled in an interview how her song (one of the few she performed which had no dancing) involved throwing rubber balls, inscribed with her name, into the audience. One night she accidentally hit a man in the eye; he took it in good sport, but 'a lady with him was quite furious'. She also remembered that the Australian Test cricketer Billy Murdoch presented her with a bat and ball as a tribute to her song. She continued to promote her 'Lady Cricketer' act until January 1891. Other artists, including Nelly Wilson and 'the Sisters Twibell', performed songs about the lady cricketers, the former's version being particularly successful. Similarly, in July, a group called 'Sam Hague's Own' performed an act at St James's Hall in Liverpool in which the OELC were parodied. If such acts cannot tell us what people thought of the team – and satire does not necessarily mean that they were objects of widespread mockery – they do indicate how much it had penetrated the public consciousness.

* * *

Finally, it is possible to discern from newspapers the faintest echo of how the women played the game. Comments on individual players were the exception rather than the rule. That exception was Violet Westbrook. For example, 'Magpie' writing in *The Globe* said that she was 'really a good all-round cricketer. She is the mould of form at the wicket, batting in good style and hitting well all round.' Her efforts to be the first OELC player to score a century were noted several times; after scoring 91 at Chiswick, 99 (run out) at Guildford, and an unbeaten 93 on a cold day at Cambridge when no other player on her team reached double figures, she finally scored 104 not out at Burnley in mid-July. For this effort, a local player (who had acted as umpire alongside Matthews) organised a collection for her; Westbrook told the *Burnley Express* she planned to buy a brooch or ornament to commemorate the occasion. Later in the season, she recorded two more unbeaten nineties, at Hastings and the Royal Military Exhibition, and a second century, 102 not out at Barnstaple. She was clearly a class above any other player, and almost always the top scorer, but even she was never subject to prolonged analysis or description beyond trivial comments.

The Heather sisters attracted some cricketing attention. Ella Heather was the only batter in 1890 other than Westbrook to score over 1,000 runs in games for which scores survive (at an average of just under 28). One report stated that she 'batted with a correctness of style and freedom which would have done credit to any team of the other sex'. She also took over 50 wickets with her slow bowling, but did not bowl regularly in the second part of the season. Her sister Ada was described as the fastest bowler for the OELC and took over 150 wickets; her 169 in recorded matches was second only to Westbrook's 222. Several reports also suggested that she could spin the ball at pace.

Comments on other individuals were few and far between. One report described Florence Hardwick batting with neither pads nor gloves, but given that she averaged under 6 with the bat and had a highest score of 25, this was apparently none too effective. Lena Parsons seems to have adopted an aggressive approach when she batted, but her average of 6.44 indicates a lack of success. Similarly, Lizzie Sanders usually attacked the bowling, such as when she scored 29 through 'hitting out very boldly' at Newport. But that remained her highest score, not least as she was frequently run out, and she averaged just under 9, despite a few promising innings.

If we cannot say much about the play of individuals, we can get a flavour from a few reports about the overall approach of the teams. For example, 'Magpie' in *The Globe* stated: 'The majority of the girls ... do not seem to be able to get any amount of swing upon the bat, and this, of course, prevents hard hitting; but this is the only general fault noticeable.' A report in mid-June said: 'One or two could [of the OELC] play very fairish cricket, but several of the larger scores were the result of adopting the "tip-and-run" principle, dangerously short ones being accomplished. In this, however, they were favoured by inability to pick the ball up promptly, a general failing with both teams.' Some of these short runs were a little *too* risky; there were a lot of run-outs, especially early in the season.

Almost all the bowling was overarm; a report in the *Manchester Weekly Times* noted the gloves and pads worn by the players were a 'necessity' because 'some of the balls were sent at a fair pace, all the bowlers who were tried on Monday despising "lobs" and bowling overhand.' Only Sophie Charles and Florence Hardwick were listed as under arm bowlers in the *Gazette* profiles; the former took only 12 wickets, although she bowled more than Hardwick who did not take any. Charles's one big success came at Maidenhead, when her lobs took four wickets for seven runs in six overs.

Different bowlers came to the fore at different points in the season. For example, Elizabeth Dempsey took over 80 wickets but barely bowled after the middle of June for reasons that are unclear. Instead, she became an exceptionally good fielder at point and took an almost unbelievable 96 catches in matches for which we have a full scorecard (the next highest were Lena Parsons with 46, the inevitable Violet Westbrook with 30, and Grace Westbrook – who was usually a wicket-keeper – with 20). Louise Daly took at least 104 wickets but disappeared from the team in mid-August. The other main bowler – with around 150 wickets – was Georgina Sheffield, but like most of the others, she had a long spell – around a month, mid-season – in which she did not bowl.

A few hints emerged over the course of the season about fielding tactics. The reporter for the *Manchester Weekly Times* observed: 'The field was set on the usual plan, but much nearer the wickets than in ordinary cricket, as the ball rarely travels far.' The only point on which almost everyone agreed was that the wicket-keeping was very good. One story suggested that the Australian wicket-keeper Jack Blackham intended to present a pair of his gloves to the two wicket-keepers (who at the time were Bessie Moss for the Blues and Adele Matthey for the Reds) but it is unclear if he ever did so. It was around this time that the wicket-keeping gloves literally changed hands; Grace Westbrook had played for the Reds until the end of May; after a game against Boston, she switched to the Blues and took over from Moss as their wicket-keeper for the rest of the season. Westbrook drew almost unanimous praise; the *Warwickshire Herald* said that her wicket-keeping was 'of such a quality that it is impossible to speak of it too highly'.[34]

If a suggestion in the *Manchester Weekly Times* that the keepers stood 'a yard behind the stumps' is accurate, this would have been further away than was usual (for a wicket-keeper 'standing up' to the bowling) and might explain a lack of stumpings. And one watcher at Clifton was critical of the wicket-keeping: 'A very noticeable error frequently made was that the wicket-keeper, in receiving a ball, stood before instead of behind the wicket, many a chance of a stumping being thus missed.'

* * *

It is extraordinary that so many of the runs, wickets and catches were concentrated among so few players. In those matches for which we have full scores, only five players (of those who batted more than three times) averaged in double figures with the bat and only eight took more than 20 wickets with the ball; Violet Westbrook, Ella Heather and Ada Heather were in both groups, meaning that ten players accounted for the majority of runs and wickets. Most of the women appear to have been merely making up the numbers on the field. For example, Bianca Seymour (batting average 2.59), Nellie Wadkin (2.44), Eva Gordon (2.55) and Marie Beckenham (2.44) seem to have done nothing except turn up every day: they did not bowl and

---

34 Matthey took up bowling after relinquishing the gloves; after the unexplained departure of Louise Daly from the team, she began to bowl with increasing effectiveness, taking over 40 wickets from the end of August.

took few catches. But for some – possibly many – cricket was not why they had come, nor was it where their expertise lay. For those players, it was only in the evenings that they came to life.

In the Evening

CRICKET WAS never the sole focus of the OELC. The evening performances were just as important; perhaps even more so. Unfortunately, we know far less about this aspect of the programme. The intention was always to have a 'theatrical' component to the OELC, and it would be safe to assume that some – perhaps many – of the recruits, like Katie Tatton, were attracted by this prospect. What is less clear is how important this was in the original concept. Were the OELC a cricket team with a sideline in musical theatre? Or a music hall act that played cricket during the daytime? Which of these visions was in the mind of Michel, and which was acceptable to Bosanquet?

The theatrical thread can be traced right back to the beginning: the October 1889 advertisement which offered 'complete entertainment for parks, cricket grounds, fetes, or large halls'. Later promises of 'Roman sports' and a spectacle 'equalled only by Barnum and Bailey' were clearly aimed more at readers of *The Era* than readers of *Wisden*. Requests for costumes, equipment and even cyclists appeared in theatrical publications, and we know that there was a trapeze – on which Georgina Sheffield and Louisa Daly had been injured – at the Wandsworth practice sessions. But by March 1890, this aspect had been considerably toned down; perhaps by Bosanquet and the other majority

In the Evening

shareholders, because the Memorandum of Association had mentioned nothing but sport. When the OELC made their debut in Liverpool that April, the whole spectacle was based around cricket.

The first weeks seemed to vindicate the decision as cricket became the sole focus of the press and public. Had theatrical plans been abandoned? Or was there a pause for some other reason? Perhaps Michel needed to persuade Bosanquet; maybe the performance needed polish. But Michel still left room for *something*: matches concluded between six o'clock and half past six, when a cricket audience might have watched a couple more hours before sunset.

Gradually, aspects of evening entertainment were introduced, perhaps testing the water. After some early games, for example at Liverpool and Southampton in early May, the players made non-performing appearances in their cricket costumes at local theatres and music halls.[35] The first recorded evening performance by the team – although newspaper coverage was not exhaustive and there may have been earlier ones – came at Taunton in early June, consisting of gymnastics and musical drill on the ground after the match. But a clearly irritated Michel told the *Taunton Courier* that 'owing to the inefficient arrangements made locally the whole performance could not be carried out'. A much fuller programme, including supporting acts, was advertised for 11 June at Pittsville Gardens at Cheltenham, when a performance at the ground after the

---

35 They continued to make occasional similar appearances throughout the season, for example when they visited the Gaiety Theatre in Hastings in September.

match consisted of 'an assault-at-arms'[36] involving the players, and 'a variety entertainment in which the Sisters Percival will introduce their Mandolin Duets and Speciality Dancess.' At Wolverhampton a few days later, the game concluded with a cycling and gymnastics display and at Northampton on 16 and 17 June, a post-game performance included Swedish Drill,[37] a banjoist called Ada Morton and a display by 'Professor Onda and his pupils' on the flying rings. A couple of hours later, there was a 300 yards flat race, an assault-at-arms, a cycling display and 'Olympic' sports including fencing and single stick.

The day after the Northampton performance came what appears to be the first time that the players relocated to an indoor venue after a game when they appeared at the Victoria Grand Circus Pavilion in Leamington Spa on 18 June. The advertising promised 'fencing, boxing, musical drill and other athletic exercises', supported by the Town Improvement Association Band (which had played during the cricket match), and the programme consisted of Ada Morton (singing), the Sisters Lallah (wire walkers), 'Happy Ashley' (a balancing act), M. Mello (a juggler), and concluded with 'musical drill by the two teams in suitable athletic costume'. But the audience was mildly unimpressed. The *Leamington Spa Courier* reported: 'There was a very large audience, but some disappointment was experienced by those present on discovering that the programme consisted mainly of performances by a troupe of inferior

---

36 An assault-at-arms usually meant displays of activities such as boxing and wrestling, but given how the programme evolved over the season it is likely the OELC version consisted of fencing and single stick, a form of combat using a stick as a weapon.

37 Swedish Drill was a form of gymnastics.

jugglers and wire-walkers, and that the appearances of the lady cricketers were few and far between.'

From this point onwards, performances became a key part of the programme, and Daisie Stanley assumed a central role in their organisation and choreography. For example, when the team returned to Liverpool for their fairly disastrous June visit, they put on an outdoor display in the evening. A report described the spectacle: 'The musical drill by sixteen ladies under the leadership of Miss Stanley, who is a splendid all-round athlete, was prettily and effectively done. The fencing with foils was good, the fair Amazons, decked with breastplates, faceguards and gauntlets, passing and slashing at each other in quite a tragic manner.' There was also a 300-yard race, won by Stanley despite giving her opponents 'many yards start'. She also told the crowd that she could run 250 yards in 28.25 seconds. Katie Tatton then rode her bicycle around the enclosure, waving a sword and pursuing a 'cavalry-man on horseback' before a half-mile bicycle race which was – of course – won by Stanley. The evening ended with a 'mandolin solo'.

* * *

Most performances took place indoors in halls and theatres, but in a crowded music-hall market, the OELC did not stand out; most newspapers stopped paying attention at 6:30 and only a few cursory reports bothered to discuss the evenings. The most reliable information comes from local advertising. For example, when the OELC visited Aston in mid-July, they played at Aston Lower Grounds between 2pm and 6pm. Then at 7:30, they appeared in the Great Hall. The programme promised 'Grand Variety Entertainment', featuring 'Assault-at-Arms by the Lady

Cricketers and other Artistes', 'aerial gymnastics', fencing and boxing. The advert said that anyone paying the 6d admission would see 'a novel, picturesque and refined athletic and variety exhibition'.

The fullest account of an evening performance came in the *Isle of Man Times*, describing the visit of the OELC to Douglas in late July. The day before the game, the team appeared at the Palace Ballroom and Theatre, next to the Castle Mona, which was then a hotel. The ballroom could hold up to 4,000 people, and was said to be the biggest in Europe; the OELC performed there rather than in the adjoining theatre (with a capacity of 2,000). The audience, according to the local newspaper, was 'large, and at times quite demonstrative'. The performance began with Fred Vetter's band playing the overture to 'The Poet and the Peasant' before the appearance of 'sixteen ladies, under the leadership of Captain Daisie Stanley, and accompanied on the piano by Miss Seymour, went through a series of beautiful evolutions.' Bessie Moss and Adele Matthey gave a fencing display after which Katie Tatton 'gave a clever performance' on her bicycle, although she struggled a little on a floor waxed for dancing: 'Though she was evidently mistress of the machine, she sustained several tumbles, but managed the sword exercise while careering round the arena.' Next up was Bianca Seymour, this time on the banjo; she also performed an encore. The final part of the first act was a single-stick combat between the Westbrook sisters and Ella Heather ('which was not pretty').

After an interval, during which the band played, the performance resumed with bouts of fencing involving Sophie Charles, Florence Hardwick, Elizabeth Dempsey and Daisie Stanley. The versatile Stanley then sang a song but a planned performance on the flying rings had to be abandoned as 'the manager explained that they were not able to get the apparatus ready'. One of the support acts, a 'champion' trick cyclist called W. G. Hurst who accompanied the team in July and August, gave a display instead, 'wielding of the Indian clubs', before he finished off with his own performance on the bicycle. There was a firework display, followed by the opportunity for the audience to dance to the band. The OELC repeated their performance the following evening, after their cricket match.

The author of the review in the *Isle of Man Times* speculated that the aim of the tour was to 'encourage ladies to cultivate ... athletic exercises' but he thought that the evening display 'is not calculated to lead ladies to follow their example'. He continued: 'For instance, we do not think that any amount of associations will ever persuade ladies to go in for cycling dressed in tights, and we do not think any amount of desire for physical exercise will induce ladies to indulge in the manly exercise of single-stick, and belabour each other, as two of the Lady Cricketers did.' But he was more appreciative of the musical drill and 'the exercises with the clubs'; he viewed the whole performance as 'interesting' and the costumes as 'pretty and effective'.

A performance at the Festival Concert Rooms in York a few weeks later was described, albeit in less detail, in the *Yorkshire Evening Press*. The report noted: 'The reputation the ladies have already attained was sufficient to draw together a large audience, and the company present had no reason to complain of the entertainment provided.' The programme had been devised by a local man, J. B. Hampson, and included roller skaters and jugglers not associated with the OELC. But 'sixteen ladies under Captain Stanley' again put on a musical drill, the fencers fenced and Bianca Seymour gave another well-received banjo performance. In fact, according to the report, the whole show 'gave universal satisfaction to all concerned'.

We also know details from an evening at Leigh Theatre in July. Advertising promised 'an attractive and varied entertainment consisting of vocal and instrumental music, humorous and dramatic recitals, musical drill and evolutions and concluding with an assault-at-arms'. The latter was 'selected from the following subjects: fencing, single stick, aerial gymnastics, boxing, vaulting, "crooketta", cycling. The whole forming a novel, athletic and variety exhibition.' Some of the adverts noted that the assault-at-arms was 'under the direction of S. Major Steel and Professor Onda'. The latter was the trapeze artist who had been with the cricketers since June.

The *Leigh Chronicle* recorded that 'a large and enthusiastic but somewhat critical crowd assembled'. The report detailed some of the show; there was the usual 'musical drill by 16 ladies', during which 'the time kept was excellent, and the various movements were gone through with precision'. There was fencing by Stanley and Dempsey, 'who are great adepts in the art'. Stanley also 'obliged with a ballad' but was upstaged by 'a lady who sang "The Song that Reached my Heart", "Daddy's Revenge" and two other songs'. Presumably this was one of the supporting acts. Ella Heather and the Westbrooks 'were applauded for a good display' with their single sticks, and the biggest attraction among the OELC again seems to have been Seymour and her banjo; she was 'enthusiastically encored'. Also well received was 'a bar-ball exercise'. The biggest hit of the night was W. G. Hurst, who put on an acrobatic cycling display which astonished the spectators.

Professor Onda, Ada Morton and W. G. Hurst were not the only acts to provide recurring support. Several troupes and individuals joined various legs of the tour, presumably having accepted some kind of short-term contract. For example, the 'burlesque trick and knockabout cyclists' called Rae and Weston (who sometimes appeared under the names the 'Bedouin Bicyclists' or the 'Wonderful Performing Weasels') accompanied the team in early July, and took out an advertisement in *The Era* to publicise their recruitment. But otherwise acts seem to have been engaged for individual venues, perhaps by the managers of theatres.

A final indication of what might have been seen appeared in an August advert for a tour of Devon and Cornwall. It listed the evening entertainment: the opening musical drill with the 16 ladies and Stanley; three bouts of fencing, including two by Moss and Matthey at the beginning and end of the evening, and one by Stanley and Dempsey; Tatton on the bicycle; Seymour on the banjo; the Westbrooks and Ella Heather at single stick; and some musical interludes.

* * *

The scanty reporting of the evening shows offered no attendance figures, and we have no indication of how popular they were, although they doubtless helped theatre managers to 'cash in' on the phenomenon of the Lady Cricketers. But this side of the operation might have been shaped by factors outside of the OELC's control because music hall entertainment was not uniformly popular. Leicester, for example, had little appetite for music hall at the time, and so the OELC did not perform there.[38] And a hint survives that the evening performances were not always a hit. In April 1891 the Exeter Victoria Hall Company took a hotel keeper to court for non-payment of costs agreed for the gas consumed during the evening performance of the OELC. The hotel keeper argued that the event had not been a success and therefore he said that the Victoria Hall Company had agreed to reduce the amount; the latter disputed this and the judge found in their favour.

Nor do we know if the shows were watched by a 'typical' music hall audience or by those who just wanted to see the cricketers. But we have one indication of unwanted attention for the women after at least one evening performance – the kind of attention perhaps more familiar to theatrical performers than cricketers. When the OELC appeared at Leamington Spa, some men caused considerable disruption. The first newspaper to mention the story, the *Birmingham Mail*, reported: 'The proceedings were characterised by the most unseemly conduct on the part of about a dozen young men of the "masher" class, who took up a position early in the evening near the orchestra.' The report explained how during the first 90 minutes, the 'mashers' had 'amused themselves, and the company too, by calling over the barrier, and throwing notes to the young lady performers who were waiting their turn behind the curtain.' But after the show, some of them waited in 'the ring' of the theatre, hoping the cricketers would pass on

---

38 However, the players appeared on the balcony of Leicester's Royal Opera House during their visit.

the way out; they only left after the gas lights were turned out and two policemen were summoned. Most of the men fled but some waited outside the front of the building, and when the performers emerged, 'pressed their company upon the young ladies in a fashion which almost amounted to molestation'. This experience was almost certainly repeated elsewhere.

There was far less interest in the costumes of the OELC during the evening, apart from the disapproving comment about Katie Tatton cycling in tights at Douglas. But theatrical costumes worn by women in music halls were far more revealing – by the standard of the time – than anything the cricketers wore on the pitch. And it seems that the OELC wore that type of costume: apart from the adverts from early 1890 that sought gymnastic outfits, leotards and tights, and the comments about Tatton in Douglas, the Leamington Spa advertising mentioned 'suitable athletic costume'. Was this Michel's original vision: scantily dressed young women on stage before large audiences?

This might also have informed his recruitment strategy. For example, although Tatton was a professional – and probably accomplished – cyclist, it is notable that more proficient cyclists often accompanied the team, such as W. G. Hurst or Rae and Weston; it is not impossible she was simply there as an attraction for men. Complaints about music hall costume and 'suggestive' performances were a common theme of the late Victorian period, and although no such criticism seems to have been attached to the OELC, this was part of the world they entered in the evening; and doubtless part of their intended appeal.

None of the OELC members ever spoke about the evenings, so we do not know how they felt. Nor do we know how many wanted to be stars of the stage rather than the sports field. Just as in the case of the cricket matches, the women were the heart of the whole story, but their thoughts are lost to us.

Signs of Trouble

MEN'S CRICKET generally ended in early September in this period, but the OELC continued to play until mid-October. They were lucky in that they were favoured by unusually good weather, but their reputation meant that the crowds continued to flock to their matches even into autumn. A tour of south-west England that took up the second half of September was slightly less-well-attended than earlier games, perhaps owing to smaller grounds, but a crowd of between 1,200 and 1,300 watched in Torquay. When the OELC returned to London, their game at Tufnell Park on 11 October drew a crowd of 5,000.

This extension of the season did not escape notice. 'Le Balafre' in *Cricket: A Weekly Record of the Game* wrote that 'the Lady Cricketers have carried the game into the enemy's country a far greater distance than have the male exponents of the summer game', although he suggested that this was because – unlike their male counterparts – women did not devote their autumn to the sport of shooting. Incidentally, this was the only mention of the OELC in *Cricket* in 1890.

The OELC's final game was a poorly attended benefit match – the proceeds would have gone to the players rather than the ECAA – at Catford Bridge which began on 15 October. Matthews and Walter Bosanquet umpired but the day was ruined by heavy rain. Bromley's *District Times* suggested a meagre attendance of 'a dozen spectators' when play began, but the crowd had grown to around 500 by the end of the day. The ground committee agreed that the game could be continued five days later – during which interval the OELC made their return visit to the Royal Military Exhibition – but even this did not help; the *District Times* said that 'very few' attended on 20 October. The players must have been disappointed, especially as the meagre takings would have to be split between so many of them.

There had been several suggestions throughout the season that the team would play overseas during the English winter. One proposal was a visit to European capitals such as Paris, Vienna and Berlin (although it is hard to imagine any interest in places such as these which did not play much men's cricket, let alone the women's game). And there was a long-standing suggestion that the team would visit Australia, dating as far back as the advertisement in *Lillywhite's*. There was certainly women's cricket in Australia in this period. Marie Beckenham, in her 1956 interview, recalled that members of the touring Australian men's team in 1890 suggested they should put on exhibition games there. But by November, it became clear that the proposed visit would not go ahead. No reason was publicly given; Beckenham said that the players' parents had refused permission but it is likely to have been more complicated than that, if it had ever been a realistic prospect at all.

While the shareholders of the ECAA sat back to count their profits from the season, and make plans to repeat the tour in 1891, others were casting greedy eyes at the success of the OELC.

The first signs of something brewing came in an October advert in *The Era*: 'Wanted, first-class lady athletes (those having a knowledge of cricket and lawn tennis preferred) to join Gardener's Original Lady Cricketers for next season. Apply, with full particulars as to abilities, &c, 40 Wellington Street, Strand.'

We know little about who was behind this rival team. At the time of the 1891 census, 40 Wellington Street was occupied by Thomas Hale, a 40-year-old married man from Lambeth who had two children. His occupation was listed as 'shop man at costumes (or costumer)', suggesting some kind of theatrical connection. He seems unlikely to have been the originator of such an ambitious scheme. Another candidate was a cricket bat company called Gardiner's, based in Hertfordshire, advertisements for which appeared in *Cricket*. And there may have been a link to *The Era* itself; the offices of that publication were to be found at 49 Wellington Street, a few doors down from number 40. But an intriguing possibility is that it could have been connected to a man called T. W. Gardiner (or his father John), who was involved in the 1870s and 1880s with a troupe called Gardiner's Clown Cricketers, which became briefly famous at the height of clown cricket.

Not long after, another announcement in *The Era* stated that 'Gardiner's [sic] Unrivalled Lady Cricketers commence their season on Whit Monday' and revealed that nine members of the OELC had joined this rival organisation. Seven of these – Beatrice Fane, E. Fane, E. Gordon, F. Gordon (who were in fact the four Barefoot sisters), Lena Parsons, Lizzie Sanders (listed as 'E. Saunders') and Sophie Charles – might have caused Michel some regret but they were hardly leading players. Only Beatrice Fane, who usually opened the batting, had averaged over 10 in 1890. A far bigger blow came with the final two names: Violet and Grace Westbrook. Grace was a capable wicket-keeper but Violet was the undisputed star of the show. Her loss would have been devastating to Michel.

As far as can be seen from newspaper coverage, Gardener's/Gardiner's Lady Cricketers never took the field, and those women who had 'transferred' never played for them; in fact, all but Grace Westbrook eventually returned to the OELC. As usual, we do not know details; it is possible the defectors never signed any contracts with the rival team, or that Michel (or Bosanquet) held them to the terms of their two-year contracts. But this episode suggests that by the end of the season the players were aware of their worth and prepared to seek better terms elsewhere. There might have been some quite intense behind-the-scenes discussions with Michel.

Ironically, the same issue of The Era which trumpeted the poaching of the nine OELC players also contained an advertisement from Michel: 'The Original English Lady Cricketers will commence their second season at Lord's Cricket Ground, Whitsuntide, 1891.' This was either a lie or the proposed game fell through, because the OELC never played at Lord's. But Michel betrayed some nervousness; the advert continued: 'The Directors of the E. C. and A. Association, Limited, beg to caution managers and owners of grounds that the only Original Lady Cricketers which have so successfully appeared this year, are those known by their registered title of the "Original English Lady Cricketers". Sole originator and manager, E. Michel. Offices 11 Queen Victoria Street, London, E. C.' Evidently, the idea of rivals worried him. Others reacted quite enthusiastically to the prospect; some newspapers suggested that the teams could oppose each other.

But Michel continued to assert the primacy of his team and enforce his rights; an advertisement which appeared in early 1891 for the OELC emphasised that their title was a registered trademark, that the 'costumes and all printing' were copyright, that only the authorised agents listed in the advert represented the OELC, and that all contracts had to be signed by the management.

* * *

For all the worry implied by Michel's reaction, only one rival seems to have made it on to the field in 1891. It was organised to publicise the products of a soap manufacturer. 'Arthur's Ideal Soap Lady Cricketers' played a series of matches throughout the 1891 summer. The Ideal Lady Cricketers faced local teams of men who adopted the time-honoured approach of batting and bowling with their wrong hand to make the matches notionally competitive. But like the OELC, the Ideal Lady Cricketers made appearances in local halls and theatres after games, and had publicity photographs taken.

Newspapers were not impressed by this blatant attempt to manufacture an advertising opportunity out of the fascination with women's cricket. Little was reported about such matters as attendances, but for the organisers this was presumably secondary to any publicity which could be generated. For example, one advert for the team stated that admission cost 6d or 'free on the production of twelve wrappers of Arthur's Ideal Soap'. The same advert claimed that it had cost more than £1,500 to 'perfect the ladies'.

One of the few longer reports of an Ideal Lady Cricketers game mentioned 'clowns and other odd folks in the field, their songs and witticisms all having reference to a particular kind of soap', and a soap stall at the ground. The same article said that there 'were large audiences' on both days, and at the evening performance, when 'the ladies displayed talent of a different kind'. Another report said that there was a 'fair attendance', but when the Ideal Cricketers appeared at Aston, there seemed to be problems finding a team to play. On the first day, a scratch side containing 'a policeman, a lamplighter and a man-of-war's man' opposed the Ideal Lady Cricketers, but on the second the women's team had to issue a challenge to 'all-comers'.

The cricket seems to have been largely played for laughs and similar to 'clown cricket'; the games were organised in conjunction with 'Ally Sloper' – a famous star of a comic strip who at the time featured in a popular publication called *Ally Sloper's Half Holiday*. Entertainment rather than sport was the primary focus; advertising for the team claimed that all the players were associated with either the Theatre Royal, Drury Lane, or the Theatre Royal Pavilion. The evening performances seem to have been relatively popular. But neither the games nor the cricketers attracted the same attention that the OELC had, and matches were largely confined to southern England.

But there seems to have been some trouble off the field. In November 1891, a case was heard before Lambeth County Court in which Marie Backhouse (wrongly identified as Marie Duckhouse in newspaper reports) claimed damages and wrongful dismissal from 'a soap company of Camberwell' which had engaged her as a professional cricketer through a manager or agent called Bozley. Her contract stated that she would be paid 15s per week while training and £1 per week while playing; she was also to receive expenses and dresses. Backhouse claimed to have been 'summarily dismissed' so she was suing (through her mother, as she was underage herself) for the wages due and for 'dresses, &c'. The defence claimed that she had been dismissed for 'bad language and intemperance'; she denied the accusation and countered that Bozley 'had misbehaved himself'. The jury believed her, awarding £13 for her wages and expenses and £30 damages for wrongful dismissal.

There was another court case concerning the Ideal Lady Cricketers when Richard J. Back took Thomas Richards to Hythe County Court on 4 April 1892 in a claim for £1 13s 6d which Back was owed for posting advertising bills. Back related how the Ideal Lady Cricketers had been invited to play at Hythe Green Cricket Club. But he had discovered that they were not all they seemed; although they 'professed to hail from Drury Lane Theatre', Back learned that they had no such connection. Unfortunately, at this point the judge prevented Back from saying more as these matters were unrelated to his case.

Back's claim was quite complicated and need not concern us too much; Richards was some kind of local secretary for the Ideal Cricketers and had asked Back to post the advertising. Back did not trust the 'agent of the Ideal Soap Company, Mr Hudgell, under whose auspices the ladies were to appear' and therefore (according to Back) Richards had guaranteed his fee. As it transpired, Hudgell had indeed refused to pay, claiming that Back had spread stories that the Ideal Cricketers had no association with Drury Lane. But Richards denied having promised to reimburse Back and therefore the matter came to court. The judge eventually found for Richards and said that if Back wanted his money, he should sue the Ideal Soap Company.

We have one piece of evidence that Michel was rattled by the appearance of the Ideal Lady Cricketers. An advert in *The Era* in May included a sly dig: 'The OELC are not soap canvassers, but legitimate players. They are Real not Ideal sportswomen … Best wishes for the success of any properly conducted rival organisations.' But another mention of copyright protection, and a comment that the managers of the OELC 'have instructed their solicitors to commence immediate proceedings against certain infringements' are more signs that Michel was worried about competition in the new season. It was not the only issue facing him.

* * *

The biggest problem for the OELC was the loss of its biggest stars. Although the other women who had supposedly signed for Gardener's Cricketers all re-joined the OELC in time to commence the 1891 season, neither Violet Westbrook nor her sister Grace returned. Instead, the pair placed advertisements in *Sporting Life*, *The Sportsman*, *The Era* and *Cricket* in April 1891 which stated: 'Miss Violet B. Westbrook, Champion Lady Cricketer (Captain of the "Red Eleven" of the Original English Lady Cricketers' Association during the whole of their tour last season) with her sister Grace will not join the Association for the coming season. They are open to engagements for coaching or playing in lady teams. Highest references.' The given address was the Lyon family home in Forest Hill. The advert was printed in many newspapers across the country in the middle of April, but a new version in late May omitted any mention of Grace and the correspondence address was Caxton Library. Perhaps by that stage, Grace had abandoned her attempts to be a cricketer. The reason for the absence of the Westbrooks was never explained, but it was later attributed to a 'dispute'. Probably Violet wanted either an increased salary or a greater say in proceedings, but her actions hint that there was a potential market other than the OELC for professional women cricketers in early 1891.

Equally concerning for the management – and given her high profile, perhaps more so – was the departure of Daisie Stanley. Her constant appearances in the newspapers, particularly in the latter part of the 1890 season, and the continuing insistence on her talent and indispensable nature might have been part of an attempt to inflate her reputation with a view to better remuneration by Michel; perhaps she was seeking a greater measure of control in the organisation. By February it was clear that there had been a rupture between Stanley and the OELC, as she decided to strike out on her own with another rival organisation.

That month, *The Era* reported that Stanley 'intends organising another twenty-two, who will do battle with the willow under the title of All England Lady Cricketers. Their season, it is expected, will open on Whit Monday.' In May, a newspaper updated the situation: 'Miss Daisie Stanley ... has transferred her knowledge of the technique of the art to two elevens of her own selection, and now only plays with amateurs at private meetings.' There are no records that Stanley's team ever played a game – and it is hard to imagine any amateur teams overcoming the objections that had prevented such games taking place in 1890 – or even existed at all, but the loss of his famous captain must have been a considerable blow to Michel. Nor did she play for the OELC again, although she made a brief return in somewhat murky circumstances later in the 1891 season.

All of this meant that the OELC would take the field for 1891 with the two captains – and the two women who had most fired the imagination of newspaper reporters – gone. Any hopes that the teams would become an attraction for the public through the quality of their cricket or the fame of their players had suffered a considerable blow.

The image that accompanied the advertisement in Lillywhite's before the 1890 season. Back row: Georgina Sheffield, Susie Fletcher, Marie Lisle, Elizabeth Dempsey, William Matthews (coach). Middle row: Sophie Charles, Lena Parsons, Beatrice Fane, Ella Heather. Front row: Flora Fane, Adele Matthey, Ada Heather (Wikimedia Commons)

The only known photograph of the OELC playing cricket, taken at the Police Athletic Grounds, Liverpool, on 7 or 8 April 1890 (National Archives)

The Red and Blue teams early in the 1890 season. Back row: Nellie Wadkin, unknown, Georgina Sheffield, Susie Fletcher, Beatrice Fane, Lena Parsons, Marie Lisle. Middle row: unknown (umpire), Bianca Seymour, Florence Woodward, Sophie Charles, Alice Grey, Daisie Stanley, Ella Heather, Flora Fane, Ada Heather, William Matthews (umpire/coach). Front row: Violet Westbrook, Adele Matthey, Georgina Westbrook, Elizabeth Dempsey, Lizzie Sanders, Edith Woodward, Bessie Moss (National Archives)

An illustration of an OELC match in 1890 (MCC)

Miss Daisie Stanley, photographed in 1890 (National Archives)

An advertisement for the OELC from 1890 (MCC)

The English Lady Cricketers: Miss Stanley Batting: *An illustration of the OELC by Lucien Davies which first appeared in the* Illustrated London News, *May 1890 (Alamy)*

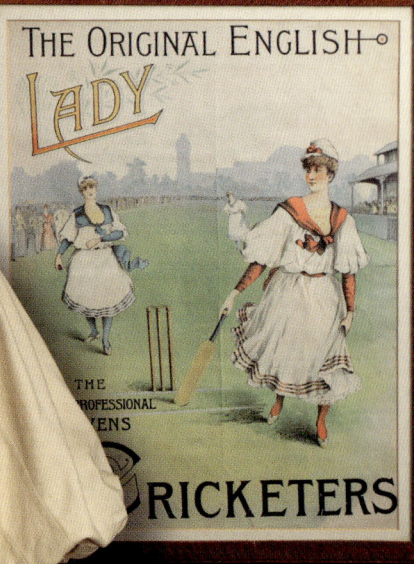

The costume of Marie Beckenham, as displayed in the MCC Museum (MCC)

The Red team from 1891. Back row: Ella Heather, May Day, E. Michel (manager), V. Martin, Caroline (?) McDonnell. Middle row: Gertrude (?) McDonnell, Lizzie Sanders, Alice Grey, Ada Heather, A. Stevens. Front row: Marie Beckenham, Lena Parsons (Peter Griffiths)

The Blue team from 1891. Back row: Nellie Wadkin, Susie Fletcher, William Matthews (coach), Mabel Emmett, M. Hood. Middle row: Flora Fane, Beatrice Fane, Elizabeth Dempsey, Sophie Charles, Ella Gordon. Front row: Lydia Hann, Adele Matthey (Peter Griffiths)

A Punch *cartoon by Edward Linley Sambourne from May 1892 depicting women cricketers confronting William Gladstone about women's suffrage (Alamy)*

The Second Season

ACCORDING TO a letter written by Michel in September 1891, the OELC continued to practise – and to be paid – over the winter of 1890–91. Although Michel had reasons for not necessarily being truthful, there is evidence to back him up. In mid-April 1891, an attendant at the grounds of Lynwood in Upper Tooting sued Matthews for £2 5s to cover the costs of 'use of dressing rooms ... and nine days' practice in the grounds' by 23 members of the OELC. Matthews pleaded that he was 'not the manager of the team, but only a professional cricketer with them', but had to pay up. No date was given by the newspapers that reported the story, but the events are most likely to have taken place over the 1890–91 winter. However, there are other indications that practices only resumed in spring. One newspaper gave a date of 24 March and an unhelpfully vague story in the *Derby Daily Telegraph* on 6 April said practices had been ongoing 'for several weeks'. The author of the latter grumbled that 'the ladies are evidently a money-making lot' as someone had been charging a shilling admission to watch the practices; photography was strictly forbidden.

As the new season drew closer, anticipation built; local newspapers began to list fixtures and report on the progress of negotiations to bring the Lady Cricketers to their town. Rumours of a potential visit by a team of Australian women drove one journalist to lament: 'The thought is too dreadful.'³⁹

Michel was more concerned about having enough players to put into the field. As well as the Westbrook sisters and Daisy Stanley, Louisa Daly and Georgina Sheffield, who had each taken over 100 wickets in 1890, did not return. Nor did Bessie Moss, Bianca Seymour and Katie Tatton, whose losses would have been felt more keenly off the field than on it.

The departure of the more 'theatrical' part of the team might explain the biggest change in 1891. The evening performances ceased almost completely. But there are a huge number of unknowns. Were the shows dropped because they were unprofitable? Because the loss of Stanley, Seymour and company made them impossible? Or did the management abandon the performances first and let the affected women go? We simply don't know. But the gap in the schedule allowed the cricket matches to continue until sunset, a considerable extension of playing hours compared to the 6:30 finishes of 1890.

There is another mystery over the 'entertainment' side of the 1891 programme. In late February 1891, an announcement appeared in *The Era* that 'the Silvani troupe of lady bicyclists have accepted an engagement to tour with the Original English Lady Cricketers for the greater part of the ensuing season'. The Silvani troupe consisted of four female cyclists who toured the country between 1887 and 1896. But there is only one mention of them appearing at

---

39 The idea seems to have arisen with reports of an Australian 'intercolonial match' between women's teams from Victoria and New South Wales; someone clearly took this as a sign that a future tour was inevitable, but no concrete plans were ever put forward.

an OELC game, during the interval at Burnley in early July. And in the meantime, the Silvani troupe continued to perform to great acclaim around the country. Perhaps there was some grand design behind these changes, but it is hard to understand.

The only remaining cricketers of proven quality were Ada and Ella Heather. Therefore replacements needed to be found and quickly coached up to standard; presumably advertisements were placed, although none have been located. Just the barest hints emerged later in 1891 that new recruits were paid less than the original players and that a divide had appeared between the two groups.

The new combinations were photographed at the beginning of the season; the Red team (with Michel) and the Blue team (with Matthews) were pictured separately in front of a painted background. But another notable difference as the new season approached was the absence of interviews or publicity material in newspapers. And the *Lady Cricketers' Gazette* was discontinued, although old issues possibly remained on sale.

The changes of focus make it hard to discern the motives of the new players; perhaps they simply loved cricket but in truth few of them excelled at it. Of those who played the whole season, only May Day averaged a fraction over 10 with the bat (although her fielding drew praise); Caroline and Gertrude McDonnell were the only new players to take any wickets but rarely bowled. The best recruit was a mysterious amateur called A. Waterfield who averaged 15.17 with the bat in a handful of appearances early in the season.

The new players are much harder to trace because they had no *Gazette* profiles. Only three newcomers can be confidently identified. Lydia Hann was the 21-year-old daughter of a provision dealer (who was wealthy enough to employ live-in shopkeepers) and one of 13 children; she helpfully listed herself as a 'lady cricketer' on the 1891 census. The sisters Gertrude (aged 22) and Caroline (aged 20) McDonnell were daughters of a widowed beerhouse keeper who had once been a sergeant in the Royal Artillery; their parents were Irish, but Gertrude was born at Woolwich and Caroline in East Looe, Cornwall.[40]

Most new recruits must have used pseudonyms; as in 1890, there is no indication why only *some* did this. Of these only Mabel Emmett, whose real name was Agnes (or possibly Annie) Rowney, ever publicly revealed her identity and even then she cannot be confidently located in any records. Possibly one or two used their actual names but these are too common to trace without more information. And further confusion arose from the haphazard reporting of names, which could have been through error or because they were using alternatives: Hann, for example, was often recorded as Hearne, and the McDonnell sisters were sometimes listed as McDonald.

* * *

The 1891 census, taken on the night of 5 April, offers a brief snapshot into the lives of those players we can identify. Most were living with their parents; two – Elizabeth Dempsey and Adele Matthey – were boarding in the same house. Most had no occupation noted, but Daisie Stanley was listed as a dressmaker and Marie Beckenham was a 'lady clerk'. Several were brave enough to give their job

---

[40] It is only the revelation of these birthplaces in some newspaper reports that allows us to identify the McDonnell sisters.

as 'lady cricketer': Sophie Charles, Elizabeth Margaret Dempsey, Lydia Hann, Adele Annie Matthey, Allina Parsons, Elizabeth Sanders, Susan Shemmonds (who played under the name Susie Fletcher) and Ellen Wadkin. While it may seem curious for so few women to admit their association with the OELC – not even 'stars' such as Violet Westbrook or the Heather sisters – it was the head of each household who filled in the census returns; perhaps some fathers preferred to be silent regarding their daughters' occupations.

The census also hints at other professional women's teams in circulation. At least 42 women had an occupation that included cricket. If we exclude those involved in the manufacture of equipment and known OELC members, we are left with some new names. Alice Thoms and Isabel Bransgrove both played for Arthur's Ideal Lady Cricketers; Elizabeth Argent and Rose Finley may have been pseudonyms for one of the OELC players or one of the Ideal Lady Cricketers.[41]

But Louisa Daly, who had stopped playing for the OELC in mid-1890 and never played for the Ideal Lady Cricketers, still listed herself as a 'lady cricketer', which would seem reasonable circumstantial evidence that at least one other team existed.[42] Perhaps she had joined Daisie Stanley, but we will never know.

---

41 Less explicable (and certainly unconnected with the OELC or any of its rivals) are two girls in Bolton – the 14-year-old Ada Proffitt (listed as a 'Cricketer', to which someone had added the word 'fancy') and the 13-year-old Hannah Greenhaigh (who is listed as what looks like 'crocketer').

42 Rafaelle Nicholson suggested to me that Daly could have retained the description 'lady cricketer' because it had become part of her identity.

* * *

The new season stuttered unconvincingly into life, with a minimum of publicity, on Easter Monday with a two-day game at the National Athletic Grounds at Kensal Rise. The match was advertised locally but no newspaper reports appeared. The coverage of other early games betrayed some of Michel's nervousness. An article in the *South Bucks Standard* featured inflated claims which must have come from the team management. The loss of Westbrook and Stanley was acknowledged but the merits of the two captains who replaced them for that game were exaggerated.

The new Red captain, Flora Fane, was praised for her seven wickets but less convincingly was described as 'a far better bat than Miss Ella Heather', even though the latter had outscored her in that game and would continue to do so all season.

The Blue captain, Lizzie Sanders, was described as 'the best lady bowler we have ever seen, and for speed and accuracy even beats Miss Westbrook. At the wicket with the bat she is equally powerful … on the previous day at Guildford she carried out her bat for over eighty.' Whether or not she was better than Westbrook, the claim about her batting was exaggerated; she had scored only 5 runs at Guildford.

Although neither Fane nor Sanders were permanent captains – the roles were rotated all season – they did more than anyone to compensate for the lost runs and wickets of Westbrook, Daly and Sheffield. Both players had averaged under 10 with the bat in 1890 and neither had taken a wicket (at least in matches for which we have a score) in

1890.[43] Both returned as vastly improved players after the winter. Fane averaged just under 20 with the bat and took over 80 wickets (despite missing a substantial part of the season with illness). Sanders did even better: she averaged around 27 with the bat and at Chiswick Park she scored 110 to become only the second OELC member after Violet Westbrook to hit a century; she also took over 100 wickets and regularly appeared to be the most threatening bowler.

Although when the season began, no one could have known that Fane and Sanders would rise so successfully to the challenge, the few publicity pieces tried to reassure readers that the departure of so many players would have little impact. An advert at the end of May stressed that 'the best players of last season [are] retained, and promising new ones added'. Later in the summer, newspaper reports bear traces of their writers being briefed about the merits of individuals who would otherwise have been unknown to them. At the start of July, a reporter for the *Sheffield Daily Telegraph* had been told, during a collapse of the Blues' batting, that 'all now depended on Miss [Caroline] McDonnell'; she was promptly bowled first ball by Sanders.

---

43 It is surprisingly difficult to be sure under what name the cricketer known as Flora Fane played in 1890. Her real name was Flora Amelia Barefoot. Someone called Flora Fane was named in the *Gazette* as one of the reserve players and 'promoted' to the full team in the update. Her sister Beatrice played regularly but 'F. Fane' only played around a third of the games for which we have full scores. Someone calling herself 'E. Fane' played more often; some of these appearances may be a mis-transcription of 'F. Fane' or another Barefoot sister: Flora and Beatrice had sisters called Ella and Ethel. To further confuse matters, Ella was Flora's twin and in a game at Sheffield, an 'E. Fane' appeared on each team. We also know that some of the sisters played under the name Gordon; 'F. Gordon' and/or 'A. Gordon' (who never played together) might have been Flora (whose middle name was Amelia) but 'F. Gordon' and 'F. Fane' played together several times. In two games (at Clifton and Bath), two people called 'F. Gordon' played, one for each side. In any case, the only Barefoot sister to average more than 10 with the bat was Beatrice.

And when Flora Fane scored 35 at Oxford, a fragment appeared in several newspapers commenting that 'Miss Fane did some capital batting at Oxford'. Assuming Michel was responsible, he was in danger of protesting too much: a man trying to sell imitations of a lost original and hoping no one would notice.

Despite the bluster, all was not well. The *Surrey Advertiser* noted that the Guildford match 'was not invested with the local interest which attended [the OELC's] appearance last year' because of the absence of the Westbrooks; and the *South Bucks Standard* reported that 'the Lady Cricketers' visit to Maidenhead was a financial failure'. In mid-May Michel himself admitted that the tour had been losing £60 a week up until then. Although he claimed that the 1890 tour recovered from a similarly poor start, it added to an impression that the OELC had lost something of their lustre.

To make matters worse, the tour was badly affected by a spell of extremely poor weather: in May a match at Tufnell Park was twice abandoned – the original game and a planned replay – owing to heavy rain; matches at Ipswich and Derby were postponed. The teams were also struck by illness, particularly an influenza epidemic sweeping the country. Player absences were usually filled in the early part of the season, but for whatever reason this became harder as the summer wore on.

Adding to the turmoil, Violet Westbrook refused to go quietly and gradually raised the pressure behind the scenes. In mid-May, when she was still advertising her cricketing services, a short piece in *Gentlewoman* observed: 'The Lady Cricketers will this year be playing without their very best player, Miss Violet Westbrook, who has withdrawn from the combination. Miss Westbrook was a wonderfully energetic and able player, and worked very hard indeed.' To reinforce the loss, the article reeled off some impressive statistics (which had never previously appeared): she had averaged 42 in 1890 and taken 377 wickets at an average of just over 8. There is no particular reason to question such figures, but they can only realistically have come from Westbrook herself,[44] suggesting that she was promoting the (admittedly accurate) narrative that the OELC had lost their best player. The most likely explanation for the article is that she wanted to promote herself; her advert reappeared at the end of May, which suggests that she had until then been unsuccessful in finding cricket employment (and her sister had seemingly given up trying as she no longer featured). Or possibly she was attempting to find a way back into the OELC on favourable terms by drawing attention to what they had lost.

* * *

As the season progressed, the OELC continued to generate far less publicity than the previous year. Although local newspapers still covered games, scorecards were much scarcer than they had been in 1890 and there was an absence of national coverage in publications such as *Sporting Life*. The theatrical press similarly paid less attention. Attendance figures were rarely given, except as vague descriptions of the crowds being 'moderate', 'good', 'large' or 'not large'. Only a handful of games were reported as being played before four-figure audiences and

---

[44] In matches for which we have a score, she averaged just over 50 with the bat and took 217 wickets, but we are missing full details for many games. The figures quoted in *Gentlewoman* are probably more accurate if she had kept her own records.

several of these came during the latter part of the season. More common was the impression that there was less interest than there had been. For example, the *Birmingham Mail* reported when the teams appeared at Stourbridge: 'Their visit did not seem to create much enthusiasm, and the attendance at their exhibition was but small.'

On a more positive note, at the venues where the OELC had played in 1890, local newspapers almost always observed that there had been a considerable improvement in standards over the winter. In some ways, the appearance of the rival Arthur's Ideal Lady Cricketers helped the OELC to become more accepted because unlike the publicity-seeking newcomers, they continued to play 'real' cricket. And although the coverage of the OELC was much reduced, it was largely positive. *The Sportsman* suggested in late May that 'nobler feelings' had overcome the initial reservations of the public when the team debuted; indeed, 'at the present time the advent of the Original Lady Cricketers to any locality is always looked forward to with almost as much interest as a county fixture'. The *Athletic News* also gave some grudging praise; although grumbling that spectators turned up 'perhaps more out of curiosity than anything else', it conceded: 'No one can fail to see that they are a set of well-trained athletes, and though "not to the manner born", their cricket is plenty good enough to put to shame many of the sterner sex.'

There were still the usual dissenting voices. The *Croydon Advertiser* trumpeted the virtues of a girls' cricket team from Croydon School, drawing unfavourable comparison with the professional teams in circulation (although the criticism was mainly aimed at the Ideal Lady Cricketers). The *Watford Observer* concluded that 'cricket is not for ladies' after watching some 'poor' batting and seeing 'a lack of smartness so essential to cricket'. Ironically, the game in question at Watford was one of the most popular of the season: 1,040 spectators paid for admittance but according to the *Herts Advertiser*, the presence of 'members, their wives and friends' boosted the attendance to around 1,800. A local journalist was similarly dismissive of the cricket he saw at Bromley; he even wondered if the players were instructed to smile when they were out to make them more appealing. Again, the large attendance – over a thousand spectators – suggested that his opinion of women's cricket was a minority view.

The largest attendance of the season came in a match which in some ways represents a high point in the story of the OELC, but could also be interpreted as a watershed. On 23 May, 3,000 people – many of whom were women – braved the continuing damp and cold to watch the OELC at the Honourable Artillery Ground in Finsbury. The widely advertised game was played to raise money for a new hospital for paralysis and epilepsy in the West End – presumably the hospital at Welbeck Street which was undergoing a controversial rebuilding programme. The fact that the OELC were an attractive option for a charity game shows how accepted they had become. But the match broke new ground for the OELC – that which they had tentatively scouted the previous season before deciding better of it – because their opponents were men. Bosanquet had disparaged such novelty cricket the previous year; this marked a distinct shift from the previous nature of the enterprise.

A team representing the best eleven members of the OELC took on a strong eleven representing the Honourable

Artillery Company. Despite predictions the previous season that they could defeat men's teams, the OELC realised they had no chance in a straight contest, so the men's team batted left-handed (their 'wrong hand'). It is unclear if the men also bowled left-handed; a limited number of extras in the first innings (11 out of a total of 71) suggests not at first, but when the women batted again, there were 20 extras out of a total of 81 which might be indicative of wides and byes surrendered by bowlers using an unfamiliar arm.

Only Ella Heather, who had been in excellent form all season, reached double figures in the first innings, with an unbeaten 46, the highest score of the day. The crowd gave her an excellent reception. She also scored 17 in the second innings, when Flora Fane top-scored with 19; again no one else reached double figures for the OELC. But the bowlers did a better job; Ada Heather was too good for men batting left-handed and took eight wickets as the Honourable Artillery Company scored 89. But a report in *Lloyd's Weekly Newspaper* – in contrast to the rest of the season, this match was widely reported nationally – suggested that the occasion was too much for the women, who 'occasionally appeared constrained and timorous, certainly less spirited than we have seen them on former occasions'.

Quite what the women thought of it all is unfortunately a mystery. But there was a strange follow-up which suggests a potential change of approach. A week after the charity game, the OELC appeared in the well-attended match at Bromley. The Blues were one player short – presumably owing to the illness ravaging the team – yet still won after scoring 61 and dismissing the full-strength Reds for 34. No one reached 20 and both Matthey and Sanders took seven wickets for their respective teams. One of the umpires was

Walter Bosanquet, who was closely associated with Bromley Cricket Club. A long report in the *Bromley and District Times* written by 'Inveterate' stated: 'Mr Bosanquet, who has taken an active interest in the formation of the teams, was quite at home with the large family [i.e. the players] at tea-time, and, in fact, seems to be looked upon quite as a father.'

Normally after the early completion of two innings, the teams would have batted again, but not this time. Instead, a combined OELC eleven faced the men of the Bromley Cricket Club, who inevitably batted, bowled and fielded left-handed. As a result, the men's bowling and fielding were horrific and the women hit up 87/4 (Flora Fane 46). The men played out time, scoring 55/5 and finding some of the bowling uncomfortably quick when using their wrong hand; one of the home team was struck painfully in the ribs. Although the crowd may have been briefly amused by men bowling wides with their wrong hand, forgetting which side was left or right, and putting one hand in their pocket to resist using it, this was dangerously close to burlesque and the antics of 'Ally Sloper' and his soap cricketers. The atmosphere was also different to that usually found at OELC games. There was heavy drinking among some of the crowd: at the end of the season, a man with the pseudonym 'Lover of the Game' wrote to the *Bromley and District Times* to say that selling of 'intoxicants' on the ground 'was the cause ... of complaints' during this match.

Given the importance Bosanquet had placed on serious cricket, why was he accepting this, at his own cricket club of all places? Perhaps it is not a coincidence that this was the last time we can be certain he accompanied the team; perhaps it is equally coincidental that this was the last match against a men's side until the final, desperate game of the 1891 tour. Around this time, a curious 'wanted' advert appeared in *The Era* which requested 'the address of the manager of any team of lady cricketers other than that designated "The Original English Lady Cricketers"'. The address given was George Vincent, the secretary of the Athletic Ground Company, Limited, of Silver Street in Hull.

At this stage of the season, there was a strangely chaotic approach to running the team. The captaincy passed from player to player with no apparent pattern or design: both Heather sisters, Sanders, Adele Matthey, both Fane sisters, Sophie Charles and Lena Parsons all took turns. The wicket-keeper also changed with dizzying regularity: Matthey performed the role when she was not needed for her bowling, but Nellie Wadkin, Alice Grey, Beatrice Fane and V. Martin all took the gloves. There was a similar disorder over the team composition. Sophie Charles, who had played for the Blues in 1890, switched to the Reds after the first few matches. A. Waterfield, the only amateur ever to appear for the OELC – something which throws up questions of its own – switched teams several times, giving the impression that she was plugging a gap when players were indisposed. She proved quite useful, playing several good innings and bowling occasionally. Other women switched sides frequently, but this may simply have been a result of the illness ravaging the team. Even so, such confusion never occurred in the first season.

Three regulars from 1890 disappeared around the time of the Bromley game. Elizabeth Dempsey had begun well with three scores over 30, but after a string of single-digit scores she vanished from the record in the week after the Honourable Artillery Company game, just before the

Bromley match, and never returned to the team. Around six weeks later, on 20 July, she married a man called Arthur John Veitch, the son of the horticulturist Arthur Veitch. Susie Fletcher also stopped playing; her last match was at Bromley (she was named in the team when the OELC played at Chiswick Park, but this could have been an error as she was absent from the surrounding games). Alice Grey lasted a bit longer, and produced several good scores (she averaged just over 18 in the games for which scores survive) but her appearances became intermittent and apparently ended completely after she scored 77 at Watford.

Some of these gaps were filled by more new recruits. Two sisters named Chessington (which probably represented their birthplace in the same way that Marie Beckenham's name did) joined around this time.[45] There were also various sisters called Stevens who came in and out of the team.[46] And almost directly filling one of the places vacated by Dempsey and Fletcher – her first game for which we have a scorecard, which took place on 1 June, came two days after Fletcher's last appearance and four after Dempsey's – was L. Douglas.

As May turned into June, it became harder to track what was happening; the publishing of full scores was increasingly infrequent. Some games can only be identified from advertising or a throwaway line in a local newspaper. Perhaps the press had lost interest, but the absence

---

[45] We only know their initials: F. Chessington and M. Chessington, although a C. Chessington appeared alongside them in one game.

[46] Among the various sisters were A. Stevens, C. Stevens and L. Stevens; as recording of initials was often erratic on scorecards, we cannot be sure how many Stevens sisters there really were. The two regulars were Mabel and Maud Stevens, but as both were usually recorded as M. Stevens, it is impossible to track who was who.

of scorecards in many match reports might indicate a breakdown in communication. Following the departure of Tatton, the only mention of a scorer in 1891 was when the *Oxford Chronicle* said that Beatrice Fane performed the role in May; as she appeared in the game in question, this was likely an error, but perhaps one of her sisters kept score.

Another curiosity about this period is that we cannot be certain who was accompanying the players. There is no mention at any point in 1891 of the matrons who were so important for establishing respectability the previous year. Matthews had umpired many early games but by the time the OELC visited Kettering in mid-June, he does not seem to have been present. In fact, he is absent from newspaper reports (which admittedly does not mean he was not at games) throughout June except when he was mentioned in passing when the teams played at Kingston, his old club; he might have been at Derby but evidence is inconclusive.

Something clearly was not working, and it might have been desperation to recapture the magic formula of 1890 which led to the return of a prodigal to the fold. In the aftermath of the game against the Honourable Artillery Company, a syndicated report on the match singled out 'the Misses Heather and Westbrook' as 'becoming quite well known up and down the country'. Lazy reporting using outdated information? Or a sign that Westbrook was expected back?

And sure enough, around 15 June, Violet Westbrook re-joined the OELC. Was this a triumph or an indication of panic? The only hint of what had been going on appeared in an advertisement in *Sporting Life* which revealed that, 'The management beg to announce that their difference with Miss Violet B. Westbrook [her name was all capitals] having been arranged, she will play in all future matches during the season.' No indication was given as to the nature of the 'difference' but it was probably financial. And she immediately began to feature prominently in advertising, alongside the Heather sisters and Lizzie Sanders, suggesting that the management knew the continued success of the team depended on recognisable personalities.

* * *

Despite these suggestions of behind-the-scenes problems, the popularity of the OELC increased after the HAC match. The *Penny Illustrated Paper* mentioned in June that 'the Lady Cricketers continue to draw good fields and still captivate spectators by their lissom style of running, batting, and bowling'. And attendances improved: 1,000 at Kingston, 1,800 at Watford; a 'good' number at Wellingborough; and a 'large number' at Kettering. But then something changed in mid-June. There was only a 'small' attendance at Stourbridge, while only around 40 watched the game at Burton and 200 at both Stafford and Derby. At the same time, coverage of the teams dwindled almost to nothing and only the barest of details of scores emerged.

Possibly the falling attendances were the cause of what followed; perhaps it was coincidence. In either case, as June ended, the OELC plunged into crisis.

Crisis

FOR ANYONE following the progress of the OELC in the newspapers, the events that took place on 24 June, and their strange aftermath, would not have been readily apparent. The only indication of any problem was a break in the fixtures after the teams played at Derby on that date. There should have been a game in Newark which never seems to have taken place, but otherwise there was nothing obviously amiss.

But unknown to the public, in the middle of June the ECAA quietly collapsed. Its exact status was murky for months, and it was not until February 1892 that Walter Bosanquet wrote to inform the Registrar of Joint Stock Companies that the company had ceased carrying on business the previous June. Part of the story emerged in September 1891, and a little more in February 1892; however, the various tellers of the tale were engaged in a bitter dispute with legal ramifications and we can't entirely trust what they were saying. What we *do* know is that the OELC continued to play after the mysterious collapse of the ECAA, under what looks like – but might not have been – new management.

To those watching, it might only have become apparent that something had changed in the weeks after the Derby game. The first sign was the return of Matthews in a new role as manager. When the team visited Burnley, it was reported that 'Wm. Matthews, the old Surrey pro, still acts as director to the team, his assistants being Mr Mitchell [*sic*], and Mr E. Ferries.' And when they reached Warrington a few days later, Matthews was identified as 'the manager in chief, he having taken that position in the place of Mr Michel ... and Mr E. C. Ferris was the business manager'. The *Burnley Express* suggested that the mysterious Ferris was 'a relation of the famous Australian fast bowler' J. J. Ferris – unwittingly adding to the growing number of fictitious backgrounds associated with the OELC. No report explained what had become of Michel.

This was not the only difference after Derby: Alice Grey, the Chessington sisters, A. Waterfield and some of the Stevens sisters permanently disappeared. And in a happy return to the practices of 1890, full scores reappeared in the press reports and attendances soared into four figures for several games. No explanation for these changes was offered; if anyone questioned – or even noticed – what was happening, the newspapers did not reflect their curiosity.

The first match after the brief hiatus took place at the Pitsmoor Ground in Sheffield on 29 and 30 June. The first day drew a relatively small crowd owing to the counterattraction of a cycling tournament at Bramall Lane, but around 2,000 attended the second day. The spectators comprised an unusually large proportion of women and some 'veteran cricketers' – presumably former Yorkshire players. An active Yorkshire – and England – cricketer was definitely involved: George Ulyett was the groundsman at Pitsmoor and umpired the match. But the game had some unusual features. On the second day, two women were absent and both teams batted with only ten players, presumably through illness (although both women, M. Stevens and Adele Matthey, played in the next game). A curious error in reporting 'wrongly credited' May Day with an unbeaten 65 on the first day, only for this to be corrected on the second when the runs were attributed to Ada Heather. And after an early finish at 6pm on the second day, the Blues – very unconventionally – batted for a third innings.

The next game was played in Dewsbury. Attendance figures were vague: the *Yorkshire Evening Post* said that there was a 'small attendance' on the first day and a 'large attendance' on the second, but the *Huddersfield Examiner* claimed that there were around 2,000 present by 4pm on the first day. Either way, there must have been a substantial crowd in total, probably over 3,000. The weather was poor on day one, but spectators saw Violet Westbrook reach an unbeaten 58 in the 90 minutes or so of play possible. The next afternoon, in better weather, she took her score to 145 before she was bowled by Lizzie Sanders. She followed up with six wickets to bowl the Blues out for 98 (in the follow-on, the Blues rattled up 101/1 against ragged bowling and fielding).

The *Huddersfield Examiner* observed that Matthews was a 'noticeable figure' at Dewsbury, even if it was not too sure who he was – the article claimed that he had played for Surrey and had been 'engaged by the manager for coaching purposes'. It noted that among the teams were 'two daughters of London clergymen'. Perhaps this was true, perhaps it was more propaganda to emphasise the respectability of the OELC, but it clearly emanated from the team management. The *Examiner* added one strange comment which aimed to be positive but hints at negative stories in circulation: 'During their stay in Dewsbury all the players by their bearing have totally belied the absurd rumours which have been set on foot about them.' Neither the nature nor the origin of these rumours was elucidated by the author, but this was their only such mention in print. Off the field, a dinner was held at the end of the game, attended by the Mayor of Dewsbury and one of his predecessors.

Between £70 and £80 was taken in gate money, of which 15 per cent went to the Dewsbury and Savile Cricket Club, leaving a profit for the OELC of between £60 and £68. The amount of gate money taken in this period would later become a source of rancour, and this is one of the few pieces of solid evidence we have regarding takings in 1891.

There was possibly a controversial incident at the game, although the teller could not vouch for the complete accuracy of his slightly contrived tale. A piece in the *Dewsbury Chronicle* at the end of August said that a local photographer called Brown had been taking photographs during play when he was stopped by the manager who said: 'You really must not do that; it is copyright.' Brown challenged him as nothing he was photographing could be copyrighted. The manager returned with a policeman to again ask Brown to 'desist from photographing the ladies'. Brown agreed, and when questioned why he had not backed down before, revealed that he had taken all the pictures he needed while the manager had gone to fetch the policeman.

Another curious story from this period – reprinted many times over the following weeks – said that a 'young lady' had been going to post a letter in Kensington one evening when a passer-by attempted to steal her watch: 'The young lady started after the thief, overtook him, and smote him so shrewdly over the wrist with a stick she was carrying that he dropped the watch and made off.' The punchline to the tale was that the young lady was actually the captain of the OELC Reds: 'With such a training it is not to be wondered at that she caught the thief red-handed.' The story seems to have been first reported in *The Globe* on 4 July and apparently dated to the evening of 2 July. The captaincy of the Reds in this period was split between Violet Westbrook and Flora Fane; unfortunately for the reliability of this tale, both women were in Dewsbury at the time of the supposed incident. Perhaps it happened in the previous week when the women were in London, but more likely it never took place at all.

The following day, 3 July, the OELC began a two-day game at Headingley, before what the *Yorkshire Post* called a 'good attendance' on day one and a 'much larger gathering' on day two. But once more there was a hint of confusion: an advertisement mistakenly proclaimed that the OELC would appear at a music hall. Nevertheless, that game ended an undoubtedly successful first week of the revived tour.

The team continued to travel around the north, heading across the Pennines into Lancashire and visiting Bury, Burnley, Warrington, Accrington and Manchester in the second week. After the return of Westbrook, another familiar name began to be mentioned in the press. The *Burnley Gazette* suggested that Daisie Stanley 'has not yet joined the team this season, but will do so shortly' (and wheeled out the old lie that she was an 'expert' player), while the *Burnley Express* took the line that 'she is at present detained on business, but is expected to join the teams very soon'. By the end of the second week, when the OELC appeared at Manchester on 10 and 11 July, Stanley was back. The *Manchester Courier* reported: 'Miss Stanley, perhaps the ablest cricketer of the lot, [has] now assumed managerial responsibility.' Once again, we are confronted with a question of where this was coming from; was Stanley, like Westbrook, doing her own publicity work? And there was no indication, then or later, of the nature of her management role.

Also at Burnley, the Silvani troupe of cyclists performed during the interval (their first such mention in the press, although they might have appeared before). But other issues abounded. Beatrice Fane was absent because her sister (not Flora, who was playing) was reported to be ill in Leeds with the influenza which had been causing so many problems. The *Burnley Express* claimed that the visit to that town was not a financial success, although the *Lancashire Evening Post* claimed the attendance had been around a thousand. The absence of Beatrice at Burnley and Warrington led to those games being played as ten-a-side, something which was to become increasingly common. Clearly it was no longer possible to cover absences with replacements. From the game at Leeds onwards, every match for which we have a full scorecard shows at least one team missing a player; at Buxton, the Blues only had nine listed on the scorecard while the Reds had ten. And throughout August, the Blues remained ten-a-side, facing eleven Reds. Oddly enough, Stanley never took to the field despite the ongoing player shortage.

Attendances remained good. At Manchester, around a thousand spectators watched the first day and between two and three hundred the second; a 'large number' came to Buxton, where it was reported that £32 9s 6d was taken at the gate, of which a fixed fee of £5 5s 6d was paid to

Buxton Cricket Club for the use of the ground. There were also suggestions that the attendance was good for a two-day match at Blackpool, but 'not large' at Warrington during more unsettled weather. The games at Blackburn and Barrow were similarly poorly attended, but the OELC's appearance at Birkenhead drew enough of a crowd to affect the attendances at nearby events; and one customer inadvertently started a small fire in a pile of dried grass on their way to the ground.

Perhaps in a bid to increase attendances, a different format was tried. Some matches were advertised as two separate games, even over the course of a single day. For example, the game at Blackpool seems to have been played as two games over two days, but the game at Cheltenham was advertised for 29 July as 'two exhibition cricket displays' and at Farnworth the OELC played two separate matches – one in the afternoon and one in the evening. The aim was presumably to attract fresh audiences in the evening who had not been able to see the afternoon game.

But after the boost of those well-attended games, the attentive reader of newspapers might have noticed another change in tone. Scores once again became irregularly reported. And then something strange took place at Barrow on 22 and 23 July. For the only time in 1891, the OELC put on evening performances – one on each night. It was like a replay of 1890 as the cricketers gave a 'calisthenics' display at the Royal Alhambra Theatre 'under the direction of Miss Daisy Stanley'; Stanley and Matthey revived their fencing act; and there was support from various acts, including a juggler, a guitarist, singers and dancers. We do not know why there had been a change of heart, nor whose heart had been changed, but that the revival coincided with Stanley's return (allowing for two weeks to rehearse) makes her its likeliest inspiration or instigator. Yet this was the only evening performance of 1891; for whatever reason, there was no repeat.

And strangest of all was the non-involvement of the Silvani Cyclists: they were prominently advertised as part of the Barrow show, but never turned up (their place was filled by 'Mr and Mrs Saker'). Two days after their non-appearance, the cyclists announced in *The Era* that they had broken off their partnership with the OELC. As far as can be seen from newspapers, they had only ever given one display – that at Burnley. The contemporary reader might have concluded that there had been a behind-the-scenes problem, whether financial or a clash of personalities, and as we have no other information, this explanation seems the most likely. Given what was to follow, we might even infer that they had not received their fee, but there is no actual evidence of that.

* * *

The events at Barrow marked another turning point as subsequent newspaper coverage dried up. Fragments appeared in the local press, such as the news that Lancaster had a 'moderate' attendance and 'a good number' watched at Rhyl as the OELC visited Wales. Of the actual cricket, hardly a word was printed, and the team suddenly began to appear in stories of a very different nature.

They had been scheduled to play at Kidderminster on 27 July but never arrived. The *County Express* reported that they had sent a telegram, signed by the manager, which simply said: 'The Lady Cricketers refuse to play today.' The indignant writer spluttered that they were 'unmanageables', 'emancipated weaker vessels' and 'sweet sinners' before lamenting another sign of the times, when a servant had won a case for unfair dismissal in Westminster after she had been sacked for refusing to wear her cap. A less outraged account appeared in *The Advertiser*, a Kidderminster newspaper, noting that although 'elaborate arrangements had been made for their appearance' and 'the town had been placarded, not only with extraordinary announcements of the coming events, but with very artistic posters showing the ladies in full chase of the leather', the telegram had been sent at midday from Liverpool announcing the 'refusal'. There were evidently some disappointed locals, and carriages drove up to the ground all afternoon only to be turned away.

After this, the teams headed west, crossing into Wales. But once again, they failed to fulfil engagements, this time at Swansea on the Friday of the same week. The *Cambria Daily Leader* said: 'The Lady Cricketers have probably found out Glamorganshire is not a cricketing county. They were, according to arrangements made early in the year, to have given an exhibition game at Swansea today, but they have not put in an appearance. They are, or rather have been advertised, to play at Cardiff next Monday and Tuesday, but there is a degree of uncertainty about the engagement coming off.' In the meantime, they had been scheduled to play in Cheltenham but may not have done so, although we know that they appeared at Rhyl.

The OELC were scheduled to visit the Isle of Man on 4 and 5 August after their trip to Wales, but nothing appeared in the press at the time. Suddenly, after the grumblings over non-appearances, there was silence. For a week, there was no indication in the press that any games were being played at all. Something was clearly afoot. Nevertheless, some kind of game took place on the Isle of Man. The balance sheet of Douglas Cricket Club the following May indicates that the club received £4 14s 6d from the 'Lady Cricketers' in 1891, although it does not mention if this was a flat fee from the management or a proportion of the gate receipts.

Whatever might have plagued the OELC off the field, Violet Westbrook in this difficult period attained heights that no other player reached in either season. Having scored 145 at Dewsbury, she scored 121 at Oldham two weeks later, 68 at Barrow, 117 at Birkenhead and 101 not out at Rhyl (the only game we can be certain was played in Wales). However, there are no surviving scorecards for these games and we only know about Westbrook's supreme form because of a list published in *Sporting Life* on 26 December of centuries scored in the 1891 season. Among the hundreds scored by players such as W. G. Grace, Arthur Shrewsbury and A. E. Stoddart were those by Miss Violet Westbrook for the Lady Cricketers; Lizzie Sanders's 110 was not mentioned, meaning that the source of this list was probably – once again – Westbrook herself.

* * *

After the post-Douglas silence, the OELC resumed touring, but their original itinerary – which had been faithfully followed until then apart from those abandonments – was scrapped: for example, games that had been advertised at Darlington, Whitby and Hastings were never played.

Instead, the OELC played a two-day game at Middlesbrough on 10 and 11 August, which marked the start of a two-week northern tour. No explanation was given for the hiatus, nor for the alteration in the programme. Those players who had been in the team since Derby remained involved, and there was even an odd piece of continuity in that the Blues could still only field ten players. The only absentee was Flora Fane; it is not clear when she disappeared because full scorecards were not printed in the second part of July. Perhaps she had fallen ill (there were no mentions of her in newspaper reports after the Buxton game) or perhaps she chose not to be involved in this third part of the season; she returned at the end of the season in slightly different circumstances. Her sister Beatrice remained in the team throughout.

Another curiosity was that, after this second break following the game at Douglas, the press reports (which again became fuller) did not name anyone in management – not Matthews, not Stanley, not Ferris, not Michel. Who was in charge?

At Middlesbrough, the OELC played before around 2,000 spectators on the first day (a Monday). After this game, the attendance at Sunderland was around 1,500, and a 'very large and fashionable attendance' watched a two-day game at Newcastle. The game at Sunderland also featured a promotion by the 'Sunderland Cricket and Football Club' (generally known as Sunderland Ashbrooke), whereby members were admitted free to the OELC game 'on the production of their tickets'. The teams may have appeared at the Shildon Great Show in Durham on the Saturday – an appearance long advertised – but there are no reports to confirm this; in any case, they were in Scarborough by the Monday.

The Scarborough game threw up another odd occurrence. Typically for the 1891 season, the match was curtailed by rain on both days and the *York Herald* commented: 'Strange to relate the enthusiasm awakened by these fair cricketers last year has somewhat waned.' This drew an outraged rebuttal the following day: 'This is calculated to create a false impression, as our takings for the first day at Scarborough were greatly in excess of last year, proving that the interest in the Lady Cricketers is on the increase. Yours truly, The Manager.' Who was this manager? As far as the public knew – had anyone been following closely – this could have been Matthews; or maybe Ferris; or even still Michel.

Around this time, a brief feature in the London *Evening News* claimed that 'a team of lady cricketers are to proceed to the Cape [South Africa]' after the season. Whether this was another of the endlessly proposed OELC tours is unclear, but the writer added: 'As there are so many eligible young men looking for wives out there it is to be feared that the teams will soon be broken up, and it is very probable that the conditions will bar marrying or being given in marriage until the close of the tour.' Was this just a piece of nonsense? It was certainly not repeated elsewhere. Although Victorian convention dictated that women gave up their jobs after marriage, at least two married women had played for the OELC in 1890. Had the author heard echoes of something such as a contract for a proposed tour? Or was it a curious distortion of something else which had happened, in which a player had married without 'permission'?

The following two games, at Hull and York, had what local newspapers called 'ordinary' and 'meagre' attendances respectively. In Hull, the OELC made a visit to the Theatre Royal to watch a performance – presumably to drum up publicity. But the York game might offer a clue as to how this last two-week tour came about. The *York Herald* reported that the visit of the OELC was 'through the efforts of Mr J. B. Hampson'. He was a local theatre manager who had been involved in the visit in 1890 and had been listed as one of the local agents of the OELC earlier in 1891. Had he arranged the last matches as part of his effort to ensure that the players came to York?

In another gimmick, the advertisement for the York game included an outright lie. It stated that the OELC had been 'twice honoured by royal patronage'. There is no evidence anywhere that the OELC met, or played in front of, royalty; the only such association was Daisie Stanley's supposed performance in front of the Princess of Wales when she was a gymnastics instructor.

Another figure apparently associated with the OELC in this part of the summer was the former Yorkshire player Billy Bates, a man who had undergone numerous trials over the previous few years and who was in considerable financial difficulty by 1891. Quite how he found himself with the OELC is unclear, but a report in the *Yorkshire Evening Post* stated: 'Bates, the ex-Yorkshire player, who has been travelling with them for some time, is enthusiastic in their praise. "I would match 15 of the ladies," he says, "against the present Yorkshire Eleven – aye, and they would win!"' Perhaps Bates did have some role, but although this story did the usual rounds of being reprinted in local newspapers, no other sources corroborate his involvement.

After appearing at York on Saturday, 22 August, the OELC played just once more before their tour was seemingly abandoned: an unusual match at Dewsbury on 25 August when a combined Lady Cricketers team faced the Dewsbury Tradesmen – their first game against men since May. The home team had 11 players and the women fielded 15. In between showers, the men scored 115/5 declared (a local man called Stott scored an unbeaten 71 and Sanders took four wickets) and reduced the women to 17/5 before rain ended matters. There is no indication whether the men batted or fielded left-handed but the mismatch suggests not. A possible explanation for the unusual nature of this game might be that it was organised after the success of the previous visit to Dewsbury; maybe the Dewsbury Tradesmen stepped in because only 15 women arrived in the town, either through illness or because they had given up. But after this match, the OELC stopped playing; subsequently, there was nothing but silence from the team.

* * *

Gradually, it occurred to people that the OELC tour must have collapsed. The team had been scheduled to play in Great Yarmouth, but a comment in the *Yarmouth Independent* – 'I see the Lady Cricketers should visit us again next week, but as nothing has been said about the visit, it looks as if there might be a disappointment' – was followed up a week later with the observation that they had not turned up because 'the club, or whatever you like to call it, which came here last year is disbanded'. The author expressed some satisfaction at the failure of the 'absurd' idea of 'feminine cricket'. The *Eastern Daily Press* stated in early September that the OELC had been rumoured to be visiting to play a 'local team of gentlemen' but nothing had come of it. The author had the impression that 'the ladies have a very keen eye for the filthy lucre; whether more so than the ordinary run of women we cannot say'.

This dose of extraordinary misogyny might have been the final word on the OELC, because nothing had otherwise been heard of them for over two weeks. And then they returned explosively as *The Star* of London shone some light on the mysterious events of the 1891 season. The repercussions were considerable.

The Star, Sympathy and Benefits

THE STAR – not to be confused with the modern publication of that name – was a London evening newspaper created in 1888. From the beginning it was designed to be populist in nature, appeal to a mass readership and to give a socialist viewpoint. It survived until 1960 when it merged with the *Evening News* (which later in turn merged with the *Evening Standard*). It had immediately leapt to prominence with its coverage of the Whitechapel murders of 1888 and a *Star* journalist might have been the author of one of the supposed letters from the killer, forged to drum up interest in the case, which gave rise to the name 'Jack the Ripper'. It was therefore no stranger to sensation.

On 10 September 1891, *The Star* published a story, prominently on page two, under the headline 'Willow Waly-O' (a line from the Gilbert and Sullivan song 'Prithee, Pretty Maiden') and a smaller subheading 'The Lady Cricketers' Story of the Disasters of their Tour'. As usual in this period, there was no byline. The article provided a detailed account of the events of the previous months, and is one of our few glimpses 'behind the curtain' of the OELC. It is the only example of any player (or players) going 'off script' and telling their own story – and one of the few sources directly from the women themselves. But it requires some careful handling because someone – either the anonymous author or the equally anonymous source – was being, if not untruthful, selective in which facts they presented.

Not that a firm grasp of the facts was too important. The story opened with a vague wave towards the events of 1890: 'For the past two or three years a troop of 22 girls – most of them girls of education and refinement – have been touring.' But it soon became obvious that these original girls were not the particular focus. The author described how an 'alluring advertisement' attracted new players to fill 'vacancies' in the team at the beginning of 1891 (although there is no trace of such an advert, there is no reason to question the point) and stated with misplaced confidence that the 1891 tour began on 1 May in Guildford (it most likely began on 30 March at Kensal Rise, and the Guildford match was actually on 5 May).

From such unpromising beginnings, the author was on firmer ground in giving the wages of the players as between 35 and 50 shillings per week, although he brushed over the first month-and-a-half of the season by saying that the tour progressed 'smoothly' until 20 June when the team played at Burton. And now he began his real story, only parts of which can be corroborated so that we cannot be sure if he continued to be loose with his facts.

According to our journalist, at Burton the players were only paid five shillings, and Michel vanished – 'the sad want of funds seems at about this time to have grieved his tender heart, and he returned to London' – so that Matthews temporarily stepped up to 'look after things in his place'. When the OELC reached Stafford, they were only paid 2s 6d and 'the girls began to live beyond their income'. At Derby, the next venue, they received an advance of 3s – which the author drily noted 'at once brought El

Dorado within easy distance'. But presumably the same day 'the tour was abandoned, they were put in the train at Derby with their fares paid, and they arrived at St Pancras, some of them without a penny in their pockets'.

This unfortunate clash between the advance of three shillings that the players received at Derby before boarding the train (with their fares paid) and their penniless state upon exiting the same train in London cannot have filled the reader with confidence regarding the rigorous accuracy of the story. Perhaps someone simply muddled up locations,[47] or the wages were paid earlier than the source remembered, and nothing was received in Derby at all. Another slight inconsistency is that the game at Burton was played on a Saturday – an obvious day to distribute money from the previous week – but then the source claims that the players were given money on Monday (Stafford) and Wednesday (Derby). Perhaps Matthews (or Michel) was simply paying them whenever he had funds, but something does not feel *quite* right whichever way we turn the story. Was our author tweaking the tale for dramatic effect?

While these events might have seemed sensational enough, the author – or his source – was just getting started. Shortly after their return to London (no date is given, but the team played at Sheffield five days after the Derby game so it must have been within a day or two) the women were summoned to Percy Hall on Tottenham Court Road in London, where Michel reappeared. At the meeting, he and a man called Henry Wood spoke to the players. The *Star* article identified Wood as one of the directors of the

---

[47] There is a curious break in the narrative after they were given the money: the game at Derby was on 24 June but the article could be read as if there was a gap between that fixture and their being bundled on to the train.

ECAA, alongside Bosanquet, and said, a little hesitantly, that he was 'something in the City'. But Wood was not on the original list of shareholders for the ECAA, nor was he on the similar document dated November 1890.

Michel and Wood told the women that 'the affairs of the association were in the Bankruptcy Court, and the contracts (which should have extended over three years) were mere waste paper, though they would get "something in the pound" for what was owing to them'. Once again, this was not quite accurate; the ECAA was never in the bankruptcy court and it was not officially dissolved until February 1892 (although Bosanquet later told the Registrar of Joint Stock Companies that the association, 'having spent all its capital ceased to carry on business' in June 1891).

But according to *The Star*, this was not the end. Michel and Wood told the players that 'a new tour was projected, with Matthews as manager'. They would receive £2 each 'as an earnest of the bona fides of the new scheme'. And after a tour of England, there would be a visit to Australia. The women signed a new contract, 'of which, however, none of them ever got a copy', and were paid 30s each. Presumably those like the Chessington sisters who ceased playing at this time chose not to sign, but the rest of the players resumed their tour under these new arrangements. Perhaps it is not coincidental that, from this time forward, with a few possible exceptions where sisters of players might temporarily have been recruited, there were no replacements to fill in for injuries or illness, resulting in the frequent ten-a-side or numerically unbalanced matches.

The Star went on to describe how, after the first week (the story mentioned the Sheffield and Leeds games, but omitted Dewsbury), the players 'were surprised to find that 10s was deducted' from their wages to repay the £2 advance they had received when the tour resumed. But the source for the story said that gates were good at this stage. And it is true that several games at this time, including those at Sheffield and Dewsbury, had attendances in the thousands.

But when the teams reached Manchester, Michel reappeared with apparently sinister motives. *The Star* rather delicately phrased what happened: he 'occupied himself with the congenial task of taking money at the gate'. At this point, the author explained that Daisie Stanley – 'who had previously been a member of the team, but now had been promoted to a position in the management' – also joined the operation (which is backed up by earlier newspaper reports), as did Wood who 'seemed much interested in the gate and other features of the tour'. Even Stanley 'was not above sitting at the payment of custom'. The implication of fraud is clear: 'Good gates were the rule, but payment of salaries was made an exception.'

The remainder of the article is a tale of decline and woe. The players had no food when they got to Barrow and by the time they reached Birkenhead, they had suffered enough. They 'struck' and refused to play until Michel – explicitly named in the article as responsible – paid them. 'He first threatened and blustered, called in the police (who told him to pay the girls' wages), and finally, as one or two good engagements were in the near future, he climbed down, promised payment, and made a small advance.' This fits with what we know: the team were in Liverpool when they sent a telegram to cancel the match at Kidderminster and this was also the period when they failed to fulfil a fixture at Swansea.

The article continued: 'On they went to Llandudno, where Michel and Miss Stanley reappeared.' This is a little odd as there was no indication in the article that either of them had left the tour, and Michel had supposedly been in Liverpool with the players. At Llandudno, Michel and Stanley paid the women 3s, and at Rhyl they were paid 5s. The only problem with this account is that we have no record of a game at Llandudno. There is just enough room in the fixture list for a Llandudno appearance – perhaps on 30 July – but evidence is lacking for what was happening that week.

The Star account says that after they had been to Rhyl, the players returned to Liverpool, where they had 'no breakfast, no money' and travelled to Douglas on the Isle of Man (for a game scheduled on 4 August). They played against a men's team drawn from a touring theatre group (probably the D'Oyly Carte Opera Company) performing *The Gondoliers*, and 'a timely feed of lemonade and biscuits provided by their opponents prevented them breaking down altogether'. The OELC had not been scheduled to play a men's team and if this part of the story is correct, it *might* indicate that not all the players travelled to Douglas, necessitating a local team providing opposition.

But Douglas represented the end of the road; they were 'absolutely without money. They had used all their resources, and some of them had to exist upon bread and butter and a pennyworth of nuts for a whole day.' According to *The Star*, the players were brought back to Derby – for no obvious reason as there were much easier ways to travel from Douglas to London, for example via a Liverpool train – where they once more were sent back to St Pancras, 'penniless'.

The author praised the conduct of 'the girls' – who 'seem to have behaved splendidly' – and 'the magnificent way in which they have stuck together and faced their difficulties'. Other 'girls' in similar situations might have 'faltered' – which could have carried a multitude of meanings – but the players 'never for a moment lost their heads, and never wavered in their determination to make the best of things and worry through their difficulties'. The article concluded with the information that the players planned to 'bring their manager to book in the courts, and *The Star* says good luck go with them'.

It was a sensational story and caused reverberations. But how true was it? There *is* circumstantial corroboration which backs up the overall thrust of the story. Coverage around the time of the Derby game dwindled to almost nothing. Attendances were meagre and Michel vanished from reports in that crucial period. He had also admitted in mid-May that the tour was losing around £60 per week. The game at Derby did take place (which is not obvious from *The Star*) but the OELC were scheduled to appear at Newark a few days after; there is no record that the latter game was played (although nor is there a record that it was cancelled). The next appearance came on 29 June at Sheffield. Newspapers similarly corroborate the arrival of Stanley in the period after Derby, as well as the continued presence of Michel. And *The Star*'s version of the non-appearances in Wales, and the problems at Liverpool, parallels the narrative reported in July.

But there are problems. *The Star* did not mention the resumption of the tour after the second collapse (although a follow-up article briefly alluded to this). And despite the suggestions that the women were so weak at Douglas that they had to be fed lemonade and biscuits, we know that some kind of match took place because it was mentioned in the accounts of Douglas Cricket Club. On the other hand, there is evidence from theatrical newspapers that a cricket team representing '*Gondoliers* B Company' played some games on the Isle of Man during August.

More questionable is the idea that, from Douglas, the players were inexplicably sent to London via Derby. Perhaps this was a narrative device to mirror the earlier collapse. And another curiosity – which will become more important as events unfold – is the complete absence from the narrative of E. C. Ferris, who had been named as a manager in July newspaper reports.

So who was the source of this exposé? The introduction gives the only clues: the story was 'poured into the sympathetic ear of a *Star* man by some sorrowing damsels, who assured him they had "nothing extenuated, nor aught set down in malice"'. There are hints that these 'damsels' were new players, not just the mention of the otherwise unknown advertisement for the 1891 season. The writer is vague on how long the OELC had been in existence and seems unaware that the 'professional named Matthews' had been involved in the OELC the previous season; a newer player would perhaps have been unfamiliar with the backstory. Another indication is that, although the article says that the players were paid 'from 35s to as much as 50s a week', the narrative says that when the money dried up, the players were not given their 'regulation 35s'; the 'damsels' were therefore presumably on the lower rate which might have been given to the less valuable new players. And a follow-up in *The Star* a few days later claimed that those who joined in 1891 did not receive the same winter pay as the original players.

None of this explains why there was no mention of the final two-week tour. Possibly the 'damsels' did not take part in that portion of the tour, but the only obvious absentee is Flora Fane (who might have been ill), a well-established and almost certainly better-paid player. Perhaps the information came from one of the other players who disappeared from the tour earlier in the season, such as Elizabeth Dempsey or the Chessington sisters, but they were not involved in the post-Derby revival at all. Another possibility is that the source spoke to the journalist before the two-week northern tour had been arranged. If the reporter or the newspaper had chosen to sit on the story for a month before printing it, perhaps there were concerns about potential legal action. Or maybe this part of the tour was simply omitted as it made for a less satisfying ending; *The Star* was not above tweaking a story for effect.

* * *

The exposé caused a huge stir. It was reproduced in many other newspapers: some merely summarised it; others quoted large sections, almost the entirety of the article in many cases. Yet apart from *The Star*, no newspaper named Wood. The relevant sections from the original were reproduced with his name blanked out: they literally said 'Mr _____'. Another excision was the section about how the women had 'behaved splendidly'. Such caution may have been advisable because two days after *The Star* published the initial story, a rebuttal appeared in that newspaper from John R. Hall, Wood's solicitor: 'Mr Wood was never either a shareholder in or a director of the association, nor did he at any time take any part in the management or control of the undertaking, and in so far as he is concerned my instructions are that the whole of the allegations in the article alluded to are wholly without foundation. Further, my client has never received one penny out of the takings either at the gates or otherwise.'

The first point was undoubtedly true: Wood had no apparent connection with the ECAA. But *The Star* stood by its argument. In a direct reply to Hall's letter, the editor questioned whether this Mr Wood was the same man whom the team had met at Percy Hall and who had visited some games. The editor added: 'The mystery will probably be cleared up when the girls' actions for the £70 to £100 of unpaid wages are heard.'

The letter from Hall was printed on a Saturday. The following Monday, two more letters appeared in *The Star*. The first was brief and unsigned except as 'the late acting manager', stating that the author, 'as a friend to the girls, can testify to the accuracy of the statements which [*The Star* account] contains. There is over £70 due to these girls alone, to say nothing of what is due to myself and others connected with the staff.' This might have been written by Matthews, but a more likely author was the man named E. C. Ferris. As we shall see, he later supported the legal claims of the women but his motives might not have been selfless.

The second letter was from Michel himself. He first addressed the collapse of the tour after the game at Derby. He suggested that poor gates – 'the novelty appearing to have worn off' – and bad weather meant that, 'for the first time full salaries could not be paid'. That was when the association (Michel was careful to avoid saying whose decision it was) chose to 'cease operations'. At this time, he claimed, 'the arrears of salary due [amounted] to about half a week after a period of nearly two years'. Michel said that 'a season (which it was anticipated would be remunerative) having been arranged by two local agents in the north, some gentlemen provided funds to place the teams "on the road" again, Mr Matthews having the direction of the tour, and I being replaced as business manager by a gentleman who continued in that position until the end of the season'. This can only have been E. C. Ferris, and there is some corroboration: Ferris was described in the press as the business manager after the 'break'.

Michel continued: 'From this time forward [after the resumption in June] I never had the control of finances and did not pay any salaries, part salaries, or advances to members, but merely visited the grounds from time to time to assist and advise the new management in any way I could.' He denied taking money at Manchester, and 'indeed I only acted in the capacity of money-taker at two, or at the most three, matches during the tour'. The incident at Birkenhead, he said, only arose when he acted in the absence of Matthews and the 'local agent'. He said that the amount due was around £13, and 'the members tried to seize the costumes and plant [equipment]'.

After that, there was a meeting in Liverpool, during which everyone decided to continue, and according to Michel, the players agreed to accept 'what salaries the management could afford to pay'. And it was 'again explained that I was no longer the manager but simply the adviser to the Company. My subsequent occasional visits to the matches were in a purely unofficial character, and from this time I was indeed rarely even consulted.' But it seems a remarkable coincidence that the only time he was directly involved, there was a strike which he had to resolve. Even less likely is his suggestion that he was not really involved afterwards. In his letter, he said he was only in Llandudno for half an hour and at Douglas he was there for only one day, 'and then only for a few minutes!' If his services were not needed (and the *Star* had not reported that he was in Douglas), why was he there at all?

Michel argued that 'in Lancashire and District a good gate was a great exception'. We have direct evidence to the contrary, independent of the OELC or its managers. Michel also denied that the players were not fed, and stated: 'Far from thinking they were destitute in the Isle of Man, I know that over £30 was paid for their board and lodging during the few days they were there.' He stated that Wood was 'not a director of, or a shareholder in, the association, and certainly took no active part in the control of the gates at any time'. He concluded: 'Everyone connected with the conduct of the tour made the welfare of the ladies the first consideration, and disastrous business alone caused whatever inconvenience they may have unfortunately experienced on one or two occasions.'

Michel also went to great pains to extricate Walter Bosanquet from any suggestion of wrongdoing. He wrote that Bosanquet had 'from time-to-time advanced various sums to the association' when money ran out during the 1890 season, and it had still not been returned to him. Michel emphasised that Bosanquet had 'lost very considerably by the speculation'. But if Bosanquet was no longer involved, and Wood was 'not a director of, or a shareholder', who was running this mysterious company which had taken over the running of the OELC and for which Michel was acting as an adviser? If the OELC name and costumes had been copyrighted, as Michel claimed in advertising, how could the new company use them if it had no connection with the

ECAA? And who were the 'gentlemen' who agreed to fund the tour after Derby?

However, Michel did confront the weakest point in the *Star* story: the omission, either deliberately or through ignorance, of any mention of the final tour in Yorkshire. He made clear that after the visit to the Isle of Man 'came a tour in Yorkshire during which I am informed by the local agent (who sacrificed his own emoluments entirely) a great amount of the arrears were paid up, and the members returned to London – after due notice had been given – with about two weeks' arrears of salary due to them.' The evidence supports him to some extent as it seems likely that J. B. Hampson was the figure behind the two-week tour.

Far less convincing was Michel's suggestion that the revived tour, once it was 'on the road again' after Derby, had no connection with the original operation. Not only his presence, but that of Daisie Stanley (whom he studiously avoided mentioning) indicated otherwise. And he did not admit that this second tour came to grief, implying that it simply ended once the originally planned fixtures had been fulfilled. There is no doubt from contemporary coverage that the tour collapsed – there were the non-appearances in Kidderminster and Wales in June, then at Yarmouth in August, as well as the abandonment of the original schedule when the 'Hampson tour' began. The latter portion was quite possibly something completely unconnected to the original ECAA arrangements.

Overall, Michel's letter was a piece of self-serving distortion designed to protect himself and Bosanquet: if the mysterious organisers were making a loss owing to poor attendances, there would have been no money for Michel, Wood or Stanley to steal; therefore they could not have been guilty of any kind of fraud. Michel's refusal to name Ferris or Stanley, and his insistence that Wood played 'no active part in the control of the gates' also suggest that he was trying to keep others out of trouble.

But the author from *The Star* was unconvinced, and put 'one or two questions' to Michel, inviting a reply. Clearly, the writer had returned to his source for more information as he had more from 'the girls' in response to Michel. He first said that Michel's 'allegation that the members were paid a weekly salary during the winter practice is only true as regards the old members of the troop. The eight or ten who joined this year received only a few pence per day to cover the cost of travelling from their homes to the practice hall.' Not only does this reinforce the notion that the story was sourced from new players, but it also implies a division within the team.

The writer went on to state that Bosanquet's 'losses and his benevolence have nothing to do with the question. He is the only director whose name appears on the card of rules and regulations handed to the girls, and he seems to have been the guiding spirit of the association, which, according to Mr Michel himself, discharged these girls without paying their salaries after failing to make a profit out of them.' The editor also made a rather sly dig. Michel had signed the letter 'E. Michel, ex-manager' and addressed it 11 Queen Victoria Street. In discussing Bosanquet, the editor noted he was 'Mr Bosanquet of 11 Queen Victoria Street'; because whatever might or might not have taken place, Michel was still using Bosanquet's office as his correspondence address.

The next point made in response to Michel was that he seemed to blame bad gates for the 'failure of the association to pay their debts' but he had 'very seriously understated the amount of arrears after the break-up at Burton. The girls only received 5s for the last week instead of 35s or 40s and got no compensation for being dismissed without the fortnight's notice provided for in their contracts. The arrears of salary amounted to about three weeks, instead of, as Mr Michel states, half a week.'

The *Star* writer then addressed the next part of Michel's letter, saying that 'his statement is not as clear as we could wish', and asked some (extremely good) questions about the revival. Who were the people who provided funds? Who replaced Michel as business manager, and was this manager the author of the letter published alongside Michel's? If Michel held no official role, how could he act as money-taker 'at several meetings' and 'bully' the players at Birkenhead, 'threatening, according to their story, to leave them helpless' and trying 'ineffectually to take from them the dresses and plant which they held in default of getting their due'? And if he had no responsibility, how could Michel exercise 'authority' at Birkenhead? The writer finally asked who appointed him as an 'adviser' and could he produce the contracts signed by the players at Percy Hall, 'copies of which were refused to them'?

The writer noted that 'some of Mr Michel's statements are contrary of the truth, and others are partially corroborated by the girls'. He/they ridiculed the notion that the players had agreed at Liverpool not to be paid their full salary. The source also revealed that £30 *had* been given to the players at Douglas to pay for food and lodgings, 'but that sum was guaranteed by Mr Leicester Barratt, a local vocalist'. And, curiously, the source said: 'It is true also that Mr Michel only saw the ladies [at Douglas] for a few minutes, but his absence was due to considerations of so pressing a character that it might be held to be involuntary.' There is no further hint at what this might mean, but it was clearly something reflecting badly on Michel. And the source added: 'No arrears were paid up by the Yorkshire local agent (agent for whom?) though he did not allow further arrears to accrue to any extent.'

The author also made another attack on Wood, suggesting that 'he will be allowed an opportunity elsewhere in explaining on oath his presence at the Percy Hall meeting when the contracts for the tour were made, and at Manchester and Sheffield, where he assumed supreme authority in matters of management'. His final point was that, if the tour *was* making a loss (and 'the girls aver that the "gates" were not so bad as represented') that should not have ended the management's liability for the wages. The whole article – the two letters and the response – took an entire column and was carried under a sub-headline 'The Managers Play a Game of Spenlow and Jorkins'. Spenlow and Jorkins were legal business partners in Charles Dickens's *David Copperfield* who each blamed the other for their own inaction.

But *The Star* still did not address the biggest weakness in its own case; even after the new information from 'the girls', there was no mention of that two-week tour except the brief mention of the mysterious agent who had paid up for those games. The comment 'agent for whom' muddies the waters even more. Did the players not know for whom Hampson was working? Or are they indicating that he was acting independently and was not the agent for the person/group Michel was representing? Perhaps we can deduce that they thought this was a different set of managers and had no part in their grievance; therefore they simply left it out of the account.

The *Star* rebuttal shied away – perhaps out of legal caution – from the claims about fraud on the gate, but the case was quite strong. Where did all the money go? Who exactly was running the show at this point? Is there anything to support the suggestion that the profits were being taken by the 'management'? Between the resumption of the tour and its collapse at Douglas, just over five weeks elapsed, comprising at least 22 matches. In that time, if the management had been paying 22 players at the rate of 30s per week, that would have cost £165. We know that the OELC took around £60 from the Dewsbury game alone, and just over £27 at Buxton; there were also several four-figure attendances. It seems highly likely that there was more than enough money to pay the players, even allowing for the lower attendances at Warrington, Lancaster or the poor gate at Burnley, particularly if Wood had provided an initial injection of cash. Therefore, the suggestion that someone was siphoning gate money into their own pocket does not seem outlandish.

Both Michel and the article's author tiptoed around why Bosanquet's involvement apparently ceased after Derby. The solicitor later claimed that money had run out – a line used and exaggerated by Michel at the Percy Hall meeting – but in 1890, he had been willing to cover early losses out of his own pocket. He was certainly wealthy enough to do so again in 1891 with the expectation of improved returns later in the season. A more likely explanation may be that he – or his fellow shareholders – had decided to distance themselves from the whole concept. Perhaps there was something of which they disapproved; maybe even those games against men. And yet there cannot have been an enormous breach with Michel, who was still able to write from Bosanquet's own offices in September; there was either a continuing partnership between the two men, or Bosanquet still employed Michel.

The Star cautiously implied that Bosanquet was still involved after Derby; but if he was, perhaps it was as a private individual. And given his wealth and respectability, he is unlikely to have been a party to any theft of gate money, even if his later vagueness about the date that the ECAA ceased operations, and his lateness in reporting this fact, might seem slightly suspicious.

* * *

Meanwhile, the carefully edited first *Star* article (but not the replies published over the following days) continued to circulate around the newspapers. The timing of this publicity was unlikely to be accidental because the story coincided with the return of the OELC to the cricket field. A benefit match for the players had been arranged for 21 September at Tufnell Park, and it is not impossible that the story was released – with a few details omitted for added effect – to foster sympathy for the plight of the women. If so, it was successful because *Sporting Life* reported on 10 September, clearly using details from the *Star* exposé, that the 1891 tour had 'ended prematurely, and the girls have found themselves in London absolutely without resources'. It suggested that they 'have returned to their homes' but that the 'proprietors of the Tufnell Park Ground have kindly offered them the opportunity of playing a benefit match there ... The girls are making all the arrangements themselves, and if they get good weather they will probably receive some compensation for their serious losses and sufferings during a very eventful season.'

Reaction both to the story in *The Star* and the benefit match was largely positive. The *Yorkshire Evening Post* judged that the story 'reflects very seriously on the managing officials, who are to be brought to book by the parents of the girls – people in good station of life'. The *Eastern Daily Press*, a week after slamming the women for their pursuit of 'filthy lucre', abruptly reversed course, admitting that they 'had no knowledge of the almost heart-rending conditions under which this band of ladies have been fulfilling their engagements' when criticising the team. It wished them success for the benefit matches that were being arranged, and suggested that 'the manner in which the gate money has previously been disposed of is shortly expected to be inquired into'.

Perhaps more usefully for the financial prospects of the players, several groups came together to support the benefit at Tufnell Park. As well as the ground being provided for free, the *Sportsman* and *Sporting Life* paid for umpires; the First City of London Artillery Band played for free, and a printer provided tickets and posters without charging.

Not everyone was so supportive. A writer in *Gentlewoman* offered some sympathy but believed that 'as a speculation the attraction of the lady cricketers began and ended with the first season. People were attracted by the novelty and not the cricket, and when the novelty wore off the money ceased to come in.' The *Southern Echo* was positively gleeful in its sarcastic account of the collapse, and said: 'This will give heart to those who have maintained that cricket is not a pastime for women ... and as there is no money in the business one may expect to see the speedy termination both of the controversy in the press and its subject as displayed in the fields.' But even the author of that piece hoped that the benefit would be a success. And the *Burnley Express* also attributed the failure to the loss of novelty after the first season, and said: 'At the end of last year they looked forward to this season with sanguine expectations, which, however, were doomed to disappointment. They have had a dismal and disheartening season, and instead of indulging in raptures over a cricketer's life now vote it a fiasco.' The *Lennox Herald* thought that 'popular sympathy' would help the benefit, and that 'if it proves successful they may be inclined to tour next year "on their own hook", without the intervention of managers or middlemen'.

The original article in *The Star* concluded with a pointed remark about the benefit game: 'The girls will make all the arrangements themselves, and will collect the money at the gate without the assistance or Mr Michel or Miss Daisy Stanley.' But the newspaper that had broken the sensational story seemed to lose interest remarkably quickly. After the letter of Michel was printed, it fell silent. It did not even cover the benefit match; there were no follow-up letters nor anything else about the OELC. Possibly there were other stories to pursue, but it is hard not to suspect the involvement of lawyers for Michel and Wood (perhaps even Bosanquet himself), or *The Star* receiving its own legal advice to let the matter drop.

* * *

The benefit game took place at Tufnell Park in terrible weather – something the players had been doubtlessly expecting bitterly – but still drew a crowd of around a thousand. There was time for Violet Westbrook to score

59 in around an hour but little else was achieved and the players looked rusty, having not taken the field for almost a month. Flora Fane returned, but Adele Matthey was absent. The Blues again had only ten players. One notable attendee was Alfred Craig, known as the 'Surrey Poet' and a famous figure at the Oval, who performed a poem about the 1891 season (which did not mention the OELC). The *Yorkshire Evening Post* chose to print a tired old tale – which the last two seasons had surely proven to be a nonsense given the number of times they played in terrible weather – that one of the players appealed to the umpire to go in during a rain shower as 'the wet is spoiling my hair'.

A less heralded – but apparently more successful – benefit match took place in Hastings later in the week. Over two days, there were half-centuries from Westbrook, Ella Heather and Sanders and wickets for Ada Heather and Flora Fane. The attendance was reported to be good, and the gate money substantial; the only problem came with the exclusion of the press from the 'scoring enclosure', although the reporter who complained about this made clear it was not at the request of the players. A few days later, photographs of groups of the lady cricketers were being advertised on sale in Hastings.

That was the OELC's final game of the year, a considerably earlier finish than in 1890. Across the 1891 season, under the various managers, Westbrook (at an average in recorded games of over 57), Ella Heather (at an average just under 50) and probably Lizzie Sanders (she had 930 in games for which we have scores, at an average of 27) had all passed 1,000 runs. Others to average between 15 and 20 with the bat in 1891 included Beatrice and Flora Fane, Alice Grey and A. Waterfield. The leading wicket-takers were Ada Heather (at least 118 wickets) and Sanders (at least 109), but Flora Fane (84), Matthey (52) and probably Westbrook (47 in recorded games) also passed 50 wickets. The leading catcher by a distance was Lena Parsons with 35 catches in recorded games; of the others, only Flora Fane (12) and Sanders (13) took more than ten catches.

Given the turmoil behind the scenes, as well as the appalling weather, it is incredible that the players achieved anything at all. And with that, the tour concluded. Most believed that this would mark the end of professional women's cricket. But they were not quite correct.

Recrimination and Revenge?

EVEN AFTER the season, the OELC remained in the public consciousness. They were mentioned in September in an odd attack on women printed in the *Birmingham Mail*, and in October the *Dundee Telegraph* proclaimed that the professional lady cricketer was 'by now happily extinct'. But that was not quite the case. The 'Lady Cricketer' continued to be a popular fancy-dress costume; during a 'high society' slander case one witness recalled losing some jewellery when she went to watch the Lady Cricketers; and Violet Westbrook's centuries appeared in the list printed in *Sporting Life* on Boxing Day.

Hanging in the air though was the expectation of legal action that the *Star* article had promised: 'The girls ... are now determined to bring their manager to book in the courts.' The intended target of this legal action was vague: Michel, Matthews, E. C. Ferris, Daisie Stanley and Henry Wood all had held some kind of position in management. Yet the only 'lady cricketer' to take her employers to court in 1891 was Marie Backhouse, whose claim against the management of Arthur's Ideal Lady Cricketers was heard in November.

It was not until 1 February 1892 that an OELC cricketer carried through the threat. Before Assistant Judge Roxburgh at the Lord Mayor's Court in London, the player known as Mabel Emmett – whose real name, the court heard, was Agnes Rowney – made a claim for payment owed. The case was reported widely in newspapers; the fullest account appeared in Dublin's *Evening Herald*, an article littered with awkward cricket metaphors. Rowney – who was named both 'Agnes' and 'Little Annie' in the *Evening Herald* – demanded £12 from Henry Wood, described as a financial agent.

Rowney's case *should* be vital evidence: the apparently unvarnished truth from an actual OELC player, given in court not long after the events in question and recorded (mostly accurately) by the press. Except that, as usual, we don't *quite* have that. For a start, Rowney's version differed in quite important respects from the story printed in *The Star*. Putting aside the real possibility that she was a source for that story, surely evidence given in court would have been more reliable than that reported in a sensationalist newspaper? Not quite, for various reasons that we shall see.

Nor do we entirely have Rowney's version of events because most of the evidence was presented by her legal representative. Therefore, once again our first-hand account has been filtered through someone else. In fact, the only words of Rowney directly reported in the press were complaints about the efforts of the court artist; her actual evidence was a secondary concern to journalists. And a final problem is that, in common with so many others involved with the OELC, Rowney may not have been an entirely trustworthy witness. In the end, the case creates as many questions as answers.

* * *

Rowney's representative, Mr Forbes Lancaster, put her claim to the court. He outlined how the OELC had been run by Michel under the 'Cricket and Athletic Company' associated with Walter Bosanquet. According to the *Evening Herald*, Forbes Lancaster said: 'If they were not equal to W. G. [Grace] they were, at all events, in the language of the prospectus, very good slow and medium bowlers, sound and stylish bats, and very smart on the field and at the wicket.' Lancaster related that in 1890, 'the ladies did very well' but in 1891 'the tour dried up' by the time they reached Derby – something for which he carefully avoided suggesting a reason. Lancaster related how Matthews had told the players that 'something had gone wrong with the syndicate', (according to *The Times*) and that there was no more money.[48] The women therefore returned to London and the tour was apparently over.

Lancaster said that in London, the women were summoned to Percy Hall (on 26 June) where they were told 'that the agreement with Mr Bosanquet on behalf of the syndicate was at an end'. But Rowney's case diverged from the newspaper story at this point. *The Star* had equally attributed the revised offer for the players to Michel and the 'director' Henry Wood. In Rowney's version, Michel vanished from the story at this point, and Wood took centre stage, informing the players that *he* would finance the tour. Wood told them that, in future, 'instead of Mr Michel being regarded as the "daddy" of the company, they would look upon [Wood] as the "daddy"'. This extraordinary claim, which drew quite a laugh from the court, passed without comment in most reports. 'Daddy' may have been a simple joke among the team – and an article early in

---

48 Some accounts of the court case suggest Matthews had been summoned to London while at Derby and informed the players of the collapse by telegram.

the 1891 season had said of Bosanquet that he was 'looked upon quite as a father' by the team – and most likely meant an authority figure, a common contemporary meaning for the word when not referring to an actual parent. It was an unfortunate choice however, as 'daddy' was sometimes used – as early as the 17th century – to refer to pimps.

After the meeting, Rowney signed a new agreement but details of the contract were slightly mysterious. According to Lancaster, Wood told the women that he did not want his name publicly associated with the team and so the contract was counter-signed by E. C. Ferris as acting manager. Wood promised to keep the tour going until the autumn and offered Rowney terms identical to the earlier deal: 35s per week[49] plus railway fares and her costume; she was expected to buy her own food and 'to provide suitable underclothing'.

Rowney's argument became a little fuzzy at this point. Lancaster made clear that the tour broke up a second time but was again reluctant to offer any explanation. According to the *Evening Herald*, Lancaster suggested that 'the tour did not pay, salaries were irregular and fragmentary'. The *Times* version was even woollier, simply saying that 'she did receive some money, but only in driblets'. As it was 'impossible to play cricket without food', the tour broke up. Neither *The Star*'s implication of fraud nor Michel's counter-explanation of poor attendances was even hinted at. Nor were these Rowney's only curious omissions: Daisie Stanley's name was not mentioned in court, nor was Michel's continued involvement after the tour was reorganised. For Rowney – at least for the purposes of her case – Wood

---

49 The same wage received by the players who spoke to *The Star*, making it possible that Rowney was one of the sources.

was solely responsible; but even here, she stopped short of the suggestion made in *The Star* that he had been taking gate money.

The final part of Lancaster's argument was that on 28 July the players 'wrote to Mr Wood for the money owing, but received no reply'. It was on 29 July that the team had refused to play at Kidderminster. Lancaster said that the women eventually returned to London on 29 August, which would tally with the last match of the tour being played in Dewsbury on 25 August, but Rowney had brushed over everything following the reorganisation on 26 June, including the second collapse, and Lancaster had dismissed crucial events with a few bland words. And Rowney's case implied that the players were unpaid between 28 July and 29 August, a period in which it is almost certain that wages were being provided by Hampson – or whoever organised the two-week northern tour.

Having presented Rowney's argument, Lancaster explained what she was claiming: 15 guineas (£15 15s) in unpaid salary, and £3 10s – two weeks of salary at 35s per week – 'in lieu of notice'. Against this, she accepted that she had already received £7 10s, and therefore requested payment of £11 15s from Wood.

At this point in proceedings, Rowney stepped into the witness box. She gave her own account, according to the *Evening Herald*, of 'how, after the first company collapsed, she was re-engaged, as she believed, by Mr Wood'. She then showed the court her contract, but there was a brief legal discussion over whether it could be admitted as it was not stamped; this too was curious as *The Star* had claimed none of the players had received copies. While discussion was ongoing, according to the report, Rowney engaged in repartee with a reporter who was attempting to draw her, claiming, 'That isn't the way to draw a hat,' and threatening to tell the judge to stop him if he did not draw her well enough.

Rowney was questioned by Wood's representative but according to the *Evening Standard*, 'stood up to his deliveries, and scored off him at a great rate'. Two other witnesses appeared to support Rowney's case. The first was Ella Heather; reports said little more about her except that she gave 'corroborative evidence' and when questioned said that 'Mr Wood expressly told her ... that he would engage her on the same terms as she had been engaged by Mr Bosanquet.' And Ferris, named as the 'acting manager', also appeared as a witness, stating that 'he looked to Mr Wood for his money'. But not all newspapers mentioned the witnesses in their reports.

Wood's defence was simple: he had no responsibility. Some newspapers were sparing in their presentation of Wood's case; although the *Evening Standard* waxed lyrical about Rowney's witnesses, it gave Wood just two sentences. *The Times* offered more detail: Wood contended that it was Michel – absent from much of the story given by Rowney – who was liable. Wood admitted that he had financed the team by advancing £150 to Michel to allow him to continue the tour 'until a colonial tour – South Africa and Australia – could be arranged'. He had not agreed to pay the salaries, had never agreed to be responsible for any aspect of the tour and 'repudiated all liability beyond having lent Mitchell [*sic*] £150, for which he received a bill. He was aware that his name appeared in the contracts with the ladies, but his name appeared without his authority.' Wood claimed to be considering legal action against Michel to recover his money. But according to the *Lancaster Gazette*, he 'admitted that he amended the agreements in his own handwriting. He was interesting himself in a suggested tour of the ladies to the colonies.'

With three witnesses against Wood, the jury found in favour of Rowney, who was awarded the full amount of £11 15s. However, this was not quite the end of the matter. On 15 March, Rowney and Wood returned to the Lord Mayor's Court in front of Assistant Judge Roxburgh. Rowney wanted the court to enforce payment of £11 which Wood still owed her. To justify his inability to pay, Wood said that he was 'an agent and undertook all sorts of business, but he was doing none just now'. According to his evidence, he had an office at George Yard in Lombard Street, which cost him a weekly rent of £7 6s, and a house at Kew for which his wife paid the annual rent of £100. He stated that he was having to give up the house as he could not afford the cost of travelling into the City, and had no way to pay Rowney. Somewhat pointlessly, he claimed that 'the case was really decided against him on perjured evidence'. The judge ordered that he should pay Rowney 8s per month.

As it happens, Wood's attempts to avoid paying Rowney allow us to identify him. The London *Post Office Directory* for 1890 lists 'Henry Wood & Co., financial agents' at 7 St Benet's Place (which was just round the corner from George Yard in Lombard Street), sharing the building with wine merchants, a timber merchant and a surgeon. There were two Henry Woods living near Kew on the 1891 census. The most likely candidate was a 53-year-old insurance broker from Shropshire who lived with his wife Mary, their three children and two servants in Hatherly House. Henry and

Mary had married in 1866, when he was a farmer; he was listed as a 'binders commission agent' (a job connected to insurance) on the 1881 census. By 1911, he had retired and was living 'on private means'. When he died in 1918, he left an estate of just under £500. It looks quite likely that he did not suffer too badly from his encounter in the courts with Rowney.[50]

* * *

The shifts in the narrative between the printing of the story in *The Star* and Rowney's account in court had a simple explanation. Rowney and her legal representative needed to prove a case against Wood. Other people involved, such as Michel, Stanley or Bosanquet, were irrelevant and would not have been discussed in court except where their actions related to Wood. Therefore Rowney's testimony featured neither fraud, financial irregularities nor strikes. Furthermore, had Rowney mentioned Michel or Stanley taking gate money, she would have provided Wood with an escape route: he could have argued that he *had* provided wages but they had been stolen by others. Although this makes the court case less useful to the historian, the absence of any claim of Fraud accusations against Wood might prove his innocence on those grounds. Rowney would likely have used any pertinent evidence against him had it existed.

---

50 The other Henry Wood in Kew was a shipbuilder, so cannot have been our Wood. The only other plausible candidate is Henry A. Wood, born around 1856 at St George's in London. The 1901 census lists him as a financial agent, married to Annie Wood, a 30-year-old from Leeds. The same man could also be found on the 1911 census, listed as a retired 'traveller'. But that Henry Wood was listed on the 1891 census as a 'licensed publican', living at 'The Crown' on Essex Street in St Clement Danes; our Wood was a financial agent at the time.

But there are several other questions which have no obvious answer. Why was there a delay before Rowney took Wood to court? And why, despite the threatening hints in *The Star*, did no other players take action against Wood, especially after the Lord Mayor's Court found against him? It seems extraordinary that Ella Heather was happy to appear as a witness against Wood but never tried to recover her own unpaid wages. The most likely, albeit unprovable, explanation is some kind of settlement, financial or otherwise, between all the concerned parties.

Why was Wood the target rather than Michel or Stanley? Despite his denials, it seems clear that he *was* involved in the 1891 tour, particularly if we can believe *The Star*, but there is no evidence that he played the leading role alleged by Rowney. For that matter, how did E. C. Ferris somehow avoid trouble even though it was his signature on the contracts? Ferris is a particularly interesting case as he also escaped mention by *The Star*, but had been openly named as the team's business manager during the season. Why was he absolved of blame so often? Was there some complex legal argument behind the scenes?

Another issue is that Wood, although he lost, had quite a good defence. His name might have appeared on the contracts (the newspaper reports are unclear), but he had not signed them. His claimed role as a distant purse-holder who provided money to Michel would have been similar to that played by Bosanquet in 1890. And Wood's argument that any blame belonged largely to Michel seems reasonable; the author of the article in *The Star* would certainly have agreed.

It is not a stretch to suggest that Wood lost simply because there were two witnesses against him, even if one was the impossibly slippery Ferris. Did a scheme exist to get money from Wood by falsely blaming him for the non-payment of wages? Or were the witnesses trying to protect whoever was genuinely responsible – whether that was Ferris himself, Michel, Stanley or even Bosanquet – by apportioning all fault to the unfortunate Wood? Perhaps Ferris, Rowney and Heather conspired to create a convincing-looking case against him which had little basis in reality. Maybe this was why no one else ever acted – not being part of the scheme, they had simply accepted the collapse. Wood's lament when taken back to court that the witnesses had perjured themselves might have been more than self-pity. In the end, however, we don't know, and none of this explains why Wood never took Michel to court.

In any case, someone in authority was clearly paying attention because just two weeks after the court case, on 15 February 1892, the Registrar of Joint Stock Companies wrote to Bosanquet concerning the status of the ECAA; Bosanquet replied the following day to assure him that the company had ceased business the previous June.

* * *

Looming over the whole tale, without ever seeming to be part of it, was the mysterious E. C. Ferris: business manager; the probable author of the corroborating letter to *The Star*; a key supporting witness for Rowney; the beneficiary of a false claim to be related to an internationally famous cricketer. And much, much more than that.

Edgar Charles Fearis (who possibly changed the spelling of his surname to match the Australian cricketer when he was associated with the OELC) was born on 29 April 1866 in London, the son of George Fearis, a linen draper. The progress of the family as recorded in census returns tells its own tale. In 1871 and 1881 they lived in the district of St George Hanover Square, an area filled with grocers and shopkeepers. On both occasions, George Ferris employed servants and had live-in apprentices and draper's assistants; in 1881 two of his children were employed by him and his second son was an architect's pupil. If not rich, the family seem vaguely prosperous. That changes in 1891, when they had moved to Battersea and George was listed as retired. One son was now a 'clerk to a house agent'; another was a ship's steward; and the architect's clerk had become a 'rate collector'. Edgar Fearis was working as a 'tea taster', a role which involved working with tea merchants, testing their product for quality. Neither servants, apprentices nor assistants lived with the family. There is a definite sense of a fall from grace. However, there is no indication that Edgar Fearis was associated with anything such as law, business, sport or theatre that might have brought him into the orbit of the OELC in 1891. How did he become involved? He had no obvious connection with Michel (unless it was through the brother who worked as a 'clerk to a house agent'), Bosanquet or Wood. But there might be an explanation.

At Chelsea Registry Office on 25 February 1892 – just over three weeks after the conclusion of Rowney's first court case – Fearis married Lizzie Sanders, the 17-year-old all-rounder who had occasionally captained the Blues during the 1891 season. Fearis gave his occupation as a 'tea taster'. Sanders gave her age as 18, an understandable lie in the circumstances, but more interesting is the fact that she already shared an address with Fearis: 9 Tetcott Road in Chelsea. The house was a large one, whose only listed resident on the 1891 census was a 16-year-old servant called

Ida Mayhew; no head of the household is named, meaning they were most likely away on census night. Fearis or Sanders could only realistically have lived at that address if they were employed there. Another curiosity is that Tetcott Road led on to the King's Road; number 476 King's Road, where the Sanders family lived in 1891, was only 400 yards from 9 Tetcott Road.

This marriage between Sanders and Fearis casts a different light on both his own motivations and the court case of Rowney. Sanders and Fearis presumably were living together when he was a witness and probably long before that. Did he become involved with the OELC through Sanders? Her mother and sister were both dressmakers, Fearis's father was a linen draper; perhaps the families knew each other before the OELC came into existence. Maybe Lizzie Sanders was Fearis's route into the OELC.

Although the venue of a registry office might hint at a desire for discretion, there was no legal issue with the wedding; marriage at the age of 17 was relatively common at the time, as were age gaps considerably larger than that between Fearis and Sanders. Nor could the wedding have taken place without the permission of Sanders's mother (Sanders was underage); one of the witnesses on the marriage certificate was Frances Sanders – either Lizzie's mother or her sister.[51] But even in 1892, it would have been frowned upon for the manager of a team to be involved romantically with one of his employees.

* * *

The murky nature of Fearis's involvement with the OELC

---

51 The other witness was a man called Ernest Millard, about whom nothing more is known.

and the court case contradicts the press interpretation that the cricketers had received justice. Rowney's day in court might have been the attempt of a small group within the OELC to extort money from a relatively innocent man. It could have involved others such as Lizzie Sanders, whose marriage to Fearis indicates a messy, complicated set of relationships in which motivations suddenly become questionable. There is even a whiff of exploitation. Had the whole affair become as disreputable as the press had feared it would be from the start?

The Last Gasp

DESPITE THE disasters of 1891, someone still believed money could be made from a professional women's cricket team. In early April 1892, newspapers reported that the former members of the OELC had 'reorganised' or 'reconstituted' themselves under new management and would be touring again, under the new name of 'The All-England Lady Cricketers' (AELC) – which coincidentally or otherwise had been the name chosen by Daisy Stanley for her own team in early 1891. One article suggested that 'Original English Lady Cricketers' was copyrighted, forcing the adoption of a different title. According to the story, 13 members of the new organisation would tour Australia in September, playing around 30 matches.

The AELC were something of a mystery. There was no indication of who the new managers were: it could have been the women themselves; it could have been Fearis (Lizzie Sanders was part of the team, making his involvement likely); or even Stanley. But it seems that neither Michel nor Bosanquet were involved; nor were many of the OELC. Of the founding members, only Lena Parsons, Lizzie Sanders, Alice Grey, Ella Heather and Ada Heather were involved. Other OELC players included Mabel Emmett, Caroline McDonnell and M. Stephens, but there could have been others: we only have two complete scorecards from the 12 known games played by the AELC.[52] The participation of everyone who had been involved in the case against Wood might be further evidence of some kind of conspiracy between them.

But there were some unfamiliar names in the team: M. Argent could have been Elizabeth Argent, listed on the 1891 census as a 'lady cricketer'; other new faces included E. Miller, B. Miller, A. Carr and G. Fortescue. None of these overlap with Arthur's Ideal Lady Cricketers, so there is no indication of how they became involved. Perhaps they were the remnants of another team – maybe even that run by Stanley – which merged with what was left of the OELC.

Nevertheless, the new team followed the old format, fielding two sides known as Reds and Blues for exhibition games. Unlike previous seasons, these attracted little attention from the press – which perhaps had grown tired of it all by now – and so we have little information. The opening game took place at Putney during the Oxford and Cambridge Boat Race; one report said that the crowds which were there for the race were drawn to the cricket, and the AELC took home plenty of gate money. But another said that, as the match had received little advertising or publicity, 'there was a very sparse attendance'.

Nor did the players show too much enthusiasm. At Guildford in late May, several of the AELC were missing owing to illness, making the usual exhibition match impossible. To give the large crowd something to watch, a team from a nearby boys' school was recruited at the last minute to play those women who *had* turned up. The

---

52 These were the only ones reported in newspapers. Again, there might have been more that were not advertised widely.

school side was less forgiving than other male opposition had been, and scored 163/3 declared before dismissing the women for 40. This was not the only occasion that the AELC proved unreliable. When they were scheduled to play against Kingston Cricket Club the following day, heavy rain delayed proceedings and only fifteen women had appeared before the weather forced an abandonment. In fact, it is not clear how many of the scheduled games took place: a fixture at Chesham on 2 June was abandoned when the AELC never showed (a local report said it was because of the 'wet and stormy' weather).

The only two games which attracted attention – and which proved to be the last serious appearances of the team – took place at the Windsor and Eton Rowing Club on 6 and 7 June. On the first day, the AELC played their signature 'Reds v Blues' game before a reported crowd of 1,500. On the second, 16 of the AELC (although only 15 were listed; Ella Heather was missing from the scorecard but this was probably an oversight by the newspaper concerned) faced a men's side representing the Windsor and Eton Rowing Club. Before a 'fairly good number of spectators', and with the accompaniment of the Windsor Volunteer and Town Band, the men took the game seriously, hitting hard to score 169/8. The women replied with 82. According to the report – which perhaps should be taken with a pinch of salt, but by this stage anything was possible – 'After the match was completed, several of the gentlemen "wet-bobs" [i.e. rowers] gave their opponents lessons in the art of rowing, the hours of tuition extending, in many cases, well into the hours of the pale moonlight.' This might have been idle gossip or someone looking for scandal (the author began his account with the words 'I learn that'), on a par with some of the earlier rumours. Or maybe the women simply did not care anymore.

Two days later, on 9 June, the AELC were scheduled to appear at Abingdon. There had been some doubt that the game would take place, and it was only confirmed when a telegram arrived from Windsor (where the women had presumably stayed after the previous game) to say that the players would arrive around 2pm (two hours late). Nevertheless, only eight of them had appeared by 2:30. Neither of the Heather sisters were there, and the unconvincing explanation was that the absent women 'had missed their way or taken the wrong train'. To make a match possible, a men's team was put together from the Abingdon Town and Early Closing clubs. There was a large attendance as the home side scored 146, and the women replied with 103, their numbers being made up with three local men; some of the women also batted twice. But it was not a contest, which is perhaps not surprising as all the best players were absent; the men switched to left-handed batting after lunch and when the women were 36/6, switched to left-handed or lob bowling. This was the last time that the OELC/AELC took the field.

A scheduled match at Caversham on 10 June never took place. A crowd was waiting but the women did not come. A local newspaper speculated that this was because of the hosting ground's demand for a payment of £3 3s, and expressed irritation that the club had cancelled a game against Christchurch to accommodate the AELC, in pursuit of 'filthy lucre'. The *Berkshire Chronicle*, on the other hand, suggested that the non-appearance related to a legal dispute over the team's name. But in reality, the last remnants of the OELC had finally collapsed.

Right there until the bitter end in Abingdon were some of the stalwarts of 1891: Mabel Emmett, the McDonnell sisters and May Day. And perhaps the most committed of all were the two survivors of the original team, Lena Parsons and Lizzie Sanders. Had this rump of players been the ones behind the ill-advised 1892 games? Maybe. Unfortunately, as with so much of the tale of the OELC, only a few wispy trails survive. For the last act of the team, which had been through so much since the beginning of 1890, to be this travesty of a match at Abingdon is somewhat unfortunate. Perhaps Windsor would have been a more satisfactory ending to the narrative, a last defiant gesture at convention as the women laughed under the moon with the rowers in their thrall. But reality is rarely so picturesque.

The Ghost of a Forgotten Idea

IN MAY 1893, the 'English Cricket and Athletic Association Limited' was struck off the Register of Joint Stock Companies, meaning that the company was officially dissolved. The Registrar had been in correspondence with Walter Bosanquet for some time, but the solicitor clearly wanted no more to do with the ECAA.

Despite the final collapse of the OELC and the disappearance of the Ideal Lady Cricketers, women cricketers remained in the public consciousness a little longer. An attempt to bring about women's suffrage in 1892 was opposed by the British Prime Minister William Gladstone; a *Punch* cartoon by Edward Linley Sambourne in May 1892 depicted two lady cricketers (with a badge saying 'WLF', probably an erroneous rendering of the Women's Franchise League) turning away from the figure of Gladstone (holding a bat labelled 'suffrage') in a cricket net, with the caption: 'A team of our own? I should think so! If we're good enough to scout for you, why shouldn't we take a turn at the bat?' Even though the women were not dressed like the OELC, the association between the women's suffrage movement and women cricketers might have been made – fearfully or hopefully – many times over the course of the previous two years. But such thoughts gradually faded and the *Daily Graphic* noted later in 1892 that 'the professional lady cricketer is less in evidence this year than she was a season or two ago'.

The professional women's game was quickly forgotten. Amateur women's cricket continued to be mentioned occasionally in the press, but journalists soon stopped paying attention. The OELC were rarely discussed except in the context of their failure. The *Globe* mentioned in September 1892 that the lady cricketers had 'passed'. In his *Kings of Cricket* (1893), the old Nottinghamshire player Richard Daft suggested that attempts to make cricket a game for women until then had 'proved a failure'. The *Glasgow Evening Post*, discussing what looks to have been a bicycle race for 'actresses' in France during 1893, said that such an idea would not catch on in Britain: 'After the miserable failure of the lady cricketers, we are hardly likely to be inflicted by a team of lady cyclists.' By 1894, the London *Evening News* was able to state (questionably) that 'the lady cricketer is now but seldom seen in the London district'.

But the ghost of an idea remained. There was one hint at a planned revival. An article in the *Tenbury Wells Advertiser* in May 1893 said: 'The Lady Cricketers are practising at Willesden, prior to going into the field in earnest. They defend their wicket with great skill and grace, and their bowling is equally creditable. No doubt they will be able to play any cricket club, not county or professional, and some hope to see them figuring at exclusive Lord's before the season wanes.' There is no indication of who this team might have been – although the description of 'The Lady Cricketers' indicates familiarity, perhaps implying OELC players – and no 'lady cricketers' appeared in 1893.

The concept of the OELC retained a certain cachet (or perhaps notoriety) for some time. In late 1893, a 36-year-old woman from Tooting called Eliza Haynes was arrested for 'defrauding tradesmen by "ringing the changes"' – a practice in which she made money from shopkeepers by claiming to have been short-changed after buying small items. Several newspapers reported her to have been one of the 'Lady Cricketers' with the clear suggestion that she was a former member of the OELC. But she was probably too old to have been picked for the team and she certainly never appeared under that name.[53] It was most likely a cry for attention, but the fact that it was picked up by newspapers demonstrated a continued interest in OELC stories.

More disturbingly, at least one person tried to use the idea of a professional women's touring team for his own gain. In 1894, a con man known as Redfern Alphonse placed an advertisement for a lady secretary to work with a team of Australian women cricketers. He claimed to be called Hawke Bryan, and a relative of Lord Hawke (who was supposedly financing the tour). A woman called Miss Huggins applied and was engaged at six guineas a month plus expenses. She ordered a dress at Alphonse's request and gave him £2 as a deposit for it; after borrowing her watch, he disappeared. He was eventually caught and sentenced to ten months' hard labour. It transpired that his real name was Ballin – he had at one time worked in Hong Kong, holding a 'government appointment' – and that he had served six months in prison the previous year after being found guilty of obtaining money fraudulently from several women, and 'committing acts of indecency' while measuring them for a costume he claimed they needed to wear.

---

53 Her solicitor suggested that she was 'not in her right mind' and so not responsible for her actions but she was sentenced to six weeks in prison without hard labour.

Other echoes of the OELC remained, such as a horse named Lady Cricketer, trained by Tom Cannon at Stockbridge, which raced in 1897 and 1898. Even W. G. Grace was drawn into the discussion. He had a conventional view of the place of women in cricket, as he told the *Pall Mall Gazette* in 1895: 'As to the innovation of ladies' cricket, I consider it only a game for school-girls, and that it ought to be abandoned when they grow up.' His daughter Bessie seems to have been a reasonable cricketer, and was adored by her father. He taught her the game from the age of five and when she joined him on a tour of Australia in 1891–92, she played deck cricket on the outward sea journey and appeared in at least one traditional 'men v ladies' match in Australia. At home, she played for the cricket team of Clifton High School for Girls and was the subject of several starry-eyed write-ups in the press. But even for her, Grace made no exception; after leaving school, Bessie's involvement in cricket was restricted to watching her father, and keeping her own scores at the ground.

Bessie died suddenly of typhoid fever in early February 1899 at the age of 20, leaving Grace grief-stricken. But financial considerations and print deadlines meant that he had to continue to work on an autobiography with a ghost-writer called Arthur Porritt. Grace by then had little interest in the project, particularly as it interrupted his mourning, but later that year, *'W. G.': Cricketing Reminiscences and Personal Recollections* was published. Within a section about the 1891 season, amid some mechanical prose about events of the year, Grace discussed 'the appearance this season of two Elevens of "Lady Cricketers"'. Perhaps he was thinking of Bessie as he dictated the passage to Porritt, but he was clearly familiar with the advertising, because he said: 'They claimed that they did play, and not burlesque, the game, but interest in their doings did not survive long. Cricket is not a game for women, and although the fair sex occasionally join in a picnic game, they are not constitutionally adapted for the sport. If the lady cricketers expected to popularise the game among women they failed dismally. At all events, they had their day and ceased to be.' A later tale, that Grace also said the OELC 'were neither cricketers nor ladies', was untrue.

Perhaps the loudest echo of the OELC came in a different sport in the mid-1890s. The British Ladies' Football Club played a series of exhibition matches around Britain between March 1895 and April 1897. Managed by a woman who called herself Nettie Honeyball (her real identity has never been firmly established) and under the patronage of Lady Florence Dixie (who in 1890 had defended the OELC from attack in the *St James's Gazette*), the women footballers – rather like their cricketing counterparts – were briefly successful. Similarly to the OELC players, they were recruited through newspaper advertisements and trained by a professional, in this case the Tottenham Hotspurs centre-half J. W. Julian. However, the football team was largely run by women, unlike the OELC, and had a more overt political motivation in promoting women's rights.

The players were split into two teams, North and South, for the games. They wore different colours – red and blue – in another link back, whether intentional or not, to the OELC. And not unlike the OELC, the team fractured in its second season; at one point, splinters included the 'Original Lady Footballers' and the 'Original British Ladies'. Some of the players, like their OELC counterparts, were very young; one was supposedly 11 years old. The echoes of the

OELC were pointed out by the *Pall Mall Gazette* during February 1895 but in the interviews she gave, Honeyball never mentioned her cricketing predecessors. The Lady Footballers have attracted more attention from historians than their cricketing counterparts, but few have noted the similarity to the OELC.

* * *

The only mentions of the OELC in the first half of the 20th century came in reprinted articles such as 'fifty years ago' pieces. But in this period, women's cricket attained a respectability that it had lacked in the 1890s. In 1926, the Women's Cricket association was formed by a group of female enthusiasts who had enjoyed playing together. By 1930, the Association was publishing *Women's Cricket* every month during the cricket season; rather more successful than the *English Lady Cricketers' Gazette*, it remained in publication until 1967. In 1934–35, the first women's Test matches were played and by the 1950s, women's cricket was more popular than it had ever been. But it had become a purely amateur affair; there was not even a hint of professionalism.

Between 1948 and 1958, the secretary of the Women's Cricket Association was Netta Rheinberg. She had previously held the position in 1945 and had managed the England women's tour of Australia and New Zealand in 1948–49, during which she played one Test match. In many ways, she was the equivalent of the archetypal amateur from the men's game, working as the secretary to her family's business when not playing cricket.

For the *Women's Cricket Autumn Annual* in 1956, Rheinberg wrote a piece called 'An Original English Lady

Cricketer'. She began by describing one of the early OELC advertisements from 1890 and named E. Michel as the man behind the idea. But she had a somewhat unique interpretation of how the OELC came about. For her, the main driving force of women's cricket at that time was the all-amateur White Heather Club which, 'despite much derision', established that women could play the game. With this heavy lifting done, Rheinberg claimed that the obvious next step was to 'commercialise' women's cricket.

The rest of the article was an interview with the 88-year-old Marie Beckenham, referred to by Rheinberg as 'Miss Beckenham', one of several OELC players still alive in the 1950s. This has the distinction of being the only known interview with a member of the OELC except those done for publicity purposes in 1890.

The visit had been organised by Beckenham's friend Mervyn Green, in whose house she was then living and who had told Rheinberg that although Beckenham's eyesight was fading, she was still sharp. Rheinberg was welcomed by the 'upright, wiry' old woman, who was wearing a cardigan and skirt. They spoke for an hour. Rheinberg came away convinced that the OELC were not the 'stunt' she had believed it to be. Beckenham also made abundantly clear that she did not want Rheinberg to call her Mary Willett. She had not used that name since her OELC days, when Matthews had insisted she use a pseudonym; since then she had been known to everyone as Miss Beckenham or 'Beckie'.

Beckenham told Rheinberg her story: how she and a friend replied to an advertisement; how she was accepted but her friend not; how they had practised both indoors at Wandsworth and outdoors at Balham, coached by George and Alec Hearne, Maurice Read and Fred Bowley. She could not remember what she had been paid, other than a shilling a day for expenses, but recalled that her father had no objection to her taking part, even attending the match at Crystal Palace.

Rheinberg supplemented Beckenham's tale with reports from the opening Liverpool match of 1890, and mentioned photographs, two of which accompanied the article, showing the Reds and Blues as they were during the 1891 season. These must have belonged to Beckenham. She had also managed to keep hold of her costume, which she had stored in a trunk; she gave it to Rheinberg (who in turn donated it to Lord's, where it is still to be found). The label revealed that they had been manufactured by Stagg and Mantle of Leicester Square. Beckenham also handed over her old bat, an Ayres International, which all the players had been given.

Beckenham thought (incorrectly) that the OELC were the first team to play at Headingley, because she remembered turf being laid. She was slightly outraged at suggestions that the women had bowled underarm; she said that she herself bowled leg-breaks (no records of her bowling in a game have survived) and fielded in the deep. And according to her recollections, the Australian tour at the end of the 1890 season was abandoned after protests from parents.

Rheinberg left the interview having been persuaded by Beckenham that the OELC had reached a high standard, and that the players were 'women of character' – 'tough, forthright, enterprising'. She noted that the teams stopped playing after two years but offered no explanation. The article concluded with a comment from Beckenham disparaging the use of cosmetics: 'My face has never been touched by them!'

* * *

Little else appeared subsequently in *Women's Cricket* about the OELC. And when an article called 'Stepping Stones' listed some key dates in women's cricket between 1745 and 1960 in a later annual, there was no mention of the OELC. In 1958, Miss Beckenham's death was reported in a brief obituary. But *Women's Cricket* did her something of an injustice because she was far more than just a cricketer from a mayfly team. Rheinberg had described fragments of Beckenham's subsequent life but these occupied just a few lines in a two-page article and deserved much more attention as Beckenham was the only member of the OELC to become relatively well-known away from the cricket field.

The 1891 census listed Beckenham (under her real name of Mary Willett) as a clerk but that was probably the only conventional thing she ever did. After the collapse of the OELC, she spent her life working in the theatre. She travelled the country, managing many small companies which mainly specialised in musical comedy; her name was constantly listed in theatrical newspapers associated with some production or other. She was soon managing the theatrical company of Benjamin Greet and James Bannister Howard;[54] her association with both men lasted many years. For a time, she worked with the lyricist George Dance and toured as his manager. She also managed a company which included Leslie Henson, who later became famous as a comedy actor; the pair continued to collaborate for 35 years. He always called her his 'first manager'. At the

---

54 Greet, later Sir Benjamin Greet, was an actor and manager who became well-known for his efforts to bring Shakespeare to as wide an audience as possible; Bannister Howard was a producer.

height of his fame after the Second World War, Henson invited her as his guest to one of his shows at the Garrick and introduced her to the audience, which gave her a warm reception.

During the First World War, Beckenham managed the New Theatre in Salisbury. She returned briefly to the limelight in 1928 when she was interviewed in the *Derby Daily Telegraph*. At the time, she was the assistant business manager at the production of 'Queen High' at Derby's Grand Theatre. She told her interviewer that she had never wanted to go on stage but was fascinated by the 'business side'; she had refused offers from several publishers for her memoirs, although she had 'some very interesting stories'. The article briefly mentioned her former association with the OELC, and noted that she had 'striven to overcome conventional prejudice, and it has been a hard fight'.

Throughout this time, she stuck with her old cricketing name: in the interview, in her copious advertising and even on the census. Marie Beckenham never married and died in 1958 at the age of 89. She was so highly regarded in the theatrical world that her obituary appeared in *The Stage*; it said: 'She managed companies at a time when few, if any, other women held that job … She was a very colourful person and popular with all who knew her.'

* * *

Eighteen years after Beckenham's death, Netta Rheinberg revisited the OELC in *Fair Play*, a book co-authored with Rachael Heyhoe Flint. As well as giving a summary of the 1956 interview with Beckenham, Rheinberg added W. G. Grace's view of the OELC's failure. However, she gave a new twist to the story: 'The teams were suddenly disbanded after two years and it is said that the managers absconded with the profits.'

Rheinberg unfortunately did not reveal from where her information came. Her source clearly took the line argued by *The Star* in 1891 but was not quoting directly from it. Nor is there any indication that Rheinberg had read that story herself or knew about the court case. And if Beckenham had told her what happened in 1956, Rheinberg would almost certainly have included it in the *Women's Cricket* article. So where did the idea of the managers absconding come from?

Rheinberg had by then spoken to others because she mentioned 'the daughter of one of the captains', whom she identified as Miss Westbrook. This daughter 'confirmed that the cricket played was of fair standard, decorous and dignified'. There are a few problems with this: Violet Westbrook's only daughter had died in 1968 (although she could feasibly have spoken to Rheinberg after 1956), had not been born when the OELC played (making her judgements of playing standards questionable), and somehow got her own mother's name wrong (Rheinberg identified Westbrook as 'Flora Blanche Lyon'). Even so, maybe she was the source of the idea that the managers took the profits. But wherever Rheinberg's information came from, someone clearly recalled with some bitterness the events of 1891.

There was one other new piece of information in *Fair Play*, hinting at what was lost. Rheinberg had been unable to find any other information about the OELC – she did not have access to online newspaper archives like modern researchers – but said that 'some years ago' a woman in the Midlands had bought a wooden box at a second-hand sale, to use as a toy chest for her children. On the outside were the letters 'OELC' and it had contained old papers and clothing. Not realising their value, the woman had destroyed them.

* * *

For many years, Rheinberg (and Beckenham) had the last words on the subject. It was not until the 21st century that historians revisited the OELC. When Isabelle Duncan wrote *Skirting the Boundary* (2013), a history of women's cricket, she told the story of the OELC, following Rheinberg's interpretation. Then, as part of a 2015 PhD thesis on the history of women's cricket in England, Judy Threlfall-Sykes investigated the OELC, using newspaper reports which had become available through the British Newspaper Archive. The OELC formed just one part of her work, so she did not delve too deeply, but she was the first person in over a century to uncover some of the events and personalities of 1890. When Rafaelle Nicholson discussed the OELC in her 2019 study *Ladies and Lords*, she largely followed Threlfall-Sykes. Neither writer departed from the view, as stated by Duncan, that 'the whole enterprise collapsed when their managers (all men) did a runner with the profits'.

Little survives today from the OELC. The National Archives hold the Memorandum of Association and a few photographs, while Beckenham's bat and costume belong to the MCC museum at Lord's. Other than Beckenham, none of the players – some of whom lived well into the 1960s – seem to have spoken of their experiences. Perhaps some, like Beckenham, had kept their bat or costume in fond remembrance of those two seasons of cricket. Or maybe they forgot all about it. Some did not live long enough to reminisce.

So what happened to the Original English Lady Cricketers?

Whatever Happened to the Original English Lady Cricketers?

APART FROM Marie Beckenham, most of the Original English Lady Cricketers seem to have led conventional lives and vanished from the public eye. We can trace many and sometimes build a remarkably full biography. And yet there are other women who cannot be identified in records; either they used unbreakable pseudonyms or had common names. Sometimes – even for those players listed in the *Gazette* – we have insufficient information to identify them confidently. To add to the problems, several women who *can* be found inexplicably vanish from census returns; perhaps they married untraceably, moved overseas or just changed their name. Therefore we cannot give anything like a full picture of the lives of every player. And yet, there is plenty of interest in what we can find.

The shortest association with the OELC was that of Annie Hampson, born in Montacute, Somerset, who played in the first game before disappearing forever. On the 1891 census, she was listed as a draper's assistant, living in St Pancras with her parents, but a few months later she married Joseph Oliver, a clerk with whom she had two children. After his death around 1908, she remarried and as Annie Wisdom worked as the forewoman of a laundry in Maidstone, although she seems to have quickly separated from her second husband. She died at Maidstone in 1926, aged 53. Another early departure – almost certainly because she was pregnant – was Beatrice Light (Annie Emma Nicholas). She and her husband, a coal porter, had 13 children, ten of whom were still alive at the time of the 1911 census, and they lived in Southampton (her birthplace) most of their lives. Their third child, Christopher, was a fireman who died aboard the *Titanic* when it sank in 1912. Annie Light died later that year, aged 43.

Marie Lisle – assuming she was the married actress identifiable by that name – also left owing to her pregnancy. She and her husband worked as actors in Scotland until at least 1901 but were back in England by 1911, when the census listed them working for a portable theatre company in Shropshire. None of the family can be traced after this date, although a widowed woman called Mary Lisle, born at the right time, was admitted to Camden Workhouse in 1924. It is possible that Lisle was a professional pseudonym associated with her acting career and which pre-dated the OELC.[55]

The Woodward sisters returned to their previous careers, far removed from the world of sport, after their early departures from the OELC. Edith Woodward worked all her life as a dance teacher and established her own academy in the late 1890s, living with her parents and later with an aunt. During the First World War, she organised several charity concerts. By the time of the 1921 census, she was also running a boarding house, and was successful enough to employ servants and assistants. The

---

55 In which case, it may also have been used by her sister Annie, who played for the OELC in 1890 but cannot be traced at all.

1939 Register, taken at the start of the Second World War, listed her as a 'Dancing Mistress', living in Cheltenham alongside several women in the dancing profession. She died in 1947 at the age of 76 and her obituary appeared in the *Gloucestershire Echo*.

Florence Woodward married Alfred Rolph, a professor of music, in 1892. By the time of the 1901 census, they had moved to London and both were listed as actors. They had two children together and later moved to Bath. Alfred died in 1917 and Florence, like her sister, became a teacher of dancing. She died at Hastings in 1937, aged 74.

Louise Daly left the OELC in August 1890 but might have played for a rival team as she was still listed on the 1891 census as a 'Lady Cricketer'. In 1893, at the age of 25, she was baptised – with no obvious explanation – in the Parish of St Clement, Notting Hill. Two years later she married James Arthur Rawlinson, a solicitor's clerk. The couple never had children and lived for a time in Southampton. Her father Patrick, the former policeman, had spells in workhouses in 1904 and 1905. After her husband died in 1923, Daly married Thomas Edward Giles in 1937. She died at Wandsworth in 1951.[56]

* * *

There are mysteries surrounding many of the women who left at the end of the 1890 season. Particularly baffling is the story of Georgina Sheffield (Emma Georgina Sheffield). Unlike many of her team-mates, the evidence does not progress smoothly to tell a cohesive story; it jumps

---

56 A woman called Louisa Giles died at Wandsworth in 1951; a Mary L. Giles died in 1963, but Daly was known by her family as Lou and lived in Wandsworth so the former seems more likely.

bafflingly from place to place. We know her husband for a time was a gas fitter called Thomas Carash but there is no actual record of the marriage; their first child Cedric was born in 1892 so it was presumably before then. A second child, Grace, was born in 1894. But neither Sheffield nor her husband appear on the 1901 census; their son was living with his maternal grandfather. By 1906, Carash was dead and Sheffield married William Henry Garner, a widower 26 years her senior; on the marriage certificate, they share the same address in London. Garner was absent on the night of the 1911 census and is untraceable; Sheffield listed herself as an actress. Our next glimpse comes in 1921; Garner presumably was dead because Sheffield was recorded as the wife of a blind-fixer called Henry Caplin. However, she and Caplin were not actually married until 1924.

Sheffield's life offers more questions than answers but there is one family tale that fleetingly brings her to life. Caplin's daughter Ellen shared the house with her father and Sheffield, living upstairs with her own husband. In later years Ellen's son told stories of how Sheffield used to complain about him and his siblings running on the stairs; he did not think that she got along with her stepdaughter. Caplin, Sheffield's third and final husband, died in 1934. By 1939, Sheffield was living with her grandchildren in Camberwell. She died in 1941, aged 73, leaving £320 in her will.

Bianca Seymour, who made more of an impression with the piano and banjo than she did on the cricket field, cannot be traced with any certainty, and it is likely she used a pseudonym. But there are some possibilities. A woman called Bianca Olimpia Cacciola was born in Paris on 4 March 1869 – the exact date given for Seymour's birth in the *English Lady Cricketers' Gazette* (although that publication gave her place of birth as Surrey). Cacciola's father was an Italian author, according to his marriage certificate from 1868. In May 1888 the 19-year-old Cacciola and her 12-year-old sister Clarinda, both of whom lived on Kender Street in London, were baptised at All Saints Church in Lewisham; their father was dead by then. On the 1891 census, she is listed as 'living on her own means' in a boarding house in Hove. Someone called Miss Cacciola, born at about the right time, is listed as a passenger sailing to Cape Town in 1898; Bianca's sister Clarinda visited Durban in 1906, hinting further at a South African connection. Two other sisters, Sylvia and Stella, are listed on the 1901 census as actresses, living in Hastings.

Even these theatrical connections do not make it certain that Cacciola was Bianca Seymour. For example, a woman called Bianca Hicks is listed on the 1891 census as a singer and was also part of a theatrical family: her father (who was dead by 1891) and two brothers were scenic painters, two other brothers were theatrical property masters and her sister was a singer. Bianca Hicks died in 1896 at the age of 27; her occupation makes her another strong possibility for our Bianca Seymour. Or the cricketer could have been Blanche Seymour, listed as a ballet dancer on the 1891 census; but there is no further trace of her.

Although there is no doubt about the identity of Katie Tatton, the 16-year-old whose previous employer had been murdered, her fate is uncertain. Tatton only ever performed as a cyclist, taking the role of scorer during matches. She did not return in 1891; instead the census lists her as a servant in the house of George Smith; he was the new husband of the former Mrs Gorin, otherwise known as

Madame Letine. Mrs Smith/Gorin/Letine was still a 'professional bicyclist' (less glamorously, her new husband was an insurance underwriter). Tatton and a 14-year-old girl called Lizzie Pocock, although classed as servants, had the occupation 'employed for bicycle performance'. The most likely explanation is that after leaving the OELC, Tatton returned to work with Madame Letine as a trick cyclist. But after this, she vanishes from the records. Possibly Catherine Tatham, an inmate in Bethnal Green Workhouse in 1901 who was listed as a 'domestic servant', could have been her. There is no other obvious trace of her, and her family are similarly elusive. They flit in and out of records without leaving a clear picture: for example, her younger sister Dora was a 'professional actress' in 1901 (two years after the death of their father) but she too is subsequently untraceable.

The last two women to leave in 1890 are thankfully easier to trace. But there are curiosities about what happened to Bessie Moss, the fencer and wicket-keeper. The 1891 census reveals that she lived in Tottenham with her father (a bookbinder; more specifically, a gold blocker), mother, and two siblings. In 1896, by which time her father was dead, she married Henry Young Benham, a hospital attendant; their marriage certificate listed them living at the same address in Southwark. Seven months after their marriage, they had their only daughter. After this we encounter another mystery: the 1901 census lists Benham as a sick nurse at St Saviour's Workhouse in Southwark, but there is no trace of Moss;[57] her four-year-old daughter inexplicably lived in Rickmansworth as a boarder with Frederick Brooks (an 'imbecile asylum attendant') and his wife; another 'boarder',

---

57 The closest we can come is an Elizabeth Moss working as a barmaid in Streatham, but that seems unlikely.

the nine-month-old Gladys Estwick, also lived there. By 1904, Benham was dead and Moss had married Lionel Montague Mortimer, a private in the Royal Marines Light Infantry, with whom she was already living at the time of their marriage. In later years, Mortimer worked as a porter and as a school caretaker, and the couple eventually moved to Welwyn Garden City, where they lived with their large extended families at the time of the 1939 Register. Bessie Moss died in 1962 at the age of 89.

Finally Florence Hardwick (Emma Florence Hardwick), a dairyman's daughter, still lived with her father in Battersea at the time of the 1891 census, working as his assistant. Her mother had died in 1890, which might explain why she gave up cricket. In 1893, she married Alfred Baker, also a dairyman, with whom she had four daughters. She died in 1929 at the age of 61.

* * *

The next departures of the regular players we can identify came in the early part of the tumultuous 1891 season. Susie Fletcher – whose real name was Susan Fletcher Shemmonds – had vanished once partway through the 1890 season, returned at the end, and played briefly in 1891. She called herself a lady cricketer on the 1891 census, at which time she was living in Islington with her mother and widowed sister. In September 1892, she married William Hambly, who called himself a journalist and author; they went on to have four children. Fletcher's husband died in 1914 and her son Arthur was killed in Flanders during the First World War. By the time of the 1939 Register, she lived with her three adult daughters in Hornsey, Middlesex. She died in 1955 at the age of 90.

Elizabeth Dempsey left around the same time as Fletcher, but her subsequent life was complicated and brief. At the time of the 1891 census (when she was another to call herself a lady cricketer), she lived in a Battersea boarding house, alongside Adele Matthey. Around six weeks after her final game, still living in the boarding house, Dempsey married Arthur John Veitch, the son of the horticulturist Arthur Veitch who had left an estate worth around £30,000 when he died in 1880. Arthur John had followed in his father's footsteps, working as a 'nurseryman' at the time of his marriage.

How had the son of a rich – almost famous – family come to marry a professional cricketer who had spent much of 1890 performing in fields and theatres? Despite Dempsey's army background, the couple were some distance apart on the Victorian social ladder. The most obvious explanation would have been an unexpected pregnancy but there is no record of Dempsey ever having children. But the marriage did not last; by 1897 Veitch was living in Canada where he bigamously married a woman from Maidstone called Laura Jeffreys, the illegitimate daughter of a chemist. They later moved to the United States. One curiosity is that American records show that Veitch and Jeffreys had a son called Guy Veitch, born in Maidstone in 1895 (before their marriage), but he was registered under the name Guy Maitland. Was he the reason that Dempsey and Veitch separated? Or was something else entirely going on?

Dempsey remained in England and the 1901 census records her boarding with the family of a caretaker; no occupation was given. Ten days after the census was taken, Dempsey died at University College Hospital from pneumonia. She was 30 years old. The death was registered by her brother-in-law Harry Veitch.

* * *

Among the many comings and goings during the chaotic 1891 season was Alice Grey, one of the more successful OELC batters, who cannot be identified, despite playing for a season-and-a-half and featuring in the *Gazette*: the name was too common for us to find the cricketer definitively in any records. Similarly, many of her team-mates, such as the Chessington sisters or L. Douglas, departed without leaving any clues about who they were. However, there are several players about whom more is known.

Adele Matthey, Dempsey's fellow boarder, played throughout the 1891 season but did not return for the final benefit games. In 1895, she married Carl Wilhelm Hammer, a waiter (and later a clerk) born in Germany – perhaps there was some connection with her father, who was a restaurant manager. They had two children, and the widowed Matthey lived with her son by the time of the 1939 Register. She died in 1947 at the age of 76.

Lydia Hann, one of the new recruits, departed at the end of the second season. On the 1891 census, where Hann is listed as a lady cricketer, she was living at the family shop in Islington, managed at the time by her brother. After that, she disappears from the census; a possible explanation might be that a Lydia Hann (no other details recorded) was admitted to Peckham Lunatic Asylum in 1898 and remained there until her death in 1922. But we don't know for sure.

Among others not to return in 1892 were Marie Beckenham and Nellie Wadkin. Ellen Frances Wadkin was born in Rotherhithe,[58] and is listed on the 1891 census as a professional cricketer who lived with her mother and stepfather in their family-run public house. In 1893, she married William Mummery, a commercial traveller with whom she had a daughter. Mummery died in 1897; Wadkin lived alone with her daughter at the time of the 1901 census but married Henry Jeves later in 1901 and had two more children. Her second husband died in 1919. In later years she moved to Beckenham, where she died at the age of 79 in 1951, leaving £180 in her will.

Sophie Blanche Charles also left after the 1891 benefit games. She was another who called herself a 'professional lady cricketer' on the census, but there was a curiosity about that record. At the time, she was lodging in Chelsea with a cab driver and his family. But her sister – Cecilia Maude Caroline Charles – still lived with her parents; and, oddly, on the census she too is listed as a 'lady cricketer'.[59] This might be an error because no other cricketers named Charles played for the OELC. But it is hard to see how Charles's father could make such a mistake when he filled in the census return. Was Cecilia playing for the OELC – or another team – under a pseudonym? Another oddity about the family is that Sophie Charles had a key role in the evening performances as a fencer; how did the daughter of a fishmonger learn such a skill? Had she been another who attended Regent Street Polytechnic?

---

58 The second version of the player profiles in the *Gazette* gave Wadkin's birthplace as Bradford, but this seems to be an invention (although the date of birth is accurate). There is little doubt about her identity because Ellen Frances Wadkin was listed as a 'lady cricketer' on the 1891 census; her birthplace was then recorded as Deptford but she was actually born in Rotherhithe.

59 The occupation had been written next to her mother's name before being crossed out.

In 1896 Charles married Frederick Moult, a photographic printer and dealer in photographic equipment. The couple lived in Hampstead and had three sons, the eldest of whom was killed in the First World War. In later years, after her husband died in 1926, Charles lived in Wembley then Loughborough. She died on 19 August 1959 at the age of 86, leaving £237 in her will.

* * *

The various Barefoot sisters, daughters of a Kent timber merchant, ended their association with the OELC at the conclusion of the 1891 season. Four – or more – of the family played for the team. But tracing them is complicated by their adoption of different pseudonyms.

Beatrice Fanny Barefoot and Flora Amelia Barefoot played under the surname Fane. In 1909, Beatrice married Eugene Hill Goddard, a widowed London solicitor; they moved to Canada where he worked as an accountant. By the time of Eugene's death in 1924, they had returned to England and lived in Devon. The 1939 Register records Beatrice living with her sister Ethel (Flora's twin) in London. She died in February 1969 at the age of 98, leaving £971 in her will.

Flora Amelia Barefoot married Archibald Wood, a stockbroker, in 1896. Her husband died in 1910 and she became a nurse. In later years, she lived with her children Margery and Chamney (who is listed as 'incapacitated' on the 1939 Register). She died in late 1970 at the age of 97.

Several other Barefoot sisters played for the OELC under the pseudonym Gordon; it is quite hard to untangle who was who, but the longest persevering was Eva Gordon, who played until the end of 1891. This was most likely

Eveline May Barefoot, who was born in March 1874 – she was aged only 16 when she played briefly in 1890. She married Alfred Clements, a 'confidential clerk', in August 1901. They had four children – all of whom lived until the 1990s. Alfred died in 1959 but Eva Gordon lived until 1971, when she was 97 years old.

Ella Gordon – Ella Marian Barefoot, Flora's twin who probably played in 1890 – never married. She was variously employed over many years as a 'lady help' and 'nurse companion'. She died in 1959 at the age of 87. Another possible player in 1890, who might have appeared under the name of E. Gordon, was their older sister Ethel. She too never married, and worked as a school governess; by 1939 she lived with her sister Beatrice. She died in 1946 at the age of 79. Other 'Gordon' sisters who played for the OELC were A. Gordon and F. Gordon, but there were no matching Barefoot sisters; possibly these were alternative names for Flora Barefoot/Fane (her middle name was Amelia) or simply errors in the scorecard. The only other Barefoot sister old enough to play was Lena, who was 25 in 1890; she married a man called Horace Martin in July 1891 and died in 1951 at the age of 86. It may not be a coincidence that someone called V. Martin played regularly for the OELC in 1891 (she is otherwise untraceable); but the only photograph we have of V. Martin bears little resemblance to the Fane sisters.

**

Apart from stray Barefoot sisters and Lydia Hann, we can only trace three other players from the 1891 intake, all of whom played until 1892. Mabel Emmett, or Agnes Rowney, whose court case may have been more than an attempt to recover unpaid wages, is hard to track down. Perhaps the most likely candidate is Agnes Gertrude Rowney, born in St Pancras in 1874, who is listed working as a clerk on the 1891 census. This Agnes Rowney lived with her mother in 1901 and her sister (along with several of her siblings) in 1911, when she worked as a clerk in the 'Union Cold Storage'. She died in 1955, leaving £2,300.

Two other sisters from 1891 were Anne Gertrude McDonnell and Caroline McDonnell. The latter was the elder, born at Woolwich in 1869. In 1901, she married the French-born William Stevenson, who called himself a 'gentleman' on the marriage certificate but the census a few weeks later listed him as a solicitor's clerk. In later years he worked as an accountant and insurance agent. The couple never had children, but were wealthy enough to employ a servant by the time of the 1921 census. Gertrude died in 1953, aged 84, leaving an estate worth £1,392 3s 11d.

Caroline McDonnell, who was born in 1870 at East Looe in Cornwall, married a schoolmaster called James Spofforth in 1898. They had a daughter together, but there is an oddity on the 1901 census. It records a visitor to the Spofforth household: the nine-year-old Adelaide Barefoot, who cannot be found in any other records. This seems a remarkable coincidence but there is no obvious link to the cricketing Barefoots. Caroline died in 1952, leaving an estate worth £2,470 9s 1d.

Lena Parsons was one of the few original players who lasted into the 1892 season. At the time of the 1891 census, when she was one of those to list herself as a 'lady cricketer', Alina Parsons lived in London in 1891, sharing – alongside her mother – a house with her sister's family. The latter was married to Luke Alexander Moody, who worked for a time as a theatrical manager. After this, Parsons lived alone and on every census return listed herself as being of 'independent means'. Yet she had no obvious way of supporting herself and she never seems to have had a job after leaving the OELC. She never married, and died in July 1950 at the age of 79.

* * *

Like Parsons, the Heather sisters stayed until almost the bitter end. And unlike some of the other families to be involved in the OELC, Ella and Ada were formidable cricketers. Both lived with their family in Chelsea at the time of the 1891 census but neither is listed as a cricketer. Several of their family worked as lightermen but their father switched to selling coal shortly after the collapse of the OELC. Eliza Heather had called herself Ella for cricketing purposes, and continued to use that name for the rest of her life: she is Eliza Ella or simply Ella in all records after 1891. In February 1893 she married Charles Leonard Clement, a coal merchant (and later an accountant) from Wantage in Berkshire. Clement came from a wealthy Berkshire farming family which had turned to coal; he had been living in Battersea in 1891 working as a commission agent. The marriage certificate describes Heather's father as a coal merchant too, which might explain how they met. The couple had three children before Clement died in 1909, after which we encounter another mystery.

The 1911 census lists two of Heather's children living apart from her: one in the National Children's Home at Edgeworth, Lancashire; the other in Crossley Sanatorium, 'for the open-air treatment of consumption' (better known today as tuberculosis), at Kingswood near Warrington.

Heather was cohabiting with a man called Charles Duhy: she was listed as his wife but they were not married; he was – inexplicably – recorded under the name Albert Thompson. Two children were also part of the household: Heather's oldest daughter (also called Ella) from her marriage to Clement and a son called Lionel, who had been born in 1903 and whose father was a man called Albert Collingwood. Heather continued living with Duhy until his death in 1937, although they seemingly never married; their movements and living arrangements are opaque. In the same period her daughter Ella embarked on a series of adventures around the world that involved several marriages and instances of bigamy. Clearly both Heather and her daughter – who were listed together on the 1939 Register – were comfortable living unconventional lives by the standard of the time. Eliza 'Ella' Heather died in 1960 at the age of 90, listed as Eliza E. Clement (there are a few other possible death records, but this seems most likely as it was registered in Bromley).

Ada Heather had a more straightforward tale. She married an engineer called Richard Jones in 1894; her husband later ran his own public houses before becoming a taxi driver. The couple had two children (only one of whom was alive at the time of the 1911 census). Ada was widowed by the time of the 1939 Register, when she was living with her sister Ella. She was listed as an 'invalid' with no explanation; it looks as if Ella was taking care of her. Assuming she remained in Bromley, she died in 1951 at the age of 78.

* * *

Perhaps only one family proved to be better cricketers than the Heathers: the Westbrooks, or to give them their real names, the Lyon sisters. Grace Evelyn Lyon, despite initially featuring alongside her sister in their 1891 advertisement, played only in 1890. She later worked as a nurse but seems to have had an interesting personal life. The 1901 and 1911 censuses record her as a boarder with William Rich (an 'artist colourman') and his wife, both of whom were two years older than her, but on the latter occasion, Grace had begun to work as a 'Bassinetic Dealer's Assistant' (presumably someone who sells bassinets). Neither Grace nor the Rich family can be found on the 1921 census, but Rich's wife died in 1931. And in 1933, Grace married William Rich. On the 1939 Register she is listed working at a shop in Lewisham selling baby carriages alongside her husband. She died in August 1961 at the age of 89, leaving nearly £4,000 in her will.

Violet Westbrook still lived with her parents in 1901, when her occupation was a 'female typist'. In 1903, she married Phillip John Seale, a clerk who had lived with her family as a 'guest' (according to the 1901 census). Seale went on to work as an importer and the couple had two children. But if she had abandoned cricket, Violet was still remembered: an article in the *Nottingham Journal* in 1919, discussing memories of the Castle Ground there, recalled the visit of the OELC and said: 'We remember one Violet Westbrook as a particularly fine figure of a girl, and a gallant hitter and bowler.' Violet's husband died in 1933 and she continued running a business without him; on the 1939 Register she worked in Billericay as a shopkeeper of the 'Fancy Shop' and lived with her daughter Phyllis. The woman who was probably the best female cricketer in the world until the 1930s died at the Runwell Emergency Hospital in 1945, aged 75, leaving an estate worth over £3,000; her final address was 'The Fancy Shop' of Wickford in Essex.

* * *

And what of Daisie Stanley? The woman who let everyone know she was the star of the show, and had a genius for self-promotion. The woman who ran the evening performances. The woman who was so essential that she returned as a manager in 1891. And the woman who was quite possibly involved in taking the gate receipts before the ignominious collapse of the tour, but apparently escaped any blame or punishment.

At the time of the 1891 census, Daisy Anita Berry lived with her family in Ramsgate. But after the cessation of her involvement with the OELC – in whatever murky circumstances – she did not give up her dreams of running a women's sports team. The Liverpool Exhibition Grounds hosted an event for the August Bank Holiday of 1892, at which there was to be music and fireworks; S. F. Cody's American Frontier Combination was also to appear, among other acts. The main attraction was a meeting of 'young lady athletes' competing for 'valuable prizes in flat and hurdle races, tug-of-war, &c'. The person in charge of this event was Daisie Stanley – 'who will be remembered in Liverpool as the captain of the "Blue" eleven of the original lady cricketers'.

A woman named Daisy Stanley appeared as a dairymaid, a part involving several songs, in a burlesque performance called *Bonny Boy Blue* at Rudge's Varieties, Ashton-under-Lyne in September 1892; the same show was also performed at the Gaiety Theatre in West Hartlepool later in the month. However, there is no certainty this was our Daisie Stanley. Perhaps she had branched out into acting and performance, but after this she faded into obscurity. In 1906 she married a sign-writer called Arthur Williams; the couple lived in Hammersmith without ever having children. Arthur died in 1924, having served in the Royal Navy during the First World War. On the 1939 Register, she was living alone in Fulham. Daisy Williams, née Berry, also known as Stanley, never remarried and died at the age of 78 in 1949, long forgotten as the leading figure in the OELC.

* * *

Through a sad chain of circumstances, the woman about whom we have the most information – and who stayed with the OELC until the absolute bitter end – was Lizzie Sanders. We can be fairly certain that she joined the cricket team to escape from a life of poverty. She had been the youngest player in 1890 and was one of the most accomplished in 1891. But it was the events of 1892 that we cannot explain. What lay behind her marriage to Edgar Fearis in February of that year? Was she involved in the court case? Were those who took Wood to court behind the attempt to resurrect the OELC for the ill-fated 1892 tour? Unfortunately we can only speculate; any evidence is lost.

However, we are on firmer ground with the next part of Sanders's story. Her marriage did not last; within a year or two she and Fearis had separated and he moved alone to New York. There are several parallels with Elizabeth Dempsey and Arthur Veitch; like the latter, Fearis bigamously married in the United States. He had two children, lived in Manhattan, and worked as a railroad clerk. But he was not a well man and in 1906 he died of tuberculosis and 'asthenia' – which meant weakness, suggesting he had been fading for some time. Although the details are unknown, the suspicion remains that Fearis treated Sanders terribly and his whole part in the OELC narrative looks uncomfortably like an opportunist exploiting an uncertain situation. But lack of evidence means that it must remain no more than a suspicion.

What happened to Lizzie Sanders over the next few years is unclear; she was present at her brother's wedding in 1896, and we pick up her trail again in March and April 1899 when she was a key witness in a case of theft. She first appeared at Westminster Police Court, when she called herself 'Tootsie' Ferris and was reluctant to give her address. But she was subsequently called to give evidence at the Old Bailey, when she confirmed that she was Elizabeth Fearis,[60] the estranged wife of Edgar Charles Fearis, whom she had left 'five or six years ago'. Several newspaper reports described her as 'stylishly attired'.

The defendant in the case was a married man called William Shinn, who had been in a relationship with Sanders since around 1896. No longer living with his wife, he had been working as a butler and secured Sanders a job as a sick nurse to his female employer. In 1898, he had stolen jewellery worth over £2,000 from a friend of his employer. Sanders told the court that he had later shown her some items that he had taken and promised her a diamond ring. But he had also threatened her with violence if she spoke out; this worried her as he had injured her several times before. At some point after this, Shinn and Sanders shared a house in Camberwell, but the relationship broke down when he moved in with another woman. Sanders therefore returned to her mother's house, where she lived when the case went to court.

---

60 The court documents spell her name as Ferris.

Shinn's defence was that Sanders was 'a revengeful and jealous woman'. It emerged in court that she had written to a friend that she would 'do anything' to get revenge after discovering that he had been keeping 'five or six women on a string'; not long after this she went to the police to report the jewellery theft. But Shinn's argument was undermined when it emerged that he had bigamously married another woman; he had never lived with the latter, only visiting occasionally. He had told the mother of his second wife about the jewel theft and she went to the police around the same time as Sanders. With two witnesses against him, Shinn was found guilty and sentenced to seven years for robbery and three concurrently for bigamy (which he had admitted).

By 1901, Sanders was still living with her mother; the census records that they shared a building at 19 Upcorne Road in Chelsea with two other families. Her mother was still a dressmaker but Sanders now gave her occupation as an actress. Given the poverty of her family (her sister at that time was a patient in the Chelsea Workhouse infirmary), her own flamboyant appearance in court, her association with Shinn and her nickname of 'Tootsie', it does beg the question of whether this was a euphemism. But again, we do not know for certain.

Sanders's mother died in 1902 and her sister Frances continued to drift in and out of workhouses. And Frances was there at 19 Upcorne Road on 17 November 1903 when Lizzie Sanders died from tuberculosis at the age of 29.[61]

---

61 Frances Sanders reported the death but gave a false name, Frances Cartridge, presumably as she was hiding her identity. Frances' life eventually settled down and she became the common-law wife of a porter called Henry Clements. She lived until 1927.

* * *

What of those who ran the team? We cannot trace William Matthews, but Walter Bosanquet continued to work as a solicitor. Despite his losses with the OELC, he remained extremely rich, although he lost his wife Penelope in May 1894. Bosanquet died at the age of 65 on 9 October 1904 just as his relation Bernard was making the family name famous for all time in cricketing circles; his estate was worth over £72,000.

What of Edward Parsons Michell, who styled himself as the French entrepreneur E. Michel and who might have been Edward Ludwig? He is a hard man to locate, missing from all census returns after 1881. But it is just about possible to track his progress. His son Henry, although born in 1882, was not baptised until 1898, when the baptismal records indicate that the family lived at 35 Reedworth Street in London; Michell's occupation was a 'commercial traveller', which would explain his absences. The family had moved by the time of the 1901 census – his wife Clara was visiting someone in Leicester on census night – but in 1911 they lived at 14 Glebe Road in Barnes (Michell was away once more). By then, Henry was a deck officer in the merchant navy and went on to be a master mariner.

On 23 April 1914, Edward Parsons Michell, of 14 Glebe Road, died at the age of 54, leaving £91 19s to his wife. Clara lived until 1947. Edward's older brother, Joseph Sanders Michell, lived until 1930; he made the news for unfortunate reasons in 1908 when his daughter died in a fire at his house.

The man who, by accident or design, provided the spelling and birthplace of Edward Parsons Michell's persona as manager of the OELC, Louis Edouard Michel, was admitted to the Holloway Sanatorium on 14 July 1894 at the request of his wife; two doctors certified that he was suffering from 'general paralysis of the insane', which today would be called tertiary syphilis. He remained a patient there until he died on 30 July 1896, leaving just over £2,500 in his will.

A Place in History?

IF WE are to evaluate the legacy or impact of the OELC, the answer depends entirely on how we frame the story.

As a cricket team, the OELC must be regarded as a failure. Popular for a time, their problem was that success was unsustainable. The same teams facing each other, day after day, would have quickly lost its appeal. And the spectacle of women playing men – batting left-handed – was never attractive, least of all to spectators asked to pay for the privilege. Such a contest, favoured by Arthur's Ideal Lady Cricketers, belonged to the sphere of clown cricket. The only chance the OELC would have had for long-term success – as Bosanquet seems to have recognised from the start – was to play competitive matches against other women. But they had no serious professional rivals, and amateur clubs refused to dirty their hands by associating with such a team.

The contemporary press insisted that there was a boom in amateur women's cricket after the OELC appeared – even if many writers were reluctant to credit the professional team – and from what evidence survives it appears that the Reds v Blues games attracted more women spectators than was customary in the 1890s. But nothing grew from the ashes of the OELC; no one was inspired to emulate them, no one rose to the top of women's cricket and proclaimed how she had been inspired by Daisy Stanley or Violet Westbrook. The team was erased from the history books. By the 1930s, when women's cricket became popular, the OELC had long been forgotten and professionalism was not even entertained as a concept. It was not until 2014 that full-time professional contracts were introduced in England for women cricketers.

But looking at the OELC like this makes the mistake of trying to understand the story from the viewpoint of today, and trying to tell a linear tale of progress from 1890 to the debut of The Hundred in 2021 or today's vast audiences for the women's World Cup, Ashes or IPL. For those who formed the OELC, it was not a purely sporting enterprise. It crossed over into music hall and theatre. By those terms, at least in 1890, the OELC had been a resounding success, achieving huge audiences and enormous publicity. Yet the OELC have never been analysed within that entertainment sphere; no history of music hall would need to cover the OELC to be complete, and yet the players deserve their small role in that story too. They offered a twist on the usual fare, albeit one which would never have set theatres alight.

In that case, should we view the OELC simply as a business enterprise, which aimed to make a profit for the shareholders of the ECAA? This results in a story of two parts: success in 1890 and catastrophe in 1891. If Bosanquet had pulled the plug in October 1890, the ECAA would have made a profit. But either greed or ambition prompted him to continue, and in those murky circumstances of June 1891, the ECAA collapsed under its own expenses until Bosanquet presumably decided enough was enough. Yet there is something unsatisfactory about looking at the

OELC in this way. Instead of being about the players or the spectacle, it becomes a tale of profit, greed and cash.

This only increases when we consider the mysterious reconstitution of the team in mid-1891. At that point, it becomes a story of exploitation. There is enough evidence to say that the managers – whoever they might have been – took the gate money during the second half of the season, with the result that the players could no longer be paid. We cannot say who was responsible as it was no longer possible to identify who was in charge. How big a part did Michel, Wood and Fearis play? And despite the narrative that the male managers 'absconded with the profits', it is not implausible that the versatile and ambitious Miss Stanley was one of those who schemed to make money from the tour at the expense of the players.

Dismissing the OELC as a fraudulent sham to take advantage of a group of young women does not quite fit the story either. Because if we consider the viewpoint of the players, a quite different picture emerges. Although so much about them remains shadowy, although their own voices are largely lost to us, we can still see an outline of their perspective. Their backgrounds were diverse, and each woman had her own reason for joining – and her own unique narrative – but we can make one broad generalisation. Almost all the women were from poorer backgrounds. At a time when women had little freedom, fewer rights, and were almost universally treated badly, being part of the OELC offered an opportunity to break the restrictions of late-Victorian society and achieve fame and fortune. Even if we concede that the plan was drawn up by men, that the tour was managed by men and that men were making the decisions, it was the women who drove the story. It was the women who achieved something approaching fame. And it was the women who travelled and did things of which few of their contemporaries could have dreamed. For this group to travel the country being paid to play sport – attracting tens of thousands of paying spectators, associating with Test cricketers such as Jack Blackham, George Ulyett or Billy Bates, and causing journalists to be fascinated to the point of obsessiveness – was unprecedented. Pursuing this interpretation takes us into the world of 'New Women'. Here, we can see the players as pioneers; not in cricket, but in a much wider movement. Even if their venture ultimately failed, or was derailed by (male) greed, this seems like a more appropriate canvas on which to view their story.

Was this therefore a story of the battle of the sexes? Of women proving themselves against the expectations of men? In this case, they doubtlessly succeeded in winning over opinions. But that falls into the trap of judging women by the standards of a contemporary male audience; we do not know how they judged themselves. Nor do we know what kind of standard they achieved; we cannot say how good Violet Westbrook or Ella Heather were. But again, we are trying to make comparisons that would never have been made in 1890 or 1891. It is unlikely Westbrook cared about her place in a cricket 'hall of fame'. The fact that those women were publicly scoring runs and taking wickets is perhaps its own positive judgement.

W. G. Grace, in his reminiscences, took their 'dismal failure' as a sign that 'cricket is not a game for women'. But in the misogynistic climate of Victorian England, the very existence of the OELC and the fame of its players was extraordinary. Perhaps one simple fact puts everything else into context: no other professional women's teams emerged in England until the 21st century. Would Stanley or Westbrook have been appalled at such a wait? Or proud to have been so far ahead of their time?

    Maybe in the end it is all these things, or none of them. Maybe it is just the story of an ambitious surveyor called Edward Michell, and one of the many schemes to emerge from Chesterfield Grove. Or an entrepreneurial solicitor called Bosanquet. Or a woman called Daisy Berry who made a name for herself for a few months in 1890. Or Violet Lyon, who showed that women could indeed bat and bowl before fading into obscurity. Or Katie Tatton, the trick cyclist who briefly found a different way to make a living after the murder of her previous employer. Or Elizabeth Dempsey, the military daughter who went her own way. Or Lizzie Sanders, whose memories of those shining days as a famous and talented cricketer might have comforted her as her life fell apart.

Appendix 1: Biographical Information on the Players

THE PROFILES printed in the *English Lady Cricketers' Gazette* were brief, and are produced here in full. Not all the information was accurate. The parts in italics are from an updated version of the profiles in circulation from July.

* * *

'Red' Eleven

Violet Blanche Westbrook, born at Godalming, Surrey, July 23rd, 1871. Sound and reliable bat, excellent and thoroughly correct style. *Has played the game from infancy. A good fast bowler, and very alert in the field.* Has been appointed captain of the 'Reds'. *Has made top score (99), and has the highest batting average.*

Grace Evelyn Westbrook, born at Godalming, Surrey, July 16th, 1872. Useful all-round cricketer. [Moved to Blue section in reprint] *Very steady bat. Is a first-rate wicket-keeper.*

Florence Hardwick, born at Battersea, Surrey, December 10th, 1869. Slow underhand bowler. *A steady bat.*

Louise Daly, born at Marylebone, June 19th, 1868. A good, fast bowler, *generally with success; speciality, break to 'leg'.*

Sophie Charles, born at Chelsea, November 17th, 1872. A fair, slow, underhand bowler *with break from the off, a smart bat*, and one of the fleetest runners in the team: *possesses exceptional strength, and is most useful in the field.*

Florence Woodward, native of Cheltenham, July 9th, 1864. Very good all-round player. [Omitted from reprint]

A. [*Adele*] Matthey, born in London, September 12th, 1870. A most active and effective bat *with excellent defence, and is a good wicket-keeper. Described as the 'Little W. G. of the OELC.'*

Edith Woodward, born at Cheltenham, April 12th, 1871. [Omitted from reprint]

Elizabeth Nora Dare [*Elizabeth Nora Dempsey*], born at Curragh, County Cork, Ireland, March 12th, 1871. Very good at point. [Last sentence replaced in reprint with: *Occasional bowler and fair bat.*]

Bianca Seymour, born at Kennington, Surrey, March 4th, 1869.

Beatrice Light, born at Southampton, July 30th, 1870. [Omitted from reprint]

[Added to Reds in reprint]

Nellie Wadkin, born at Bradford, Yorkshire, October 1871.
Eva Gordon, born at Dulwich, Surrey, 1871.
Flora Fane, born at Erith, Kent, June 20th, 1872.

'Blue' Eleven

Ella Heather, born at Chelsea, July 10th, 1871, one of the best bats, playing in correct style with good defence; a very useful slow bowler. *Made 63 in first match at Liverpool,*

Appendix 1: Biographical Information on the Players

Easter Monday 1890. Has been presented with bat by Mr W. H. Bosanquet, Managing Director of the Association.

Ada Heather, born at Chelsea, November 10th, 1872. An excellent over-arm bowler on all wickets; *varies her pace and pitch with judgement; breaks from 'leg' and from the 'off';* is a very fair bat, and good field. *Has been presented with bat by Wm Matthews, the Surrey professional.*

Daisie Stanley, born at Chetnole, Dorsetshire, October 27th, 1870. Successful left hand over-arm bowler. *Very dangerous when the ground helps.* Possesses a thorough knowledge of the technique of cricket and is Captain of the 'Blue' Eleven. Was formerly an Instructress at Alexandra House Gymnasium, Kennington Gore, *and is now editor of* The English Lady Cricketers' Gazette.

Susie Fletcher, born at Lichfield, Staffordshire, September 17th, 1868. Most valuable at the wicket. [Sentence omitted from reprint]

Lizzie Sanders, born at Chelsea, August 1st, 1872. Bats well, with plenty of hitting power.

Bessie Moss, born at Finsbury, June 22nd, 1873. A very agile wicket-keeper, *and at times successful with the ball; quick in the field*, and a good all-round player.

Lena Parsons, born at Oban, Scotland, October 2nd, 1870. *Good at point.*

Alice Grey, born at Camberwell, December 31st, 1868. Good round arm bowler, *occasionally good bat, and an excellent field.*

Georgina Sheffield, born at Bermondsey, December 4th, 1868. Bowls over-arm. [Last sentence replaced in reprint with: *Good over-arm bowler and promising bat.*]

Marie Lisle, born at Harborne, Staffordshire, January 27th, 1868. [Omitted from reprint]

Beatrice Fane, born at Erith, Kent, October 24th, 1870.

[Added to Blues in reprint]

Marie Beckenham, *born near Bromley, Kent, August 20th, 1868.*

Odds: Annie Hampson (Somerset), **Katie Tatton** (Surrey), **Annie Lisle** (Staffordshire), **Flora Fane** (Kent). [This section omitted from reprint; Flora Fane added to main profiles]

Appendix 1: Biographical Information on the Players

Professional Name Real Name	Date of Birth	Place of Birth	Marriage	Date of Death	Place of Death	Father's Occupation (Own occupation)
N. Aldwell			No further details			
Marie Beckenham Mary Willett	20/8/1868[a]	Beckenham, Kent	N/A	15/3/1958 Aged 89	Bromley, Kent	Coachman (Clerk; theatrical manager)
Miss Bailey			No further details			
Sophie Charles Sophia Blanche Charles	12/11/1872[b] or 19/11/1872[a] or 4/12/1872[c]	Chelsea	2/1/1896 in St Pancras to Frederick John Moult	19/8/1959 Aged 86	Loughborough, Leicestershire	Fishmonger
C. Chessington						
F. Chessington			Probably sisters from Chessington, but no further details available			
M. Chessington						
Elizabeth Nora Dare Elizabeth Margaret Dempsey	12/3/1871	Carragh, County Cork, Ireland[b] or Fermoy, County Cork, Ireland[a]	20/7/1891 in Battersea to Arthur John Veitch	11/04/1901 Aged 30	Tottenham Court, Pancras	Sergeant in the British Army
Louise Daly Maria Louisa Daly	17/6/1868[c] or 19/6/1868[b]	Marylebone	1895 in Lambeth to Arthur James Rawlinson; 1937 in Lambeth to Thomas E. Giles	1951 Aged 82	Wandsworth	Metropolitan policeman; milk carrier

Professional Name Real Name	Date of Birth	Place of Birth	Marriage	Date of Death	Place of Death	Father's Occupation (Own occupation)
May Day			No further details			
L. Douglas			No further details			
Mabel Emmett 1) Annie Rowney 2) Agnes Gertrude Rowney	1) 1868 2) 14/2/1874	1) Coventry 2) St Pancras	1) 30/10/1893 in Hackney to Alfred Bawden Wills 2) N/A	1) No details 2) 9/12/1955 Aged 81	1) No details 2) Battersea?	1) Watchmaker (Waitress) Printer? (Clerk)
L. Ernest			No further details			
Beatrice Fane Beatrice Fanny Barefoot	24/10/1870	Erith, Kent	29/5/1909 in City of London to Eugene Hill Goddard	2/2/1969 Aged 98	Sutton, Greater London	Timber merchant
Flora Fane (possibly played as F. Gordon and A. Gordon) Flora Amelia Barefoot	5/12/1872	Erith, Kent	23/8/1896 in Dulwich to Archibald Wood	1/12/1970 Aged 97	Aldershot	Timber merchant
Susie Fletcher Susan Fletcher Shemmonds	17/9/1864[c] or 19/9/1864[a] or 17/9/1868[b]	Lichfield, Staffordshire	19/9/1892 in Islington to William Treliving Hambly	4/1955 Aged 90	Wood Green, Middlesex	Druggist and grocer
C. Fletcher 1) Caroline Sophia Shemmonds?	1) 1862	1) Lichfield, Staffordshire	1) N/A	1) 1928 Aged 66	Loughborough	1) Druggist and grocer (Sick nurse)

Appendix 1: Biographical Information on the Players

Professional Name / Real Name	Date of Birth	Place of Birth	Marriage	Date of Death	Place of Death	Father's Occupation (Own occupation)
Ella Gordon Ella Marion Barefoot	5/12/1872	Erith, Kent	N/A	23/12/1959 Aged 87	Carshalton, Surrey	Timber merchant ('Lady help', nurse companion)
Eva Gordon Eveline May Barefoot	19/3/1874	Erith, Kent	21/1/1901 in Southwark to Alfred Vivian Clements	1971 Aged 97	Sutton, Greater London	Timber merchant
E. Gordon (alternative) Ethel Maud Barefoot	17/4/1867	Peckham	N/A	23/11/1946 Aged 79	Camberwell	Timber merchant (School governess)
Alice Grey	31/12/1868[b]	Camberwell[b]	No further details			
Annie Hampson Annie Titiana Hampson	1872	Montacute, Somerset	20/4/1891 in Islington to Joseph Oliver; 1909 in Maidstone to George John Wisdom	1926 Aged 53	Maidstone, Kent	Mason (Draper's assistant, forewoman of laundry)
Lydia Hann (sometimes L. Hearne)	1870	Islington	No further details			Provision dealer
Florence Hardwick Emma Florence Hardwick	16/12/1868[a] or 10/12/1869[b]	Battersea	1/2/1893 in Battersea to Alfred William Baker	1929 Aged 61	West Ham, Essex	Dairyman (Dairyman's assistant, dairymaid)

279

Forgotten Pioneers

Professional Name / Real Name	Date of Birth	Place of Birth	Marriage	Date of Death	Place of Death	Father's Occupation (Own occupation)
Ada Heather	10/11/1872[b] or 20/11/1872[c]	Chelsea	15/7/1894 in Kensington to Richard Jones	1951 Aged 78	Bromley, Kent	Lighterman
Ella Heather Eliza Heather	10/7/1870	Chelsea	2/2/1893 in Wantage, Berkshire to Charles Leonard Clement	1960 Aged 90	Bromley, Kent	Lighterman
M. Hood			No further details			
Beatrice Light Annie Emma Nicholas	30/7/1870[b]	Southampton	1887 in Southampton to James John Light	1912 Aged 43	Southampton	General/ agricultural labourer
Annie Lisle	No details	Staffordshire[b]	No further details			
Marie Lisle	27/5/1868[b]	Harborne, Staffordshire[b] (Wolverhampton?)[d]	1888 to Joseph Carter Lisle[d]	No further details		
B. Lisle						
C. Lisle	Possibly sisters connected with Annie Lisle and Marie Lisle but they were never listed as playing together and all might be mis-transcriptions of Annie Lisle					
L. Lisle						
N. Lisle						
V. Martin	No further details					

Appendix 1: Biographical Information on the Players

Professional Name Real Name	Date of Birth	Place of Birth	Marriage	Date of Death	Place of Death	Father's Occupation (Own occupation)
Adele Matthey (sometimes Annie Matthey)) (Annie Adele Josephine Matthey)	12/9/1870	London[b] or Lambeth[a]	1895 in St George Hanover Square to Carl Wilhelm F. Hammer	1947 Aged 76	Mid-Eastern Surrey	Restaurant manager
A. McDonnell Alice Mary McDonnell	6/3/1873	Plymouth, Devon	1898 in Croydon to Henry Smith	No further details		Sergeant in the Royal Artillery, beer-house keeper
Caroline McDonnell	22/11/1870	Looe, Cornwall	4/8/1898 in West Croydon to James Archibald Hope Spofforth	1/7/1952 Aged 81	Mid-Eastern Surrey	Sergeant in the Royal Artillery, beer-house keeper
Gertrude McDonnell Anna Gertrude McDonnell	24/2/1869	Woolwich, Kent	28/1/1901 in Kensington to William Albert Stevenson	5/8/1953 Aged 84	Islington	Sergeant in the Royal Artillery, beer-house keeper
Bessie Moss Elizabeth Moss	22/6/1872[c] or 22/6/1873[b]	Finsbury[b] or Peckham[d]	12/6/1896 in Southwark to Henry Young Benham 29/11/1904 in Hackney to Lionel Montague Mortimer	1962 Aged 89	Hatfield, Hertfordshire	Bookbinder
C. V. Oldbrook	No further details					

281

Professional Name Real Name	Date of Birth	Place of Birth	Marriage	Date of Death	Place of Death	Father's Occupation (Own occupation)
Lena Parsons Allina Parsons	2/10/1870	Oban, Argyll, Scotland	N/A	17/7/1950 Aged 79	Bromley, Kent	Surveyor
N. Percival	No further details					
A. Robinson	No further details					
Lizzie Sanders Elizabeth Talitha Sanders	(1/8/1872)[b] 1/8/1874[a]	Chelsea	25/2/1892 in Chelsea to Edgar Charles Fearis	17/11/1903 Aged 29	Chelsea	Portmanteau maker (Nurse/maid, actress)
Bianca Seymour Bianca Olimpia Cacciola Bianca Hicks	4/3/1869[b] 4/3/1869 1868	Kennington[b] Paris, France Peckham	No details N/A	No details 1896 Aged 27	No details Pancras	Author Scenic artist (Singer)
Georgina Sheffield Emma Georgina Sheffield	4/12/1867[ac] (4/12/1868)[b]	Bermondsey[b] or Camberwell[d]	? to Thomas Henry Carash 15/4/1906 in Lambeth to William Henry Garner 4/12/1924 in Camberwell to Henry Caplin	19/6/1941 Aged 73	Fulwood, Lancashire	Fishmonger (Actress)
Daisie Stanley Daisy Anita Berry	27/10/1870	Chetnole, Dorset[b] or Fulham	27/8/1906 in Wandsworth to George Matthew Berry	1949 Aged 78	Fulham	Bricklayer, clerk of works (Dressmaker; gym instructor?)

Appendix 1: Biographical Information on the Players

Professional Name / Real Name	Date of Birth	Place of Birth	Marriage	Date of Death	Place of Death	Father's Occupation (Own occupation)
A. Stevens						
C. Stevens						
L. Stevens	Probably sisters; they did not all play together, so there could be some overlap or mis-transcription					
Mabel Stevens						
Maud Stevens						
Katie Tatton (sometimes **Katie Letine**) Catherina Tatton	Baptised 10/3/1873 (School record gives date of birth as 27/3/1874)	Lambeth	No further details			Baker, copper plate printer (Cyclist)
L. Wadkin Elizabeth Wadkin?	1869	Deptford or Rotherhithe	1890 in Dover to Barrington Albert Nichols	1927 Aged 58	Fulham	Timber merchant
Nellie Wadkin Ellen Frances Wadkin	10/10/1871	Bradford, Yorkshire[b] or Rotherhithe[d]	16/11/1893 in Camden to William Alfred Mummery; 14/8/1901 in Putney to Henry John Jeves	15/1/1951 Aged 79	Beckenham, Kent	Timber merchant
A. Waterfield	No further details					

Professional Name / Real Name	Date of Birth	Place of Birth	Marriage	Date of Death	Place of Death	Father's Occupation (Own occupation)
Grace Evelyn Westbrook / Grace Evelyn Lyon	16/7/1872	Godalming, Surrey	1932 in Willesden to William Rich	14/8/1961 Aged 89	Ealing, Middlesex	Manager of Westbrook Mills; auctioneer; stationer (Hospital sick nurse; bassinette dealers' assistant; shop assistant)
Violet Blanche Westbrook / Violet Blanche Lyon	23/7/1870[ac] (23/7/1871)[b]	Godalming, Surrey	1/7/1903 in Hampstead to Philip John Seale	8/8/1945 Aged 75	Chelmsford, Essex	Manager of Westbrook Mills; auctioneer; stationer ('Lady typist'; shopkeeper)
Edith Woodward	12/4/1871	Cheltenham	N/A	25/10/1947 Aged 76	Cheltenham	Music dealer; instructor of music (Music teacher; dance teacher; owner of a dancing academy)
Florence Woodward / Florence Amelia Woodward	July 1863[a] or 9/7/1864[b] (Possibly 29/7/1863)	Cheltenham	13/7/1892 in Cheltenham to Alfred Rolph	1937 Aged 74	Hastings, Sussex	Music dealer; instructor of music (Musician's assistant; actress; teacher of dancing)

Appendix 1: Biographical Information on the Players

Appeared for the All-England Lady Cricketers only

M. Argent 1) Elizabeth Helena Argent?	1) 1/5/1870	1) Perth, Scotland	1) 20/11/1895 in St George Hanover Square to William Henry Potter	1) 1957 Aged 86	1) West Cheshire	1) Domestic coachman
A. Carr			No further details			
G. Fortescue			No further details			
D. Gordon			No further details			
B. Miller			No further details			
E. Miller			No further details			

Key: [a] Birth or baptismal record
 [b] English Lady Cricketers' Gazette
 [c] 1939 Register of England and Wales
 [d] 1911 census

If no source is specified for date or place of birth, there are multiple attestations.

Where there are numbered options, identification is uncertain; each number is an alternative or, if there is just one option, it is far from certain that this is the cricketer.

Appendix 2: Matches Played by the OELC

	Date	Venue	Scores	Attendance
1	7 and 8 April 1890	Police Athletic Grounds, Liverpool	Reds 111 and 117/5, Blues 130 (Ella Heather 63); Blues won by 19 runs on first innings	15,000
2	9 or 10 April	Rugby	*Private engagement*	
3	23 April 1890	Victoria Ground, Ashford	Reds 110 (Violet Westbrook 53), Blues 32/4; drawn	
4	30 April 1890	Dolphin Cricket Ground, Slough	Blues 69, Reds 80; Reds won by 11 runs	'A fashionable audience'
5	2 and 3 May 1890	Antelope Ground, Southampton	Reds 117 (Violet Westbrook 68) and 50, Blues 128 and 97; Blues won by 57 runs	First day 'moderate'; second day: 4,000
6	7 May 1890	Reigate Priory Cricket Club, Reigate	Blues 80, Reds 109 (Violet Westbrook 72); Reds won by 29 runs	
7	12 May 1890	Linslade Cricket Ground, Leighton Buzzard	Blues 27; Reds 90 (Violet Westbrook 56 not out). Reds won by 63 runs	Between 500 and 700

Appendix 2: Matches Played by the OELC

	Date	Venue	Scores	Attendance
8	13 May 1890	Paddington Recreation Ground, Paddington	*No details in newspapers; this may have been a match between two teams of 'lady cricketers' unconnected with the OELC*	
9	15 May 1890	Maidenhead	Reds 70, Blues 114; Blues won by 44 runs *Postponed from 10 May because of rain*	Between 300 and 500
10	17 May 1890	Chiswick Park, Chiswick	Reds 157 (Violet Westbrook 91), Blues 99; Reds won by 58 runs	Between 2,000 and 3,000
11	21 May 1890	Cricket Field, Guildford	Blues 150 (Ella Heather 50 not out; Alice Grey 57), Reds 169 (Violet Westbrook 99); Reds won by 19 runs *Violet Westbrook was run out going for her hundredth run from the final ball of the match*	300
12	22 May 1890	Institute Ground, Aldershot	Blues 127 (Ella Heather 58 not out), Reds 70/4; drawn	'Small', noted as being small for the ground
13	26 and 27 May 1890	Cricket Ground, Skegness	*No details in newspapers*	
14	29 May 1890	Lord Nelson Ground, Boston	Blues 43 and 49/8, Reds 111; Reds won by 68 on first innings *Played at football ground on coconut matting*	
15	30 May 1890	Clough Hall Park and Gardens, Harecastle, Kidsgrove	Reds 63 and 124/8, Blues 93; Blues won by 30 runs on first innings *Part of the week-long celebrations to mark the opening of Clough Hall, which as a whole were attended by an estimated 40,000 to 60,000 visitors.*	3,000
16	2 and 3 June 1890	Zoological Gardens, Clifton	Reds 76 and 109, Blues 103 and 117; Blues won by seven wickets and 35 runs	First day 1,000; second day between 700 and 800

	Date	Venue	Scores	Attendance
17	4 June 1890	Kensington Meadows, Bath	Blues 46 and 36/3, Reds 51; Reds won by five runs on first innings	Lower than expected owing to a nearby tennis tournament and the 'awkward' location of the ground
18	5 June 1890	County Cricket Ground, Taunton	Blues 68 and 24/4, Reds 109; Reds won by 41 runs on first innings	2,000
19	7 June 1890	Newport F. C. and A. C. Ground, Newport	Reds 36, Blues 125; Blues won by 89 runs	Either 1,200 or 15,000
20	9 June 1890	Recreation Grounds, Weston-super-Mare	Blues 106, Reds 61; Blues won by 45 runs	
21	11 June 1890	Pittville Gardens, Cheltenham	Reds 50, Blues 40; Reds won by 10 runs	2,000 (including 'many gentry')
22	13 June 1890	Bulman's Field, Cambridge	Reds 132 (Violet Westbrook 93 not out), Blues 97; Reds won by 35 runs	1,000
23	14 June 1890	Molineux Grounds, Wolverhampton	Blues 83, Reds 131/5 (Violet Westbrook 52); Reds won by 48 runs	3,000
24	16 and 17 June 1890	Franklin's Gardens, Northampton	Blues 71 and 13/5, Reds 64; Blues won by seven runs on first innings	
25	18 June 1890	Parish Church Cricket Ground, Leamington Spa	Reds 93 (Violet Westbrook 60), Blues 46/8; drawn	2,000

Appendix 2: Matches Played by the OELC

	Date	Venue	Scores	Attendance
26	19 June 1890	Castle Ground, Nottingham	Blues 83 and 102, Reds 131 (Violet Westbrook 88) and 59; Reds won by four runs	First day 'fair'; second day between 1,500 and 2,000
27	21 June 1890	Police Recreation Ground, Liverpool	Reds 20, Blues 91; Blues won by 71 runs	'No more than 300'
28	23 and 24 June 1890	County Ground, Leicester	Blues 124 and 82, Reds 117 and 36/5; Blues won by seven runs on first innings	First day 'large and fashionable'
29	27 and 28 June 1890	Deepdale, Preston	Reds 97 and 112 (Violet Westbrook 55), Blues 66 and 20/5; Reds won by 31 runs on first innings *Played on coconut matting*	First day 'moderate', possibly no more than 50
30	30 June, 1 and 2 July 1890	Royal Palace Gardens, Blackpool	Blues 78, Reds 41; result unknown *First day rained off; no scores recorded for third day*	
31	3 July 1890	Bury	*No details in newspapers*	
32	5 July 1890	St Helens	*No details in newspapers*	4,000
33	7 and 8 July 1890	Athletic Ground, Old Trafford, Manchester	Blues 77 and 82, Reds 76 and 76; Blues won by seven runs	First day 7,000; second day 6,000
34	12 July 1890	Warrington Cricket Club, Arpley Cricket Ground, Warrington	Reds 48/7	'Unusually large'
35	14 and 15 July 1890	Aston Lower Grounds, Aston	Blues 78 and 117, Reds 88 and 81; Blues won by 26 runs *Possibly played as two separate matches*	First day 5,000; second day 3,000

	Date	Venue	Scores	Attendance
36	17 July 1890	Churckery Grounds, Walsall	No details in newspapers	'Satisfactory'
37	18 and 19 July 1890	Turf Moor, Burnley	Reds 177/8 declared (Violet Westbrook 104 not out), Blues 126 (Ella Heather 55); Reds won by 51 runs	Second day 5,000
38	23 July 1890	Pulrose Cricket Ground, Douglas	Reds 82, Blues 94; Blues won by 12 runs Played ten-a-side	2,000
39	25 July 1890	Morecambe	No scores in newspapers, but Louisa Daly did the hat-trick	
40	26 July 1890	Down Croft Cricket Ground, Leigh	Blues 73, Reds 37/9; drawn	'Not so large as might have been anticipated'
41	28 July 1890	Perth	No details in newspapers (May not have taken place)	
42	30 July 1890	Wigan Cricket Ground, Frog Lane, Wigan	No details in newspapers; postponed from 16 July	
43	31 July, 1 and 2 August 1890	International Exhibition, Edinburgh	Blues 44/5; result unknown No details except for first day, but Violet Westbrook scored 68 not out for the Reds	
44	4 and 5 August 1890	Shaw Lane Cricket Ground, Barnsley	Blues 103, Reds 74/6; result unknown No details except for first day	'Large'
45	6 and 7 August 1890	Pitsmoor Ground, Sheffield	Reds 62 and 110 (Violet Westbrook 63), Blues 66 and 101; Reds won by five runs The Yorkshire County Cricket Club team watched the first day's play	First day 2,000; second day 2,500

Appendix 2: Matches Played by the OELC

	Date	Venue	Scores	Attendance
46	8 and 9 August 1890	County Cricket Ground, Derby	Blues 98 (Alice Grey 60 not out) and 75; Reds 93 (Violet Westbrook 64 not out) and 63/3; Blues won by five runs on first innings	First day 3,000
47	11 and 12 August 1890	Aylestone Road, Leicester	Blues 192 (Ella Heather 91 not out), Reds 66; Blues won by 126 runs	First day 800; second day 800
48	14 and 15 August 1890	Manningham Football Field, Bradford	Blues 37 and 35; Reds 67 and 68 Violet Westbrook took fourteen wickets in the match	First day 1,000
49	16 August 1890	Whitby	No details in newspapers (May not have taken place)	
50	18 August 1890	Bootham Crescent, York	Reds 115 (Violet Westbrook 59), Blues 98/4; drawn	1,000
51	19 August 1890	Harrogate	Reds 65 (Violet Westbrook 52), Blues 52/4; drawn	'Large gathering'
52	22 and 23 August 1890	Scarborough	No details in newspapers	
53	25 and 26 August 1890	Great Yarmouth Recreation Ground, Great Yarmouth	Reds 172 (Violet Westbrook 75), Blues 127; Reds won by 45 runs on first innings The Reds batted again and declared with one wicket down, but the scores were unrecorded	'Large'
54	27 August 1890	Bat and Ball Ground, Gravesend	Blues 150 (Ella Heather 72 not out); drawn The Reds batted briefly but no score was recorded	'Large number'
55	28 August 1890	Finn's Ground, Wincheap, Canterbury	Reds 104, Blues 37; Reds won by 67 runs	'Very small'
56	29 August 1890	Dover	No details in newspapers Originally scheduled to play men's team	

	Date	Venue	Scores	Attendance
57	2 and 3 September 1890	Devonshire Park, Eastbourne	Blues 104 (Ella Heather 69 not out) and 101, Reds 134 (Violet Westbrook 54) and 69/5; Reds won by 30 runs on first innings	First day between 5,000 and 6,000
58	4 and 5 September 1890	Central Ground, Hastings	Reds 140 (Violet Westbrook 94 not out) and 109 (Violet Westbrook 66); Blues 106; Reds won by 34 runs on first innings	'Tremendous' crowd, 'the ring all the way round being, at the very least, two and three deep'
59	6 September 1890	Angel Ground, Tonbridge	Blues 161 (Ella Heather 64), Reds 38/1; drawn	
60	8 September 1890	Crystal Palace	Blues 128 (Ella Heather 64 not out), Reds 70/3; drawn	Between 5,000 and 7,000
61	9 and 10 September 1890	Preston Park, Brighton	Blues 142 and 107, Reds 77; Blues won by 65 runs on first innings	First day 'large and fashionable gathering'; second day more than 3,000
62	11 September 1890	Chesham	Reds 36 and 31/3, Blues 62; Blues won by 26 runs on first innings	2,000
63	13 September 1890	Royal Military Exhibition, Chelsea	Reds 61 and 38/3, Blues 160 (Ella Heather 65); Blues won by 99 runs on first innings	Between 12,000 and 16,000
64	15 September 1890	Ilfracombe	Reds 65, Blues 61/5; result unknown *Scores incomplete*	700
65	16 September 1890	Barnstaple Cricket Ground, Barnstaple	Reds 147/7 declared (Violet Westbrook 102 not out), Blues 12/1; drawn	300
66	17 September 1890	Bitton, Teignmouth	*Rained off*	

Appendix 2: Matches Played by the OELC

	Date	Venue	Scores	Attendance
67	18 September 1890	South Devon Cricket Ground, Newton Abbot	Blues 89, Reds 79/2; drawn *Originally scheduled to play men's team*	Between 400 and 500
68	19 September 1890	Recreation Ground, Torquay	Blues 120 (Ella Heather 54 not out), Reds 35/5; drawn	Between 1,200 and 1,300
69	20 September 1890	Exeter	*Cancelled when team withdrew at the last minute*	
70	22 September 1890	Truro	*No details in newspapers*	
71	23 September 1890	Penzance Cricket Club, Penzance	Reds 48, Blues 83/7; Blues won by 35 runs	'Large'
72	24 September 1890	Falmouth	Reds 58, Blues 44/4; drawn	'Considerable number'
73	26 and 27 September 1890	South Devon Place Cricket Ground, Plymouth	*No details in newspapers*	
74	29 September 1890	Weymouth Cricket Club, Weymouth	Reds 158/1 declared (Beatrice Fane 58 not out, Violet Westbrook 73 not out), Blues 80/2; drawn	
75	11 October 1890	Tufnell Park Grounds, Holloway	Reds 85, Blues 56; Reds won by 29 runs	5,000
76	15 and 20 October 1890	Private Banks Cricket Ground, Catford Bridge	Reds 101 and 109/9, Blues 65; Reds won by 36 runs on first innings *Arranged as a benefit match for the players; extended into a second day after rain on the first*	First day 500, second day 'very few'

	Date	Venue	Scores	Attendance
77	18 October 1890	Royal Military Exhibition, Chelsea	Blues 111/7 declared, Reds 154 (Violet Westbrook 91 not out); Reds won by 43 runs *Teams were invited back after success of first appearance*	3,000
78	30 and 31 March 1891	National Athletic Grounds, Kensal Rise Station, London	*Part of an Easter Fete; no details of match in newspapers*	
79	5 May 1891	Cricket Ground, Guildford	Blues 129 (Alice Grey 57), Reds 121; Blues won by eight runs	'Goodly number'
80	6 May 1891	Dolphin Ground, Slough	Reds 121 (Eva Gordon 51 not out), Blues 128 (Ella Heather 56 not out); Blues won by eight runs	'Very good attendance'
81	7 May 1891	South Wilts Ground, Salisbury	(Ella Heather 82, Lizzie Sanders 69) *No team scores recorded in newspapers, result unknown*	
82	8 and 9 May 1891	Antelope Ground, Southampton	Reds 159 (Flora Fane 59) and 13/3, Blues 90; Reds won by 69 runs on first innings	
83	12 May 1891	Maidenhead	Blues 49 and 64/2, Reds 93; Reds won by 44 runs on first innings	'Not a large attendance'
84	13 May 1891	White Horse Ground, Oxford	Blues 96, Reds 93; Blues won by three runs	
85	14 May 1891	Vale Ground, New Road, Aylesbury	Blues 100, Reds 68; Blues won by 32 runs	

Appendix 2: Matches Played by the OELC

	Date	Venue	Scores	Attendance
86	19 and 20 May 1891	Richmond Town Athletic Grounds, Old Deer Park, Richmond	Blues 151 (Lizzie Sanders 53 not out) and 115 (Ella Heather 57 not out), Reds 144 (Beatrice Fane 51) and 64; Blues won by 58 runs *Flora Fane took seventeen wickets in the game, including all ten in the Blues' second innings*	First day 'small' or 'moderate', lower on second day
87	21 May 1891	Ealing Cricket Club Ground, Ealing	*No details in newspapers*	
88	23 May 1891	The Honourable Artillery Ground, Finsbury Square	Original English Lady Cricketers 71 and 81, Honourable Artillery Company 89; Honourable Artillery Company won by 18 runs on first innings *Charity game to raise money for the West End Hospital for Paralysis and Epilepsy; the men's team batted left-handed; Ada Heather took eight wickets*	3,000
89	25 May 1891	Tufnell Park Grounds, Holloway	*Rained off; the game had already been postponed from 18 May owing to rain*	
90	28 May 1891	Cambridge Road Cricket Ground, Colchester	Reds 35, Blues 129 (Ella Heather 60, Alice Grey 51); Blues won by 94 runs	'A large number of spectators' but 'not so good as had been expected'
91	30 May 1891	Bromley	Blues 61, Reds 34; Blues won by 27 runs *Blues had ten players; Reds had eleven*	1,000
92	30 May 1891	Bromley	Lady Cricketers XI 85/4 declared, Bromley Cricket Club 55/5; drawn *After the first game, eleven of the OELC played the men's cricket club, which had to bat, bowl and field left-handed.*	

	Date	Venue	Scores	Attendance
93	1 June 1891	Angel Ground, Tonbridge	Blues 62, Reds 110/6 (Flora Fane 50 not out); Reds won by 48 runs	'Not as many present as might have been expected'
94	2 June 1891	Bat and Ball Grounds, Gravesend	Reds 55, Blues 65/6, Blues won by 10 runs *Postponed from 27 May owing to rain; Blues had ten players, Reds had eleven*	'Fair'
95	3 June 1891	Priory Cricket Club Ground, Reigate	Reds 60 and 30/1, Blues 103 (Ella Heather 54); Blues won by 43 runs	'A good many' but fewer than previous season
96	4 June 1891	Dartford	*No details in newspapers*	
97	5 June 1891	Ipswich and East Suffolk Cricket Ground, Ipswich	*No details in newspapers; game postponed from 26 May owing to rain*	
98	6 June 1891	Chiswick Park Club, Chiswick	Reds 38, Blues 200 (Lizzie Sanders 110 not out); Blues won by 162 runs	'Very fair attendance ... not as many as might have been expected'
99	8 June 1891	Kensington Park Club Ground, Wormwood Scrubs	*No details in newspapers*	
100	9 June 1891	Kingston Town Cricket Club, Richmond Road, Kingston	Blues 54 and 63/1, Reds 101; Reds won by 47 runs on first innings	1,000
101	10 June 1891	West Herts Ground, Watford	Reds 98, Blues 184/6 (Alice Grey 77)	1,040 paid for admission, attendance around 1,800 including members

Appendix 2: Matches Played by the OELC

	Date	Venue	Scores	Attendance
102	11 June 1891	Wellingborough Town Cricket Club, Wellingborough	No details in newspapers	'Good'
103	12 June 1891	Town Ground, Kettering	No details in newspapers	'Moderately large', 'good' or 'large'
104	13 June 1891	Stourbridge	No details in newspapers	'Small'
105	15 and 16 June 1891	County Ground, Leicester	Reds 44; Blues won by five wickets *Very few details recorded but the Blues passed the Reds with five wickets down; Violet Westbrook's first game of 1891*	'Not large' or 'large number'
106	18 (and 19?) June 1891	Castle Ground, Nottingham	No details in newspapers	'Fair assemblage'
107	20 June 1891	Wanderers' Football Club Ground, Derby Turn, Burton	Reds 123/6 declared, Blues 127; Blues won by four runs	Poor, possibly only 40
108	22 June 1891	Lammascotes, Stafford	Blues 58; Reds won by six wickets *Only details recorded*	200
109	24 June 1891	County Ground, Derby	No details in newspapers	200
110	27 June 1891	Kelham Cricket Ground, Newark	Almost certainly abandoned	
111	29 and 30 June 1891	Pitsmoor Ground, Sheffield	Blues 117 (Ada Heather 65 not out) and 109 (Ella Heather 56), Reds 81 and 92; Blues won by 53 runs *Two players absent from each team on second day; first game after 'reorganisation'*	First day 'moderate'; second day 2,000

	Date	Venue	Scores	Attendance
112	1 and 2 July 1891	Dewsbury and Savile Cricket Club Ground, Savile Town, Dewsbury	Reds 210 (Violet Westbrook 145), Blues 98 and 101/1 (Lena Parsons 53); Reds won by 112 runs on first innings	First day 'small'; second day 2,000
113	3 and 4 July 1891	Headingley Cricket Ground, Leeds	Reds 133 (Violet Westbrook 65) and 127 (Violet Westbrook 65), Blues 95 and 77; Reds won by 88 runs Ella Heather took nine wickets in the Reds' second innings (with one player absent) and 13 in the game	First day 'good'; second day 'much larger'
114	6 July 1891	Turf Moor, Burnley	Reds 74, Blues 121/5 (Ella Heather 55 not out); Blues won by 47 runs Reds had ten players; not known how many were on the Blues team	1,000
115	7 July 1891	Bury	No details in newspapers	
116	8 July 1891	Warrington Cricket Ground, Warrington	Reds 57 and 35, Blues 72; Blues won by 15 runs on first innings Both teams ten-a-side as one player was still in Manchester	'Hundreds'
117	9 July 1891	Accrington	No details in newspapers	
118	10 and 11 July 1891	Athletic Club Ground, Old Trafford, Manchester	No details in newspapers; Daisie Stanley assumed role in management	First day 1,000; second day between 200 and 300
119	13 July 1891	Park Ground, Buxton	Blues 72, Reds 88; Reds won by 16 runs Reds had ten players; Blues had nine	Large number, unusually large gate for the ground
120	14 July 1891	Oldham Borough Cricket Club, Nether Hey, Oldham	No details in newspapers; one match played in the afternoon, another in the evening; Violet Westbrook scored 121	

Appendix 2: Matches Played by the OELC

	Date	Venue	Scores	Attendance
121	15 and 16 July 1891	Blackpool	Reds 65 and 59, Blues 55 and 76; Blues won by seven runs *Possibly played as two separate matches on each day*	
122	17 and 18 July 1891	Rovers' Athletic Ground, Ewood, Blackburn	Reds 45, Blues 73/8; result unknown *No details of second day's play reported in newspapers*	'… deserving of a larger assemblage of spectators than there was'
123	21 July 1891	Farnworth Cricket Ground, Farnworth	*No details in newspapers; one match played in the afternoon, another in the evening*	'Gratifying gates'
124	22 and 23 July 1891	Cavendish Park, Barrow	Blues 132 (Lizzie Sanders 52), Reds 133 (Violet Westbrook 68); Reds won by one run	'Meagre'; a few hundred
125	24 July 1891	Lune Road Ground, Lancaster	*No details in newspapers*	'Moderate'
126	25 July 1891	Birkenhead, Liverpool	*No details in newspapers; Violet Westbrook scored 137*	
127	27 July 1891	Kidderminster	*Refused to play, match abandoned*	
128	29 July 1891	Montpellier Gardens, Cheltenham	*No details in newspapers; may not have been played*	
129	31 July 1891	Swansea	*Teams did not appear*	
130	1 August 1891	Rhyl	*No details in newspapers; Violet Westbrook scored 101*	'A good number'

	Date	Venue	Scores	Attendance
131	3 and 4 August 1891	Cardiff	'Not expected to appear'; the dates given here clash with those given for the Douglas game which followed	
132	Before 4 August 1891	Llandudno	No details in newspapers	
133	4 and 5 August 1891	Pulrose Park, Douglas, Isle of Man	No details in newspapers but the dates come from a newspaper advertisement; may have played a local men's team of the 'Gondoliers Company'	
134	10 and 11 August 1891	Middlesbrough Cricket Club, Middlesbrough	Blues 103 (May Day 50) and 156 (Lizzie Sanders 90 not out), Reds 97 and 73/4; Blues won by six runs on first innings *First game under new management; Blues had ten players; Reds had eleven*	First day 2,000
135	12 August 1891	Ashbrooke Ground, Sunderland	Reds 63, Blues 110; Blues won by 47 runs *Blues had ten players; Reds had eleven*	1,500
136	13 and 14 August 1891	Constabulary Ground, Jesmond, Newcastle	Blues 101 and 96/3, Reds 40; result unknown *No details of second day's play reported in newspapers*	'Very large and fashionable attendance'
137	15 August 1891	Shildon Great Show, Shildon	May not have taken place	
138	17 and 18 August 1891	Scarborough	Reds 83 and 70/6, Blues 147; Blues won by 64 runs on first innings *Blues had ten players; Reds had eleven*	
139	20 and 21 August 1891	Hull	Reds 89, Blues 82; Reds won by seven runs *Scorecard possibly incomplete; one player batted twice for the Reds*	'Ordinary'

Appendix 2: Matches Played by the OELC

	Date	Venue	Scores	Attendance
140	22 August 1891	York Cricket Club, Bootham	Reds 63/6; drawn *Blues had ten players; Reds had eleven; had originally been advertised to play in Whitby on this date*	'Meagre'
141	25 August 1891	Dewsbury	Dewsbury Tradesmen XI 115/5 declared (Stott 71 not out), Lady Cricketers XV 17/5; drawn *Played against a local men's team; the Lady Cricketers had fifteen players*	
142	21 September 1891	Tufnell Park Grounds, Holloway	Reds 96/8 declared (Violet Westbrook 59), Blues 31/3; drawn *Benefit match for the players; Blues had ten players; Reds had eleven*	1,000
143	24 and 25 September 1891	Central Cricket and Recreation Ground, Queen's Road, Hastings	Reds 157 (Violet Westbrook 73 not out) and 135, Blues 201/4 declared (Ella Heather 62, Lizzie Sanders 66) and 64; Reds won by 27 runs *Benefit match for the players; both teams had ten players*	'Excellent' both days

301

Games played by the All-England Lady Cricketers in 1892

144	9 April 1892	Putney Athletic Ground	No details in newspapers; played as part of Boat Race Day	Good takings on the gate
145	18 April 1892	Dartford	No details in newspapers	
146	30 April 1892	Stamford Bridge	Reds 60, Blues 143/5; Blues won by 83 runs	
147	25 May 1892	Guildford Cricket Club, Guildford	Castle School 163/3 declared, All-England Lady Cricketers 40; Castle School won by 123 runs *Several of the players were missing owing to illness so a game was arranged against a local boys' school*	
148	26 May 1892	Kingston Town Cricket Club, Kingston	Match rained off, but only 15 players turned up	
149	27 May 1892	Ealing Cricket Club	No details in newspapers	
150	1 June 1892	Bat and Ball County Cricket Ground, Gravesend	No details in newspapers	
151	2 June 1892	Chesham	Teams did not appear owing to rain	
152	6 June 1892	Windsor and Eton Recreation Ground, Windsor	No details in newspapers	

Appendix 2: Matches Played by the OELC

153	7 June 1892	Windsor and Eton Recreation Ground, Windsor	Windsor and Eton Rowing Club 169/8 declared (C. Lorraine 55), All-England Lady Cricketers 82; Windsor and Eton Rowing Club won by 87 runs *AELC team had 15 players*	1,500
154	9 June 1892	Abingdon	Abingdon Town and Early Closing Clubs 146, All-England Lady Cricketers 103; Abingdon Town and Early Closing Clubs won by 43 runs *Only eight women appeared to numbers made up by locals to play a men's team; in latter stages, men batted and fielded left-handed*	
155	11 June 1892	Caversham	*Teams did not appear*	

Appendix 3: Averages for the OELC

THE FOLLOWING figures are the statistics for all the players who appeared for the OELC. The table is not a complete record as there are many games for which we do not have a full scorecard and others for which we have only a partial one. These figures reflect only these games for which the scores of individual players survive (as opposed to numbers reported in newspapers, such as those for Violet Westbrook). This means that some averages may be inflated as there are several matches in which only high scores were recorded; some smaller scores are therefore missing. Wickets and catches are particularly unrepresentative as there are many games, particularly in 1891, for which there is no record of successful bowlers and fielders: only batting scores were published. There are also several games in which sisters who played together were not distinguished by their initial in taking wickets or catches; these have been omitted. Finally, some of the players who share a surname in this list might be the same person; particularly in the case of the Gordon and Stevens sisters, it is not always certain which family member was playing either owing to inconsistent use of initials, probable mistakes in transcription or flexible identities (especially for the Fane/Gordon sisters).

Appendix 3: Averages for the OELC

Player	Season	Innings	Not out	Runs	Average	High Score	50s/100s	Wickets	5wi/10wm	Catches/Stumpings
N. Aldwell	1890	3	0	24	8.00	15	0	-	-	0
Marie Beckenham	1890	50	9	100	2.44	13*	0	-	-	0
Marie Beckenham	1891	25	6	67	3.53	15*	0	-	-	1
Marie Beckenham	Total	75	15	167	2.78	15*	0	-	-	1
Miss Bailey	1890	1	0	0	0.00	0	0	-	-	0
Sophie Charles	1890	60	2	348	6.00	22	0	12	0	6
Sophie Charles	1891	39	2	212	5.73	22	0	8	0	4
Sophie Charles	Total	99	4	560	5.89	22	0	20	0	10
C. Chessington[62]	1891	-	-	-	-	-	-	-	-	-
F. Chessington	1891	4	1	16	5.33	13*	0	-	-	0
M. Chessington	1891	2	0	0	0.00	0	0	-	-	0
Louisa Daly	1890	37	5	183	5.72	28	0	104	7	12
May Day	1891	30	10	227	11.35	50	1	-	-	0
Elizabeth Dempsey (L. Dempsey)	1890	64	1	556	8.83	47	0	80	6/1	96
Elizabeth Dempsey (L. Dempsey)	1891	9	0	130	14.44	40	0	24	3	2
Elizabeth Dempsey (L. Dempsey)	Total	73	1	686	9.53	47	0	104	9/1	98
L. Douglas	1891	16	3	57	4.38	16*	0	-	-	4
Mabel Emmett	1891	34	1	224	6.79	33*	0	-	-	1
L. Ernest	1890	1	1	15	-	15*	0	-	-	0
Beatrice Fane	1890	60	3	732	12.84	58*	1	-	-	13/1
Beatrice Fane	1891	30	1	444	15.31	51	1	-	-	8/3
Beatrice Fane	Total	90	4	1176	13.67	58*	2	-	-	21/4

---

62 C. Chessington played in one match but did not bat

Forgotten Pioneers

Player	Season	Innings	Not out	Runs	Average	High Score	50s/ 100s	Wickets	5wi/ 10wm	Catches/ Stumpings
E. Fane (Blues)	1890	4	1	2	0.67	2	0	-	-	3
E. Fane (Reds)	1890	30	10	68	3.40	16*	0	-	-	2
Flora Fane	1890	19	3	82	5.13	15	0	-	-	1
Flora Fane	1891	29	2	523	19.37	59	2	84	8/1	12
Flora Fane	Total	48	5	605	14.07	59	2	84	8/1	13
Susie Fletcher	1890	30	4	139	5.35	19	0	-	-	2
Susie Fletcher	1891	5	0	45	9.00	19	0	-	-	1
Susie Fletcher	Total	35	4	184	5.94	19	0	-	-	3
C. Fletcher	1890	2	1	6	6.00	6*	0	-	-	0
E. Gordon (Probably Eva Gordon)	1890	30	8	56	2.55	12	0	-	-	7
Ella Gordon	1890	2	0	6	3.00	4	0	-	-	0
Eva Gordon	1890	1	0	3	3.00	3	0	-	-	0
Eva Gordon	1891	32	5	276	10.22	51*	1	1	0	6
Eva Gordon	Total	33	5	279	9.96	51*	1	1	0	6
A. Gordon	1890	4	1	25	8.33	18	0	-	-	0
F. Gordon (Blues)	1890	3	2	10	10.00	6*	0	-	-	0
F. Gordon (Reds)	1890	52	2	278	5.56	29	0	4	0	3
Alice Grey	1890	56	2	652	12.07	60*	2	19	1	19
Alice Grey	1891	17	1	271	16.94	77	3	1	0	4
Alice Grey	Total	73	3	923	13.19	77	5	20	1	23

Appendix 3: Averages for the OELC

Player	Season	Innings	Not out	Runs	Average	High Score	50s/100s	Wickets	5wi/10wm	Catches/Stumpings
Annie Hampson[63]	1890	-	-	-	-	-	-	-	-	-
Lydia Hann	1891	33	2	184	5.94	23	0	-	-	1
Florence Hardwick	1890	59	4	328	5.96	25*	0	-	-	4
Ada Heather	1890	66	2	702	10.97	45*	0	169	10/1	8
	1891	34	3	421	13.58	65*	1	118	10/1	6
	1892	1	0	39	39.00	39	0	-	-	-
	Total	101	5	1162	12.10	65*	1	287	20/2	14
Ella Heather	1890	68	15	1520	28.68	91*	11	64	3	16/1
	1891	41	14	1257	46.56	82	8	15	1/1	5
	1892	1	0	40	40.00	40	0	-	-	-
	Total	110	29	2817	34.78	91*	19	79	4/1	21/1
M. Hood	1891	21	0	40	1.90	8	0	-	-	1
Beatrice Light (M. Light)	1890	1	0	24	24.00	24	0	3	0	0
Annie Lisle	1890	5	1	8	2.00	7	0	-	-	0
B. Lisle	1890	1	0	0	0.00	0	0	-	-	0
C. Lisle	1890	1	0	0	0.00	0	0	-	-	0
L. Lisle	1890	1	0	3	3.00	3	0	-	-	0
Marie Lisle	1890	8	2	14	2.33	7*	0	-	-	0
N. Lisle	1890	1	0	0	0.00	0	0	-	-	0
V. Martin	1891	30	1	118	4.07	19	0	-	-	5

---

63 Annie Hampson played in one match but did not bat

Player	Season	Innings	Not out	Runs	Average	High Score	50s/ 100s	Wickets	5wi/ 10wm	Catches/ Stumpings
Annie Matthey (Adele Matthey)	1890	60	2	310	5.34	41	0	44	3	15
	1891	33	1	138	4.31	27	0	56	3	5
	Total	93	3	448	4.98	41	0	100	6	20
A. McDonnell	1891	2	1	10	10.00	10	0	-	-	1
Caroline McDonnell	1891	33	0	121	3.67	23	0	19	1	5
Gertrude McDonnell	1891	27	0	99	3.67	26	0	2	0	3
Bessie Moss	1890	54	5	303	6.18	27*	0	5	0	8
C. V. Oldbrook[64]	1890	-	-	-	-	-	-	-	-	-
Lena Parsons	1890	63	2	393	6.44	28	0	-	-	46
	1891	37	3	359	10.56	53	1	-	-	35
	1892	1	0	22	22.00	22	0	-	-	-
	Total	101	5	774	8.06	53	1	-	-	81
N. Percival	1890	4	3	19	19.00	19	0	0	0	0
A. Robinson	1890	2	0	9	4.50	6	0	1	0	0
Lizzie Sanders	1890	64	7	495	8.68	29	0	-	-	9
	1891	41	5	947	26.31	110*	5/1	109	6/2	13
	1892	2	0	52	26.00	40	0	-	-	-
	Total	107	12	1494	15.73	110*	5/1	109	6/2	22
Bianca Seymour	1890	53	7	119	2.59	10	0	-	-	1
Georgina Sheffield	1890	65	4	561	9.20	39*	0	149	15/1	9

---

64 C. V. Oldbrook appeared in one game but did not bat

Appendix 3: Averages for the OELC

Player	Season	Innings	Not out	Runs	Average	High Score	50s/100s	Wickets	5wi/10wm	Catches/Stumpings
Daisie Stanley	1890	46	1	173	3.84	23	0	42	2	7
A. Stevens	1891	2	1	2	2.00	2	0	-	-	0
C. Stevens	1891	10	1	23	2.56	9	0	-	-	0
L. Stevens	1891	5	0	10	2.00	4	0	-	-	0
M. Stevens (Reds)	1891	3	0	23	7.67	12	0	-	-	0
M. Stevens (Blues)	1891	20	1	78	4.11	41	0	-	-	2
Mabel Stevens (Blues)	1891	3	0	6	2.00	5	0	-	-	0
Maud Stevens (Blues)	1891	3	0	4	1.33	3	0	-	-	0
L. Wadkin	1891	1	0	9	9.00	9	0	-	-	0
Nellie Wadkin	1890	44	12	78	2.44	10*	0	-	-	7
Nellie Wadkin	1891	30	12	66	3.67	7	0	-	-	7
Nellie Wadkin	Total	74	24	144	2.88	10*	0	-	-	14
A. Waterfield	1891	9	3	91	15.17	23	0	-	-	0
Grace Westbrook	1890	67	5	499	8.05	33	0	-	-	20/3
Violet Westbrook	1890	69	16	2614	49.32	104*	23/2	222	18/5	30
Violet Westbrook	1891	24	4	1146	57.30	145	5/4	47	5/2	4
Violet Westbrook	Total	93	20	3760	51.51	145	28/6	269	23/7	34
Edith Woodward	1890	7	2	14	2.80	7	0	-	-	1
Florence Woodward	1890	8	3	12	2.40	3	0	-	-	5

Acknowledgements

I WOULD like to thank the staff at the Boston Spa Reading Room of the British Library, whose patient help has been invaluable. The staff at Manchester Central Library were similarly accommodating. I would also like to thank Alan Cobb, Anita Howarth, Tina Griffin, Suzanne Moult and Sue Moody (distant relatives of Georgina Sheffield, Mary Louisa Daly, the Veitch family, Sophia Charles and Lena Parsons respectively), as well as distant relatives of the Heather and Lyon families, who were able to provide some family stories and information.

Peter Griffiths, whose many roles include running the excellent website womenscrickethistory.org, was extremely helpful throughout, not least for providing advice, contacts and copies of the team photographs printed in the *Women's Cricket Annual*. Thanks also go to Alan Rees, the manager of the MCC Library and Archive, for providing material held there. Similarly Paul Johnson, the Image Library manager at the National Archives, gave a lot of assistance in locating photographs of the teams.

Dr Victoria Clarke at the University of York was able to suggest some good background material. Also from York, Dr Mark Roodhouse was invaluable in locating information on the sporting context for late-Victorian

Acknowledgements

Britain. Siobhen Brown at Queen Alexandra House was also extremely helpful.

Dr Rafaelle Nicholson provided a few pointers early in this process and very kindly gave some excellent suggestions after reading a nearly complete version of the book. Ben Timmo also made helpful suggestions having read the text. And I would like to thank everyone at Pitch Publishing for their assistance in putting this book together.

Bibliography

Archival

'Company No: 29978'. English Cricket and Athletic Association Ltd. Incorporated in 1889. Dissolved before 1916. BT 31/4579/29978; Board of Trade: Companies Registration Office: Files of Dissolved Companies; National Archives, Kew.

Census returns (up to 1911), dates for births, marriages and deaths, baptismal information and details from the 1939 Register were all accessed using Ancestry.com, Provo, UT, USA: Ancestry.com Operations Inc, 2005. Other details – particularly 1921 census information – was taken from FindmyPast.com.

Books

Baker, Richard Anthony. *Music Hall: An Illustrated History*. Barnsley: Pen and Sword, 2014.

Bailey, Peter. 'Introduction: Making Sense of Music Hall' in *Music Hall: The Business of Pleasure*, edited by Peter Bailey. Milton Keynes: Oxford University Press, 1986.

Crump, Jeremy. 'Provincial Music Hall: Promoters and Public in Leicester, 1863–1929' in *Music Hall: The Business of Pleasure*, edited by Peter Bailey. Milton Keynes: Oxford University Press, 1986.

Duncan, Isabelle. *Skirting the Boundary: A History of Women's Cricket*. London: The Robson Press, 2013.

Grace, William Gilbert. *'W. G.': Cricketing Reminiscences and Personal Recollections*. London: James Bowden, 1899.

Höher, Dagmar. 'The Composition of Music Hall Audiences 1950–1900', in *Music Hall: The Business of Pleasure*, edited by Peter Bailey. Milton Keynes: Oxford University Press, 1986.

Holt, Richard. *Sport and the British*. Oxford: Clarendon Press, 1989.

Huggins, Mike. *The Victorians and Sport*. London: Hambledon and London, 2004.

Ledger, Sally. *The New Woman: Fiction and Feminism at the Fin de Siècle*. Manchester: University Press, 1997.

Nicholson, Rafaelle. *Ladies and Lords: A History of Women's Cricket in Britain*. Oxford: Peter Lang, 2019.

Pope, Mick. *Headingley Ghosts: A Collection of Yorkshire Cricket Tragedies*. Leeds: Scratching Shed Publishing, 2013.

Pullin, Alfred William. *Talks with Old English Cricketers*. Edinburgh: W. Blackwood, 1900.

Rae, Simon. *W. G. Grace: A Life*. London: Faber and Faber, 1998.

Rheinberg, Netta. 'An Original English Lady Cricketer'. *Women's Cricket Annual*, October 1956, pp. 173–76.

Rheinberg, Netta and Heyhoe Flint, Rachael. *Fair Play: The Story of Women's Cricket*. London: Angus and Robertson, 1976.

Showalter, Elaine. *Sexual Anarchy: Gender and Culture at the Fin de Siècle*. Viking: New York, 1990.

Sissons, Ric. *The Players: A Social History of the Professional Cricketer*. London: The Kingswood Press, 1988.

Threlfall-Sykes, Judy. *A History of English Women's Cricket, 1880–1939*. PhD thesis, De Montfort University, October 2015.

Tomlinson, Richard. *Amazing Grace: The Man who was WG.* London: Abacus, 2015.

Newspapers

The Telegraph Historical Archive via Gale.com, accessed through the British Library

The Times via https://www.thetimes.co.uk/archive

Women's Cricket via https://womenscrickethistory.org/Magazine/index.html

All other newspapers viewed at the British Library or via the British Newspaper Archive at https://www.britishnewspaperarchive.co.uk

References

For reasons of space, it has not been possible to include detailed references. However, these are available online at https://oldebor.wordpress.com/the-forgotten-pioneers/.

Index

admission price 114, 116, 144, 155, 161
Alexandra House 85, 87–89, 275
'Ally Sloper' 156, 173
Alphonse, Redfern 235
amateurism 23–24, 39, 67, 105–07, 109, 121, 159, 163, 174, 234, 238–39, 268
'Arthur's Ideal Soap Lady Cricketers' 155–58, 165, 170, 215, 229, 233, 268

Backhouse, Marie 156, 215
background of players 12, 16, 44–49, 53, 58, 60, 69, 82, 85–86, 88, 94–96, 164, 253, 270,
Barefoot, Beatrice: see Fane, Beatrice
Barefoot, Flora: see Fane, Flora
Barefoot sisters: see Gordon sisters
Bates, Billy 190, 271
Beckenham, Marie 49, 54, 56, 59, 77, 83, 96, 100, 138, 152, 164, 175, 239–44, 246, 254–55, 277, 305
Berry, Daisy: see Stanley, Daisie
Billett, Charles 56
Blackham, Jack 137, 271
'British Ladies Football Club' 237–38
Boat Race 66, 229, 302
Bosanquet, Walter Henry 23–26, 28, 31–32, 34–36, 38–41, 50, 54–56, 103, 105, 118, 140–41, 151, 154, 171, 173, 178, 196, 204–06, 209–10, 212, 217–18, 220, 222–225, 228, 233, 266, 268–69, 272, 274
Bowley, Fred 56–57, 240

Cave, Charles 63
Charles, Sophie 47, 53, 73, 84, 136–37, 144, 153, 165, 174, 255–56, 274, 277, 305
Chessington sisters 175, 179, 196, 201, 254, 277, 305
Chesterfield Grove 13, 19–20, 22–24, 26–28, 30, 272
clown cricket 40–41, 153, 155–56, 268
contracts 49, 154, 189, 196, 207–08, 219–20, 223
costume 12, 28–29, 66, 70, 72–73, 77, 82, 108, 126–28, 133, 140–42, 145, 149, 155, 203–04, 215, 218, 240, 244

Daft, Richard 234
Daly, Louise 13, 46, 58, 73, 84, 90, 100, 104, 137–38, 140, 162, 165–66, 248, 273, 277, 290, 305
Day, May 163, 180, 232, 278, 300, 305
de Broke, Lord Willoughby 91–92
Dempsey, Lizzie 47–48, 53, 60, 73, 79, 120, 137, 144, 146–47, 164–65, 174–75, 201, 253–54, 263, 272, 274, 277, 305
Dixie, Lady Florence 129–30, 237
Douglas, L. 175, 254, 278, 305
Duckhouse, Marie: see Backhouse, Marie

Emmett, Mabel 164, 215–28, 232, 257–58, 278, 305
English Cricket and Athletic Association (ECAA) 24–27, 30–31, 33–34, 61, 63–65, 72, 81, 99, 113, 115–17, 151–52, 178, 196, 202, 205, 210, 216–17, 224, 233, 269

Fane, Beatrice 100, 153, 167, 174, 176, 183, 213, 256, 275, 278, 293, 295, 304–05
Fane, Flora 100, 166–68, 172–74, 182–83, 188, 201, 213–14, 256–57, 274, 276, 278, 294–96, 304, 306
Fearis, Edgar Charles: see Ferris, E. C.
feminism 51–52, 124, 129
Ferris, E. C 179, 188–89, 200, 202–03, 206, 215, 218, 220, 223–228, 263–64, 270, 282
Frith, Henry 25
Fletcher, Susie 46, 59, 73, 100, 165, 175, 252–53, 275, 278, 306

'Gardener's Original Lady Cricketers' 152–54, 158
Gordon sisters 100, 138, 153, 167, 256–57, 274, 278–79, 294, 304, 306

Index

Gorin, George 32, 42–43
Gorin, Olga 42–43, 250–51
Grace, Bessie 37, 236
Grace, W. G 15, 36, 37, 69, 75, 84, 123, 187, 217, 236–37, 242, 271
Grey, Alice 13, 174–75, 179, 213, 228, 254, 275, 279, 287, 291, 294, 296, 306

Hampson, Annie 46, 73–74, 96–97, 246–47, 276, 279, 307
Hampson, J. B. 145–46, 189–90, 205, 208, 219
Hann, Lydia 164–65, 254, 257, 279, 307
Hardwick, Florence 47, 53, 135–37, 144, 252, 273, 279, 307
Haynes, Eliza 234–35
Hearne, Alec 56–57, 240
Hearne, George 56–59, 66–67, 70, 239–40,
Heather, Ada 12, 47, 58, 68, 73, 79, 90, 120, 135, 138, 163, 165, 172, 174, 176–77, 180, 213–14, 228, 231, 259–60, 275, 280, 295, 297, 307
Heather, Ella 13–15, 47, 53, 59, 73–74, 79, 84, 92, 104, 135, 138, 144, 146–47, 163, 165–66, 172, 174, 176–77, 213, 220, 223–24, 228, 230–31, 259–60, 271, 274, 280, 286–87, 290–98, 301, 307
Honeyball, Nettie 237–38
Hurst, W. G. 145, 147, 149

'Lady Footballers' (1889) 75–76
Lancaster, Forbes 216–19
Letine, Madame: see Gorin, Olga
Letine, Professor: see Gorin, George
Light, Beatrice 71, 97, 247, 274, 280, 307
Lillywhite's 66–68, 72, 152
Lisle, Annie 98–99, 276, 280, 307
Lisle, Marie 48, 53, 98–99, 247, 275, 280, 307
local agents for the ECAA 63–65, 116, 155–57, 190, 202–03, 205, 208–09
Lohmann, George 55, 102–03
Lohmann, Stewart 56
Ludwig, Edward 19–20, 22–23, 266
Lyon, Grace: see Westbrook, Grace
Lyon, Violet: see Westbrook, Violet

Martin, Thomas 65
Martin, V. 174, 257, 281, 307
mashers 17, 133, 148–49
matrons 13, 67, 83, 103, 176
Matthews, William 13, 55–59, 66–67, 77, 86, 95, 103, 135, 151, 161, 163, 176, 178–80, 188–89, 194–96, 200, 202–03, 215, 217, 239, 266, 275
Matthey, Adele 48, 53, 58–59, 73, 78, 137–38, 144, 147, 164–65, 172, 174, 180, 184, 213, 214, 253–54, 274, 281, 308
McDonnell, Caroline 163–64, 167, 228, 232, 258, 281, 308
McDonnell, Gertrude 163–64, 232, 258, 281, 308
Memorandum of Association 24–28, 31, 141, 244
merchandise 22, 34, 64, 77, 81, 133, 213
Michel, Mr. E. 13, 19–28, 30–32, 35, 39, 41, 43–45, 49–50, 54–57, 59, 61–65, 70, 72, 75–77, 81–83, 85–86, 90, 92–93, 95, 103, 113, 115, 117–18, 126, 140–41, 149, 153–55, 158–59, 161–63, 166, 168, 179, 188–89, 194–99, 202–10, 212, 215, 217–18, 220, 222–25, 228, 239, 266–67, 270, 272
Michell, Joseph Sanders 20, 22, 24, 266
Michel, Louis Edouard 22–23, 266–67
Michell, Edward Parsons: see Michel, E.
Morton, Ada 142, 147
Morgan, Henry 64, 116
Moss, Bessie 49, 53, 58, 73, 127, 137–38, 144, 147, 162, 251–52, 275, 281, 308
music hall 15, 31–34, 41–42, 70, 79, 134, 140–50, 182, 269

Navette, Nellie 134
'New Women' 50–53, 86, 124, 271
Nichols, Annie: see Light, Beatrice
xNorris, Ernest 63

Onda, Professor 142, 146–47

Parsons, Lena 46, 53, 73, 124, 136–37, 153, 165, 174, 214, 228, 232, 258–59, 266, 275, 282, 298, 308
Percival, N. 142, 282, 308
practices 28–29, 33, 39, 49, 56–60, 66, 68–70, 95, 116–18, 140, 161, 206

Index

profits 113–18, 152, 181, 204–06, 209, 243–44, 269–70
pseudonyms 20, 22, 40, 59–60, 100, 164–65, 239, 246–47, 249, 256
publicity 11–12, 22, 29, 48, 55, 57, 59–60, 63–67, 70, 73, 76, 79, 81–84, 88, 96, 116, 122, 155–56, 163, 166–67, 169, 189, 210, 229, 269

Queen Victoria Street 13, 24–25, 34, 154, 206

Rae and Weston 147
Read, Maurice 56, 58, 66–67, 240
recruitment 28–30, 43, 49–50, 54–55, 68–69, 100, 149, 163–64, 194
Regent Street Polytechnic 58, 255
Rheinberg, Netta 54, 77, 83, 238–44
Robinson, A. 97, 282, 308
Rowney, Agnes: see Emmett, Mabel

St George's Hall 30, 57, 66
Sanders, Lizzie 14–15, 45–46, 52, 78, 84, 136, 153, 165–67, 172, 174, 177, 180, 187, 191, 213–14, 225–28, 232, 263–65, 272, 282, 294–96, 299–301, 308
Seymour, Bianca 12–13, 53, 138, 144, 146–47, 162, 249–50, 274, 282, 308
Shaw, Alfred 25
Sheffield, Georgina 12, 47, 58–59, 73, 79, 90, 104, 137, 140, 162, 166, 248–49, 275, 282, 308
Shemmonds, Susan: see Fletcher, Susie
Silvani Cyclists 162–63, 183, 185
Stanley, Daisie 13, 15, 49, 53, 69–71, 73, 77, 80–94, 96, 122, 127, 143–47, 159, 162, 164–66, 182–84, 188, 190, 197–99, 205–06, 212, 215, 218, 222–24, 228–29, 262–63, 269–70, 272, 275, 282
Stevens sisters 175, 179–80, 283, 304, 309

Tatton, Katie 43–44, 52, 59, 77, 117, 127, 140, 143–44, 147, 149, 162, 176, 250–51, 272, 276, 283
theatre: see music hall
training: see practices

Ulyett, George 179, 271

Veitch, Arthur 175, 253–54, 263, 277

Wadkin, Nellie 48, 96–97, 100, 138, 165, 174, 254–55, 274, 283, 309
wages 49–50, 116–17, 156–57, 194–95, 197, 202, 208, 218–19, 222–24, 257–58
Walden, F. W 63
Waterfield, A. 163, 174, 179, 212, 283, 309
Westbrook, Grace 59, 71, 73, 137–38, 144, 146–47, 153–54, 158–59, 162, 168, 260–61, 284, 309
Westbrook, Violet 12–15, 59–60, 68–71, 73, 75, 77–79, 82, 84, 89–96, 104–05, 120, 123, 134–35, 137–38, 144, 146–47, 153–54, 158–59, 162, 165–69, 176–77, 180, 182–83, 187, 212–15, 243, 260–61, 269, 271–73, 284, 286–94, 297–99, 301, 304, 309
White Heather Club 38, 239
Willet, Mary: see Beckenham, Marie
Wood, Henry 195–97, 201–02, 204–06, 208–09, 212, 215–25, 229, 263, 270
Woodward, Edith 49, 53, 99–100, 247–48, 274, 284, 309
Woodward, Florence 49, 53, 74, 97, 99–100, 247–48, 274, 284, 309